THE
BOTANICAL ATLAS

THE BOTANICAL ATLAS

THE
BOTANICAL ATLAS

A Guide to the
Practical Study of Plants

DANIEL M^CALPINE

Introduction
by
DR. S. M. WALTERS
University Botanic Garden, Cambridge

PORTLAND HOUSE
New York

Previously published in 1883 by
W. & A. K. Johnston, Edinburgh

This 1989 edition published by Portland House, a division of dilithium Press, Ltd.
distributed by Crown Publishers, Inc., 225 Park Avenue South,
New York, New York 10003

Printed and bound in Hong Kong

ISBN 0-517-68132-3

h g f e d c b a

Publisher's Note

As Dr Walters' Introduction explains, *The Botanical Atlas* is a remarkable product of late Victorian scientific educational literature. The facsimile that we present has an explanatory text for each of the 53 plates reproduced *verbatim.* Inevitably, botanical scholarship in the intervening century has advanced to a varied extent. In general the greatest advances in knowledge have occurred in the smallest of the 'Lower Plants' so that the Cryptogams appear more dated than other areas of botanical work. At the other extreme it could be said that, with relatively little change to some technical terms, the Phanerogam plates and their accompanying text remain valid. The reasons for this difference are themselves of general interest and are explained in the Introduction.

CONTENTS

INTRODUCTION

This remarkable example of Victorian book production can be appreciated at two levels. The full-page illustrations speak for themselves, from the microscopic enlargement of the speck-like *Volvox* (Cryptogams, Plate IX) to the fascinating detail of the Plate (Phanerogams, Plate V) devoted to the Martagon Lily and the Crown Imperial. They can be studied as minor works of art, impressive both for the skill and care of the original artists. But they are much more than that: they represent the flowering of what is recognisably modern botany which the late Victorian educational expansion brought in its train, and it is the background to this story that we must first sketch in.

The history of botanical science can be traced back to the teachings of Aristotle and his pupil Theophrastus in Ancient Greece, and this venerable tradition is obvious to the present day in that, by international agreement, we use classical, Latin- or Greek-based names for all plants (and animals). Fascinating though these classical roots are, we must confine ourselves for the present purpose to the briefest mention of botany over nearly 2000 years from the time of Aristotle to the rise of what is recognisably modern science in Europe in the seventeenth century. Risking a broad generalization, we can say that throughout this stretch of the Christian era what botany there was flourished as a handmaid of medicine. The struggle to break away from the 'herbal' tradition and to observe and to study plants for their own sake is epitomized in Britain, as elswhere in Europe, by the history of Botanic Gardens.

Originally institutions devoted very largely to the cultivation of medicinal plants, they gradually emerged from this restriction in the seventeenth and eighteenth centuries and took on their modern shape. In the case of Edinburgh, where our book originated, this history is excellently told in the book by Fletcher and Brown, 'The Royal Botanic Garden, Edinburgh' published in 1970 to commemorate the tercentenary of this famous Garden. In London the remarkable Chelsea Physic Garden, also more than 300 years old, can still be visited and its collections admired on its original site by the river in Chelsea. (The dominance of Kew over Chelsea and indeed all other Botanic Gardens is a late eighteenth and nineteenth-century phenomenon.)

The pioneers of empirical, observational and experimental botany were, in Britain, men like John Ray (1627-1705) who were Fellows of the newly-formed Royal Society, and the complex history of our subject unfolds over three centuries. A glance at the second half of our book, devoted to 'Phanerogams', mainly what we would commonly call 'Flowering Plants', reminds us that one strand of accurate observation developed early. This concerned the detailed description of the structures of flowers and fruits. In spite of fundamental advances undreamt of by Ray in the seventeenth century or the great Swedish naturalist Linnaeus in the eighteenth, which would make much of what is studied in a modern Department of Botany totally incomprehensible to those great botanists, the basic comparative morphology of the flower remains unaltered from the eighteenth century. The original wall-diagrams (see below) from which the illustrations of the flowers of Sage (*Salvia*) are taken (Phanerogams, Plate XXIII) are, for example, usable in any lecture on the adaptations of flowers for insect pollination, as I know from my own teaching experience.

What then has changed, and why? The changes all refer to Part I of the book, devoted to the Cryptogams, or 'Lower Plants' as we still commonly call them. In nearly all general botanical works up to 1840, very little of the text was devoted to the 'Lower Plants', for the reason that an elucidation of their structural relationships to each other and to the Flowering Plants could not be made until better microscopes were available. The old-fashioned term 'Cryptogam', meaning in Greek 'hidden union', refers to this lack of knowledge of the details of their reproductive processes. By 1883, when our book first appeared, this revolutionary advance had happened, and an exciting new evolutionary picture of the whole Plant Kingdom and its essential unity of basic structure is presented here, for the first time, to British students in English. Cryptogams, Plate XXVI and the accompanying text set out the whole story, which was almost entirely the product of Germanic scholarship mainly in the new scientifically and technologically-minded Universities which sprang up and flourished in Germany between the end of the Napoleonic Wars and the foundation of a unified German State in 1871. An excellent account of this important period in the history of botany is available in the later chapters of Professor A. G. Morton's 'History of Botanical Science' (1981) — a book, incidentally, written in Edinburgh by a man whose breadth of knowledge is, as so often, a tribute to Scottish education.

This total supremacy of German botany is, of course, part of a much wider cultural and scientific phenomenon of the Victorian period, and the story cannot be told here. Perhaps it is sufficient to remind the curious reader that much of the impetus which underlay the British industrial and scientific drive in the late Victorian period came *via* the personal dedication of the German Prince Albert, Prince Consort to Queen Victoria, who was committed to a vision of rational scientific and technological progress involving wide popular education. It is impossible to understand the shape of British science if this crucial influence is ignored. So far as botany is concerned, it soon became obvious to the brighter students attracted to plant studies that a period of study in a German University under one of the great Professors — among them, De Bary (Strasburg), von Nägeli (Munich), Pringsheim (Berlin), Sachs (Würzburg) and Strasburger (Jena) — was a necessary part of their education. By 1872, however, when Thomas Henry Huxley transferred his science department (originally the Royal School of Mines and Science) to South Kensington, modern German-style biology was being taught in English in an atmosphere of intellectual excitement difficult for us to recapture. Here Huxley, the zoologist, and Thiselton-Dyer and Vines, the botanists, were producing a new generation of biologists to teach their science in the new National Schools introduced after the Education Act of 1870. This new curriculum was explicitly evolutionary, presenting the range of plants and animals from the lowest unicellular forms to the flowering plants and man himself in terms of common ground-plans against an evolutionary time-scale. Nothing has essentially changed in the way we teach elementary biology of organisms today — if we still teach any: what the twentieth century has seen is an enormous increase in what is now usually distinguished as 'cell biology', until there is real danger that comparative studies of anatomy and morphology drop out of the modern University syllabus.

Against this background we can understand the author of our book and his contribution to botanical education. Born in Ayrshire, Scotland, in 1848, he studied botany in London under Huxley and Thiselton-Dyer, and returned to Scotland to lecture at Heriot Watt College in Edinburgh in 1877. He held this post for seven years, and during this period produced the two major related works which interest us. 'The Botanical Atlas' is the derivative product of his earlier work entitled 'Anatomical and Physiological Atlas of Botany', which needs some explanation. One of the educational by-products of German botanical scholarship was the publication of sets of large 'wall-diagrams' (Wandtafeln) for use in the lecture-room. Most British University Departments of Botany dating from the period before the first World War probably had at least one of these sets. In my own Department I have used these excellent diagrams occasionally, realising that they combined clarity, size and accuracy to an unrivalled extent. Such diagrams must have been an integral part of the teaching received by the young McAlpine, and in 1880 he arranged for a famous set to be published by Johnston's of Edinburgh, together with three small 'Handbooks' in which he gave an edited text in English to accompany each diagram. In the 'Preface to the English edition' he states:

'In translating the text I have endeavoured to make it serviceable for all classes of students by adopting such technical terms as are met with in the best modern works, and by giving the "English literature" alone under each subject.'

The literature cited includes as appropriate works by Charles Darwin, T. H. Huxley and others, as also Sachs' 'Text-book of Botany' recently translated into English. The Preface to *The Botanical Atlas* explains the relation to this earlier publication, in paying tribute to the author of the original German edition, Professor Dodel-Port, of the University of Zurich, 'who allowed me free and full use of the beautiful figures.' A detailed comparison of the two works confirms, however, that much of the 'Botanical Atlas', though interestingly derivative in origin, represents the talents of a brilliant and inspired young lecturer, McAlpine himself.

Daniel McAlpine's later career was in Australian Universities, where he became widely known as a specialist in mycology and fungus diseases of commercial crop plants. He died in Victoria in 1932.

Dr. S. M. WALTERS
University Botanic Garden
Cambridge
12 · 1 · 1989

PREFACE

This work is intended as a guide to the practical study of Flowering Plants—and to this end selected types of the principal Natural Orders are dissected, drawn, and briefly described. Practical work requires to be *encouraged* for we have been so long accustomed to obtain our knowledge of Nature entirely through the agency of books, that the "book of Nature" has become to many the printed page and not the living reality. The inducements here offered are—the selection of Common Forms; the Dissection of Parts in their regular order, usually with just sufficient detail to illustrate their leading characteristics; the Drawings in their natural colour, for ready comparison with the natural object; and the necessary Explanation opposite of what is seen and how to see it.

In using this book the Student may either practically examine the forms figured or their equivalents—thus, the Shepherd's Purse may be chosen instead of the Wall-flower; the Garden Pea instead of the Sweet Pea, and so on. He may then examine, with less detail, other Plants belonging to the same Natural Order, noting chiefly peculiarities or differences. Some may take exception to many of the examples, on the ground that they are already sufficiently illustrated in the ordinary Text-books; but it may suffice to point out that, even in two such common forms as Buttercups and Daisies, careful examination will reveal new features of interest. Thus, the Buttercup shows beautifully the gradual passage of the *compound* Foliage-leaves into the *simple*, green Floral-leaves or Sepals; and the Daisy will be found to exhibit occasionally the Five-lobed Corolla and the Five-lobed Stigma, although it is invariably figured as having two only in each case.

It will be observed that the Flower and its various parts passing into fruit and Seed are mainly considered in the Volume; and the Leaves are merely introduced, copied from Nature, for purposes of comparison with the Floral-leaves. This forms the best introduction to a course of Practical Botany, since the eye and hand trained to dissect and distinguish these comparatively conspicuous structures, then can more readily pass to the consideration of Root and Stem and Leaf, and their minute structure. In the next Volume the minuter forms of Plant Life are dealt with, where niceties of manipulation and the use of the highest powers of the microscope are required.

The style of Botany that is too much the fashion at present, and the kind of Botany which it is the purpose of this Work to encourage, are strikingly shown, in a recent Report by the Examiner in Botany for the Science and Art Department, who says:-

'The candidates have displayed a good deal of knowledge, but as far as I can see if is of a purely literary kind. It has been obtained from books and not from study of the objects themselves. The result is the exhibition of much confusion of ideas which could scarcely have arisen if the candidates had ever attentively examined the things they have written about.'

DANIEL MᶜALPINE

EDINBURGH, *December 1882*

CRYPTOGAMS

PLATE I.

GLŒOCAPSA, OSCILLATORIA, SCYTONEMA, RIVULARIA, NOSTOC, PALMELLA, EUGLENA, and YEAST.

(Figs. 1b, 5, and 6a after Luerssen; Figs 3 and 4 after Dr Welwitsch.)

GLŒOCAPSA.

Glœocapsa (Gr. *glia,* glue; *capsa,* a case) occurs in damp places, and may be conveniently had for examination from the glass of damp green-houses, here it forms in gelatinous masses.

The single rounded cell consists of a small protoplasmic mass surrounded by a gelatinous cell-wall, and divides in all the directions of space till it forms a little colony. Division takes place within the parent envelope, and each daughter-cell forms for itself a new cell-wall. The original envelope, stretched in this way, absorbs more and more water until, towards the exterior, it gradually shades off into the surrounding liquid.

Fig. 1a Examine under highest power: 1*st,* as it naturally occurs; 2*nd,* stained with magenta; and 3*rd,* with iodine to bring out cell-wall distinctly.

The young cell stains deeply, showing the protoplasm to be dense; the next is undergoing division lengthways, and the third shows transverse division.

Fig. 1b Showing different stages of division, ending in the formation of a colony.

OSCILLATORIA.

Oscillatoria (so named from its oscillating or pendulum-like movement) occurs in various situations, either in water or on damp earth; but it may be found at any season of the year by the roadside, where it forms those spreading green patches at the bottom of damp walls, etc.

Under the microscope it is seen to consist of long filaments, each with a distinct colourless sheath of cellulose, containing protoplasm coloured bottle-green. The protoplasmic contents are marked by transverse lines, with alternate lines only faintly indicated. The power of growth is equally distributed over the whole filament, and any one of the segments can divide into two new ones.

Under the influence of light these filaments exhibit movement. They have a slow, swinging movement from side to side, the stiff filament giving the idea of a pendulum in motion.

Fig. 2a Mount a small quantity in a drop of water, and examine under highest power.
Long filaments, with their contents divided by numerous transverse lines.
Fig. 2b Press upon cover-glass so as to

crush the filaments.
The contents are seen to be little discs wrapped in a sheath of cellulose, which lies about to be ruptured.
Fig. 2c The faint lines between the more decided transverse markings are

the expression of the incipient division of each disc into two.
At the base a single disc is shown.
Fig. 2d The moving filament swings from side to side, at the same time going forward.

SCYTONEMA.

Scytonema (Gr. *skutos,* a whip; *nema,* a thread) occurs usually in dense tufts on moist rocks, sometimes in sufficient quantity to disguise the natural brownish or blackish colour of the rocks. This particular kind is of a shining black colour.

Instead of growth going on regularly throughout the filament, as in Oscillatoria, there are some points at which growth is more vigorous, and this bulging gives rise to side filaments or branches.

Fig. 3 Shows a small tuft in its natural size.

Fig. 4 Shows a small filament magnified. There is the common

sheath wrapping round the discs, and branches going off at particular spots.

RIVULARIA.

Rivularia (Lat. *rivulus,* a rill) may be found in mountain streams, coating the surfaces of submerged stones or water-plants.

It forms dark-green cushions, which are often incrusted with carbonate of lime, thus giving the whole a peculiar hardened look.

It departs from the uniform characters exhibited by the plants already considered in several respects. 1. Whereas, in Oscillatoria, the filaments of jointed protoplasm could evidently go on growing to any extent, here growth seems to die out at one end, giving rise to a tapering whip-lash filament. 2. Whereas, in Oscillatoria, the filaments were of equal diameter throughout, here not only is there a tapering at one end of the filament, but there is a globular development at the other end, in the form of a Basal-cell or Heterocyst, incapable of further sub-division. 3. Whereas each segment of Oscillatoria had the power of division, and a detached disc could give rise to a new plant, here certain cells, in the course of a filament, only possess that power. One of the cells becomes a Basal-cell, and the cell immediately above that grows out into a new filament. As the whip ends of the filaments are all directed outwards, there is a radiating appearance presented, with a Basal-cell at the bottom of each filament.   4. The large cell above the Basal-cell may grow till it is fully ten times longer than broad, thus becoming capable of persisting during the winter when the rest of the plant has decayed, and producing a new Rivularia in the spring.

Fig. 5 A single filament with Basal-cell or Heterocyst (Gr. *heteros,* different) at one end, and pointed cell at the other.

THE COMMON NOSTOC.

The Common Nostoc is to be looked for after rain, as it readily dries up. It occurs as dark, shapeless, jelly-like masses on garden walks or grass plots.

Under the microscope there is seen to be imbedded in the jelly long convoluted filaments, composed of little globular cells, forming a beautiful beaded neck-lace arrangement, with larger cells every here and there—the Heterocysts. The neck-lace is composed of distinct cells, and not mere discs of protoplasm embedded in a sheath, as in Oscillatoria. The embedding jelly is probably the cell walls softened with excess of water and run together.

The mode of multiplication varies. The portion of the old colony, between two heterocysts, breaks away from the jelly, and in the water the cells stretch themselves transversely and divide repeatedly, *parallel* to the long axis of the chain. In this way a number of short filaments are formed, side by side, which afterwards arrange themselves end to end, and so form the long meandering chain. In rare cases spores are formed generally between two heterocysts, and persisting after the rest of the filament has decayed, they give rise to a new chain.

6a Examine small portion of the jelly under highest power, and observe the beautiful twistings of the chain, with larger cells occurring at intervals. *Fig. 6b* Stain with Iodine and Sulphuric acid to show the cellulose coat investing each cell.

PALMELLA CRUENTA.

Palmella Cruenta (Gr. *palmos,* a shuddering; Lat. *cruentus,* bloody), or "Gory Dew" occurs towards the bottom of damp walls, and may frequently be observed even in the thoroughfares of towns. It is readily recognised by its bloody hue, and in cold water it yields a beautiful, pale pink colour.

The cells are embedded in gelatinous matter, and are sometimes angular from pressure.

Fig. 7a, b Examine, under highest power, in a drop of water. It peels off the walls in flakes, and only a small clean speck from the surface need be mounted for examination.

EUGLENA.

Euglena (Gr. *eu,* great ; *glene,* the eye-ball), unlike the preceding, is of a brilliant green hue, yet with a touch of red in it. It occurs commonly in the black water draining from manure heaps, which is known to be rich in Nitrogen.

Euglena is a motile organism, moving freely about by means of a long vibratile cilium, at least the length of the body. It is reckoned by some zoologists as an animal belonging to the Infusoria; but there are many points in its character which bear out its vegetable nature, so that if an animal, it is a vegetating one.

It consists of a spindle-shaped body, tapering at both ends, but as it moves about the outline varies and assumes all possible shapes. There is a red spot, called the eye-spot, towards one end. The contents are distinctly granular and for the most part tinged with the green colouring matter chlorophyll. In the presence of sunlight, oxygen is evolved as a result of the decomposition of carbonic anhydride.

It multiplies by internal division. When about to do so it gradually becomes still and rounded, drops its cilium, and encloses itself in a structureless case or cyst. The contents divide into numerous portions, each of which, on being set free by the rupture of the cyst, becomes a new Euglena.

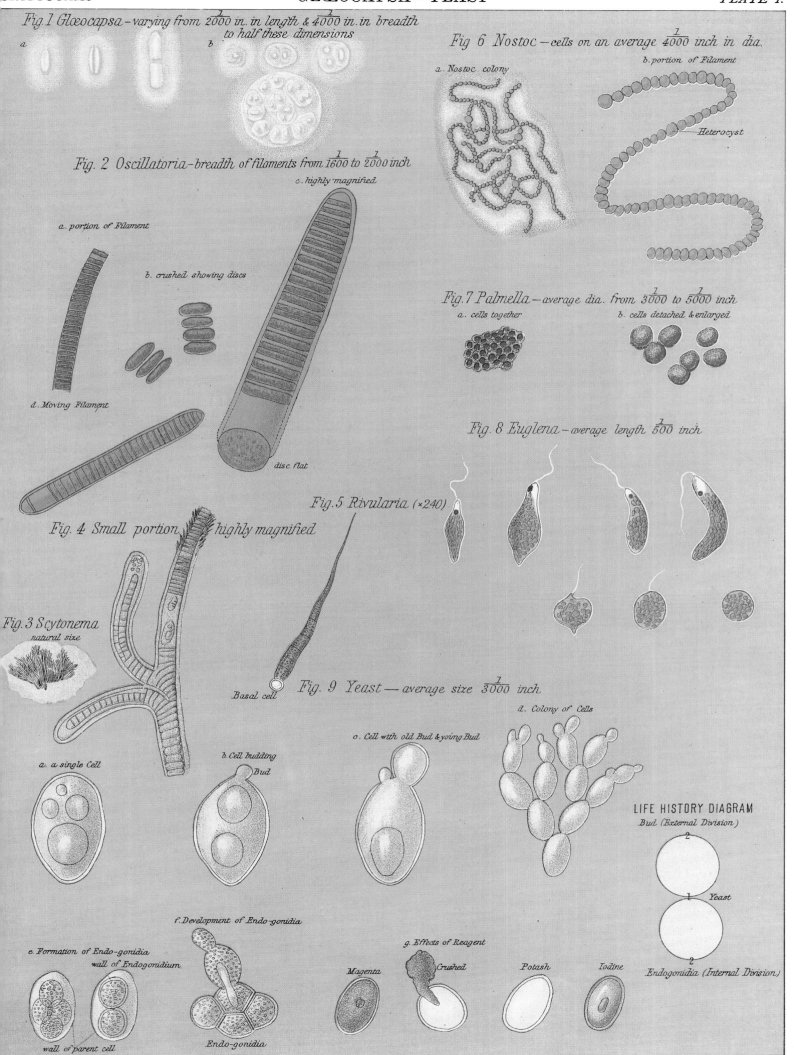

Fig. 1 Glœocapsa –varying from $\frac{1}{2000}$ in. in length & $\frac{1}{4000}$ in. in breadth to half these dimensions

a

b

Fig. 2 Oscillatoria–breadth of filaments from $\frac{1}{1600}$ to $\frac{1}{2000}$ inch

a. portion of Filament

b. crushed showing discs

c. highly magnified

d. Moving Filament

disc flat

Fig. 4 Small portion highly magnified

Fig. 3 Scytonema

natural size

a. a single Cell

b. Cell budding

Bud

Fig. 5 Rivularia (×240)

Basal cell

Fig 6 Nostoc –cells on an average $\frac{1}{4000}$ inch in dia.

a. Nostoc colony

b. portion of Filament

Heterocyst

Fig. 7 Palmella –average dia. from $\frac{1}{3000}$ to $\frac{1}{5000}$ inch

a. cells together

b. cells detached & enlarged

Fig. 8 Euglena –average length $\frac{1}{500}$ inch

Fig. 9 Yeast – average size $\frac{1}{3000}$ inch

d. Colony of Cells

c. Cell with old Bud & young Bud

LIFE HISTORY DIAGRAM

Bud (External Division)

Yeast

f. Development of Endo-gonidia

e. Formation of Endo-gonidia

wall of Endogonidium

Magenta

g. Effects of Reagent

Crushed

Potash

Iodine

Endogonidia (Internal Division)

wall of parent cell

Endo-gonidia

Engraved, Printed and Published by W. & A.K. Johnston, Edinburgh & London.

Fig. 8 Dip a glass rod into the green scum, and leave the smallest possible portion on a slide, and examine under highest power. This shows the encysted or encysting stage.
Examine a drop of the blackish water for the fully developed forms.

They will be seen moving about leisurely and twisting themselves into all conceivable shapes. By the application of iodine, the cilium will be rendered apparent ; and it is curious to note that Euglena is not propelled behind by its cilium but is actually dragged along by it.
In the same liquid there will be a variety of organisms, but the red eye-spot will mark out Euglena even when it is rounded and motionless.

YEAST (Saccharomyces—Lat. *saccharum,* sugar; Gr. *mukes,* fungus).

Yeast may be obtained at any brewer's establishment.

Fig. 9a, b, c, and *d* Take up a little yeast with pipette, and drop on to slide, and examine under highest power.
In every position the granules appear round, hence they are not flat, like a coin, but globular.
Cell-wall.
Protoplasmic contents.
Vacuoles filled with cell-sap.

Buds produced, and this process may be repeated, as in *d,* until an aggregation is formed.
Fig. 9e, f Starve some yeast by laying it out on a piece of plaster-of-Paris, and keep it moist with wet blotting-paper under a bell-jar. Under these circumstances the yeast is unable to throw off buds, so it breaks up internally in about a week into four portions, which have the power of reproducing the yeast under favourable conditions.
Fig. 9g The vacuole is seen to be less stained than the rest.
In the larger cells the staining material may bring out a dark or denser spot, which is the Nucleus.

Life History—The Yeast under ordinary circumstances multiplies by budding, and this may go on indefinitely as long as nourishment is supplied, but when nourishment fails, it can divide internally, and so prolong its existence by means of Endogonidia (Gr. *endon,* within ; *gone,* seed).

NOTE—The term *Gonidium* will be used to denote cells non-sexually produced, capable of reproducing the plant. On the other hand, the term *Spore* will be applied to such cells as result from sexual reproduction.

PLATE II.

BACTERIA, or SCHIZOMYCETES (Gr. *schisis,* a splitting).

(Fig. 8 is after Ewart, the rest after Dodel-Port, based on Dr Koch's photographs.)

Bacteria are those organisms which produce the change in organic bodies known as Putrefaction. Hay Bacteria, developed in an infusion of hay, may be profitably examined first. Take some fresh hay, pour hot water upon it, and allow to stand. In the course of a day or two the liquid becomes turbid, due to the presence of Bacteria, and latterly it has the smell of decaying organic matter. If a drop of this liquid be examined under the highest power of the microscope, it will be found to contain Bacteria of simple form.

Figures X 3000 except Fig. 8.

Fig. 1 Micrococci (Gr. *mikros,* little; *kokkos,* a berry) are simply small, round, or oval cells, occurring free, or in chain-like rows, or united into a gelatinous mass. They are remarkable for the bright colouring matters with which they are tinged—red, blue, etc. Micrococcus prodigiosus—the blood-red Micrococcus—is a spherical form, appearing as blood-red, slimy drops on stale potatoes, bread, damp wafers, and the like. From its sudden appearance (often arising in the course of a single night) it has often been superstitiously regarded as an evil omen, as stories of "bleeding bread" or "bleeding wafers" testify. The colouring matter is insoluble in water, but may be extracted by alcohol or ether.

Fig. 2 A chain of Micrococci found in putrefying blood.
This chain has probably originated from the repeated division of a single individual. The single cell lengthens as it grows, then forms a sort of figure of 8 preliminary to division, and this repeated again and again would give rise to the chain.

Fig. 3 A gelatinous film or Zoogloea. This film or scum forms on the surface of putrefying fluids, and consists of a number of Micrococci embedded in rows in a gelatinous material. This arrangement in rows has probably been produced, as in *Fig. 2,* by repeated division, as some are found in that condition.

Fig. 4 Bacteria (Gr. *bakterion,* a staff), or Cylindrical Forms—the two red blood-corpuscles are merely represented to show relative size.
These forms are the first found in the body after death. They are short or long rods, multiplying by transverse division.

Fig. 5 Rods from putrefying vegetable matter, with a vibratile cilium at each end, by means of which they wriggle about.

Fig. 6 Spirochoete (Gr. *chaite,* hair), or Relapsing Fever Bacteria, occurring in the blood of fever patients.
The spiral filaments are flexible and exhibit wave-like movements, which are often revealed by the motion imparted to the blood-corpuscles in the neighbourhood.

Fig. 7 Spirillum—to be found in puddles in summer where there is decaying vegetable matter.
They form inflexible spiral filaments, of one or several turns, and have a vibratile cilium at each end.

Fig. 8 Development of Spirillum—*a* to *i.*
(a.) Zoogloea-stage—motionless forms embedded in gelatinous material.
(b.) Vibrio-stage—bow-shaped forms passing into spiral forms.
(c.) Filamentous-stage—the last elongated.
(d.) Filamentous-stage—further developed forms, in which the filament is long and motionless.
(e.) Filamentous-stage—Spore-producing filament.
(f.) Filamentous-stage—ripe and motile filament.
(g.) Filamentous-stage—filament breaking up.
(h.) Spores which encyst and divide to form sporules.
(i.) Spores germinating—little comma-shaped bodies which reproduce the original Spirillum.

Life History Diagram.— The stages are here given through which Spirillum passes in order to complete the cycle of its life.

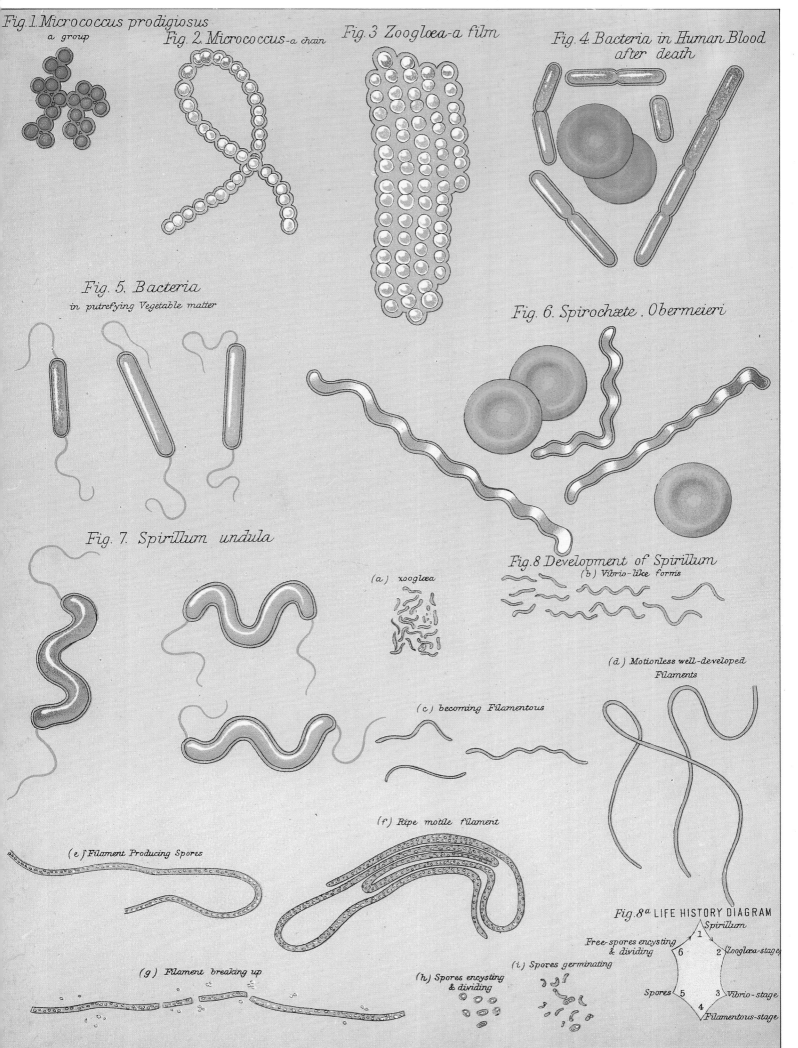

Fig.1.*Micrococcus prodigiosus*
a group

Fig. 2. *Micrococcus* - a chain

Fig.3 *Zoogloea* - a film

Fig. 4 *Bacteria in Human Blood after death*

Fig. 5. *Bacteria*
in putrefying Vegetable matter

Fig. 6. *Spirochæte . Obermeieri*

Fig. 7. *Spirillum undula*

Fig.8 *Development of Spirillum*
(b) *Vibrio-like forms*

(a) *xoogloea*

(d) *Motionless well-developed Filaments*

(c) *becoming Filamentous*

(f) *Ripe motile filament*

(e) *Filament Producing Spores*

Fig.8ª LIFE HISTORY DIAGRAM
Spirillum
1
Free-spores encysting & dividing   6   2 *Zooglœa-stage*
Spores   5   3 *Vibrio-stage*
4
Filamentous-stage

(g) *Filament breaking up*

(h) *Spores encysting & dividing*

(i) *Spores germinating*

Engraved, Printed and Published by W. & A.K. Johnston, Edinburgh & London.

PLATE III.

BACTERIUM ANTHRACIS. or
BACILLUS ANTHRACIS, COHN.

(After Dodel-Port.)

Splenic Fever Bacterium, or Bacillus Anthracis (Lat. *bacillum,* a little staff; *anthrax, anthracis,* coal), may be taken as the type of those contagious disease germs which have been so destructive in their effects upon the human race, and which are only now being carefully studied The principal facts made out concerning it may serve as a guide to other forms. It is interesting to note that it has been made to lose its infecting power by frequently changing it in a solution of extract of meat; and one of the triumphs of science at the present day has been to render this and such-like deadly organisms comparatively harmless, by appropriate treatment. The minute size and immense numbers of the spores readily explain the spread of the infection, and as it has been proved that they may retain their vitality for years, the disease may break out quite unexpectedly. It is also a matter of experimental proof that the fever ensues when the germs are taken in with the air breathed in the form of a dry dust, and thus reach the blood in the Lungs; or they may reach the blood through scratches or other means.

Figures X 3000.

Fig. 1 Transparent rods, straight and bent, and of various lengths.
These rods are colourless and motionless. They divide transversely, and the joints adhere to form longer or shorter rods.

Fig. 2 Filament produced by the elongation of the rods.
These filaments may attain a length several hundred times that of the original rods, and when fully developed, their contents break up into numberless spores or endogonidia.

Figs. 3 and 4 Spores placed obliquely or perpendicular to the long axis of the filament.
The spores are oval or elliptical, with highly refractive contents and a dark outline

Fig. 5 Gelatinous scum containing spores arranged in rows. The gelatinous material gradually dissolves in the water, thus setting the spores free.

Fig. 6 Clusters of spores set free—either as above, or by the deliquescence of a gelatinous filament.

Fig. 7 Development.
(*a.*) Oval spore.
(*b.*) Oval spore, lengthening and dividing.
(*c.*) Short rod lengthening and dividing further.
(*d.*) Longer rods formed.
(*e.*) Long jointed rod, as in Fig. 1.

Life History. — The original short *rods* grow and lengthen in an appropriate medium, such as blood-serum or the aqueous humour of the eye. The *filaments*, thus produced, having attained their full development soon begin to show in their interior numerous bright spots, which latterly become the *spores*, and the rest of the filament passes into a jelly-like mass. Several of the filaments may lay themselves together and so produce a gelatinous scum with the spores embedded and arranged in rows. The spores are set free by the dissolution of this gelatinous material, and are then ready to begin anew their course of development.

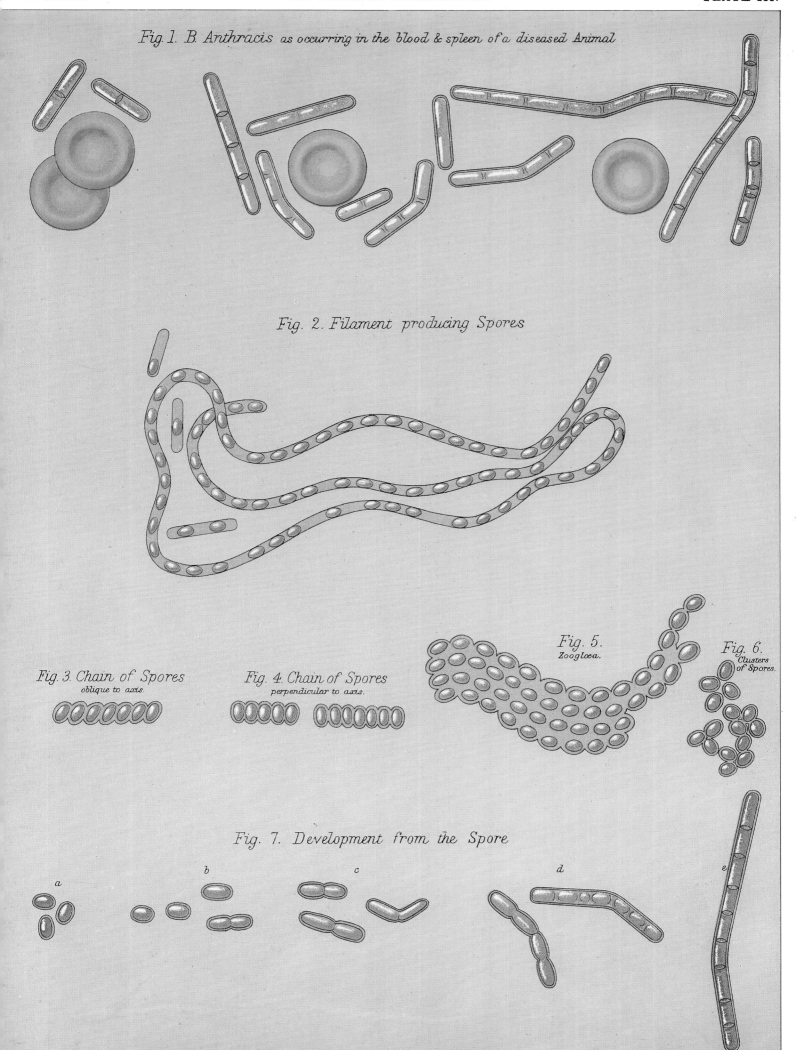

Fig. 1. B. Anthracis as occurring in the blood & spleen of a diseased Animal

Fig. 2. Filament producing Spores

Fig. 3. Chain of Spores oblique to axis.

Fig. 4. Chain of Spores perpendicular to axis.

Fig. 5. Zoogloea.

Fig. 6. Clusters of Spores.

Fig. 7. Development from the Spore

a   b   c   d   e

Engraved, Printed and Published by W. & A.K. Johnston, Edinburgh & London.

PLATE IV.

PROTOCOCCUS, PANDORINA, ULOTHRIX, and HYDRODICTYON.

PROTOCOCCUS VULGARIS.

Protococcus Vulgaris (Gr. *protos,* first; *kokkos,* a berry), or Pleurococcus, is well—known as the green scum on the bark of trees. It is so widely diffused that its means of multiplication must be very perfect. In fact it is like a continuous growing point, ever dividing and ever ready to divide.

Under the microscope it is seen to consist of rounded cells, usually having a nucleus. This nucleus is a denser portion of the protoplasm and stains more deeply than the rest. The cells are also seen to be divided into two, three, or four portions. But towards the end of autumn another process of division takes place. The contents of the cell break up into a great number of little masses which, on escaping by the rupture of the cell-wall, are seen to consist of naked bits of protoplasm, with two threads of it propelling them rapidly through the water. This naked moving protoplasm afterwards forms a cell-wall.

Fig. 1 Take a little bit of the bark of a tree, with this green scum upon it, and scrape off some of it into a drop of water on a slide. Examine under highest power.

(a.) Ordinary resting-form consisting of Cell-wall and green-coloured contents.

(b.) Iodine brings out Nucleus—seen as a small dark spot in the centre of the cell.

Iodine and Sulphuric acid together—the cell-wall becomes blue and the protoplasm coagulates.

Crushed—to distinguish clearly between the tough cell-wall and the semi-fluid protoplasm.

Potash—dissolving the protoplasm.

(c.) Multiplication by Division into four. The protoplasm first of all separates into two masses, and cell-wall forms in the partition between. Next, each half behaves like the original whole so that four divisions are formed. These divisions separate, become rounded, and each forms a new Protococcus.

(d.) Endogenous Division producing motile forms. The protoplasmic contents begin to divide in the same way as before, but instead of stopping at four, there is division into numerous segments of naked protoplasm. The particles become rounded and escape as *motile forms* through the rupture of the original case. The motile ciliated forms, non-sexually produced, are called Zoogonidia (Gr. *zoon,* an animal). In the resting-forms it will be noticed, that they were clothed with a cell-wall before *being* set free, whereas the motile forms only assume a cellulose covering afterwards.

Life History.—Multiplication takes place either by simple division into four portions, or into numerous motile forms, which afterwards settle down and return to the ordinary resting-form.

PROTOCOCCUS PLUVIALIS.

Protococcus Pluvialis (Lat. *pluvia,* rain) as the specific name denotes, occurs in places where rain-water collects.

Fig. 2 Take some of the muddy sediment from rain-water, mount with clean water and examine under highest power.

Observe motionless and motile forms. The motile forms may either be clothed with a wall or naked.

PANDORINA.

Pandorina (Gr. *Pandora,* a beautiful woman) occurs in ponds and ditches, but it may be had for examination from certain Natural History dealers.

There are sixteen cells united into a free-swimming colony of globular shape by a gelatinous investment. Each of these sixteen cells may give rise to a new colony. The cilia are withdrawn, whereby the whole comes to rest, and each individual divides into sixteen portions like the parent. In other cases, however, a single cell does not reproduce the colony. Two cells from different individuals fuse together and the common mass ultimately forms a young colony. This process is called Conjugation, where the two uniting elements closely resemble each other, and the result of it may be traced in the Figures.

Fig. 3a Colony or Cœnobium (Gr. *koine,* in common; *bios,* life) consisting of sixteen cells or Zoogonidia. Each Zoogonidium has a red eye-spot and two projecting cilia, by the collective and harmonious action of them all a rolling motion is imparted to the whole family.

(b, c) Male and Female Zoospores. These reproductive cells are produced from different colonies, the smaller being reckoned the Male, and the larger the Female element.

(d, e) In conjugation, the two elements first come into contact by their ciliated ends, then they gradually swing round side by side and fuse completely.

(f, g) The single body resulting from conjugation is called a Zygospore (Gr. *zugos,* a yoke; *spora,* a seed). This zygospore bursts its case and begins to germinate.

(h.) The germinating Zygospore draws in its cilia, rounds itself off and divides into sixteen cells, forming a colony.

Life History.—Each Zoogonidium of the Pandorina-colony divides into sixteen portions—like the original—and then escapes through the gelatinous wall. This is the non-sexual mode of multiplication. The sexual reproduction consists in the production of cells

PROTOCOCCUS—WATER-NET *PLATE IV.*

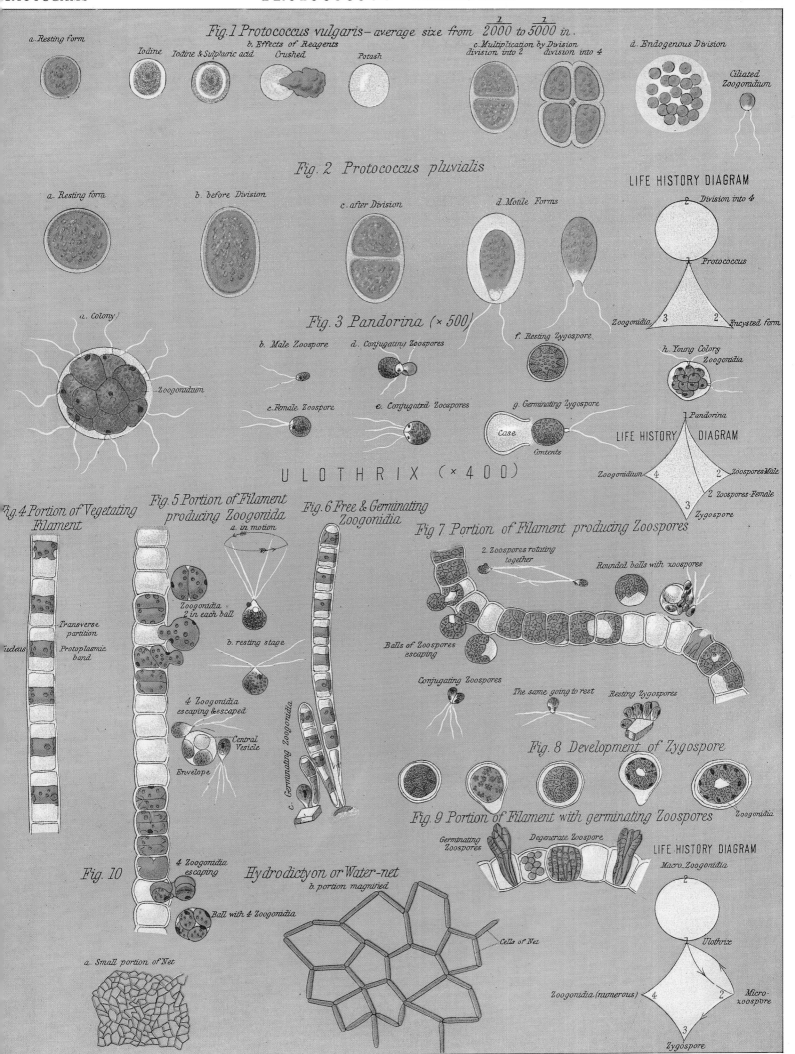

Fig.1 Protococcus vulgaris – average size from $\frac{1}{2000}$ to $\frac{1}{5000}$ in.

a. Resting form
b. Effects of Reagents — Iodine — Iodine & Sulphuric acid — Crushed — Potash
c. Multiplication by Division — division into 2 — division into 4
d. Endogenous Division — Ciliated Zoogonidium

Fig. 2 Protococcus pluvialis

a. Resting form
b. before Division
c. after Division
d. Motile Forms

LIFE HISTORY DIAGRAM

a. Colony
Zoogonidium

Fig. 3 Pandorina (× 500)
b. Male Zoospore
d. Conjugating Zoospores
f. Resting Zygospore
c. Female Zoospore
e. Conjugated Zoospores
g. Germinating Zygospore — Case — Contents
h. Young Colony — Zoogonidia

LIFE HISTORY DIAGRAM

ULOTHRIX (× 400)

Fig.4 Portion of Vegetating Filament — Transverse partition — Nucleus — Protoplasmic band

Fig. 5 Portion of Filament producing Zoogonida — Zoogonidia 2 in each ball — a. in motion — b. resting stage — 4 Zoogonidia escaping & escaped — Central Vesicle — Envelope

Fig. 6 Free & Germinating Zoogonidia — c. Germinating Zoogonidia

Fig 7 Portion of Filament producing Zoospores — 2. Zoospores rotating together — Rounded balls with zoospores — Balls of Zoospores escaping — Conjugating Zoospores — The same going to rest — Resting Zygospores

Fig. 8 Development of Zygospore

Fig. 9 Portion of Filament with germinating Zoospores — Germinating Zoospores — Degenerate Zoospore — Zoogonidia

LIFE HISTORY DIAGRAM — Macro-Zoogonidia

Fig. 10 — 4 Zoogonidia escaping — Ball with 4 Zoogonidia

Hydrodictyon or Water-net — b. portion magnified — Cells of Net — a. Small portion of Net

Ulothrix — Zoogonidia (numerous) — Micro-zoospore — Zygospore

Engraved, Printed and Published by W. & A.K. Johnston, Edinburgh & London.

which are called Zoospores, one colony forming sixteen small (male) Zoospores, another sixteen larger (female) Zoospores. Two unite to form a Zygospore, which germinates and produces a new colony.

ULOTHRIX ZONATA.

(after Dodel-Port.)

Ulothrix Zonata (Gr. *oulos,* woolly or curly; *thrix,* hair), or Curly-hair Alga, may be found in fresh waters, such as brooks, drinking fountains and the like. It occurs in green tufts attached to some fixed body.

It is a simple filamentous Alga, reproducing itself non-sexually during winter and sexually during summer, but if the sexually reproductive cells fail to conjugate, they may still grow into a new plant.

NON-SEXUAL STAGE

Fig. 4 Portion of Filament in vegetating condition.
The cylindrical cells are placed end to end, and in each there is a green protoplasmic band about the middle containing a nucleus.
Fig. 5 Portion of Filament exclusively producing Zoogonidia. A mother-cell may produce one, two, four, or eight zoogonidia. The inner wall of the cell passes out as an envelope surrounding them, and afterwards deliquesces to allow their escape.
Fig. 6 The Zoogonidium is pear-shaped, with four cilia and a red eye-spot and a contractile vacuole.
(*a.*) In motion, it rotates round its long axis by means of the four cilia.
(*b.*) On coming to rest, the cilia become stiff and fall off, and the zoogonidium fixes itself, by its tapering end, to some object.
(*c.*) The zoogonidium now germinates and, by repeated division, produces a filament, as in Fig. 4.

PLATE V.

CONFERVACEÆ, ULVACEÆ, and MYXOMYCETES.

(Reproduction and Development principally after Oersted.)

CONFERVACEÆ (Lat. *confervere,* to unite) are filamentous Algæ, occurring plentifully in every stagnant water, usually in great abundance round the margin. The filaments grow in length by the individual cells dividing into two. Multiplication takes place by Zoogonidia, and Conjugation has been observed in Cladophora.

Figs. 1 and 2 Cladophora (Gr. *klados,* a branch; *phoreo,* I bear), so named from its being branched, is a very common form.
Examine a small portion in water.
Filament with alternate branches forming. The top of the cell puts forth a little pocket at one side, which grows and divides like the parent filament. Secondary branches may likewise be formed, thus giving rise to bushy tufts. One or more nuclei may be present in each cell.

Fig. 3 Treatment with Iodine, showing starch granules.
The contents are seen to be broken up into little ovoid masses called chlorophyll-corpuscles, and it is in these the starch is formed.
Yellowish—brown colour indicates protoplasm.
The darker spots are in reality dark-blue, indicating their starchy nature. The cellulose wall is clearly differentiated from the contents.
Fig. 4 Multiplication by Zoogonidia.

The contents of the cells break up into little masses, which round themselves off, acquire cilia, and escape by a break in the side of the wall.
Fig. 5 Zoogonidia germinating. They lose their cilia, begin to elongate, and grow to a filament.

ULVACEÆ form flat expansions of cells, and are commonly met with on the seashore. The common green Laver (U. latissima) may be a foot square, and is so puckered and folded that it seems branched. Enteromorpha may be regarded as a tubular Ulva; and as Conjugation has been clearly observed in it, the process will be described in that connection.

Fig. 6 Mount a small piece in water and examine.
The cells are angular from pressure, and dark spots appear in each.

Fig. 7 Highly magnified portion. A number of the cells contain Zoogonidia. The Zoogonidia escape

by small openings on the surface, and move about in the water by means of cilia.

ENTEROMORPHA (Gr. *enteron,* intestine; *morphe,* shape), instead of being flat, like Ulva, forms a slender tube. It occurs plentifully on the seashore, attached to stones, rocks, or even seaweed, and also forms those slimy, green growths so common on the posts of piers etc. In the autumn particularly the cells give rise to innumerable actively moving Zoospores. These come together in the water, and Conjugation takes place. The result is a Zygospore, which is believed to germinate in the ensuing spring and become a new Enteromorpha.

Fig. 8 It consists of a tapering attached end, giving off numerous small branches, then expanding till it reaches the apex, where a slender forked portion branches off a little to one side. The surface of this specimen is puckered, and here and there delicate branches are formed.
Figs. 9 and 10 Take a small portion and examine under microscope.

The tube is seen to consist of a single layer of cells, and when spread out as in Fig.9, quite resembles the frond of Ulva.
Fig. 11 Portion highly magnified. Some of the cells are still in the vegetative condition, others are full of Zoospores, in some the contents have escaped, and on the left side the

Zoospores are seen in the act of escaping, enveloped by the inner membrane of the cell.
Figs. 12 and 13 Micro-zoospores free and conjugating.
Two Zoospores meet by their pointed ends, then swing round side by side, blend, lose their cilia, and become a pear-shaped Zygospore.

Life History of Confervaceæ and Ulvaceæ—The cells either produce Zoogondia, which grow into a new plant, or Zoospores, which conjugate, thereby forming Zygospores to reproduce the plant.

MYXOMYCETES (Gr. *muxa,* slime, *mukes* a fungus), or Slime-fungi, as their name denotes, are slimy bodies found on rotten wood, decaying leaves, etc.; and the specimen chosen—Aethalium septicum, or "flowers of tan"—occurs on spent tan. It is of a creamy, yellow colour; and in nurseries, where spent tan is used for bottom heat, it may be found in the autumn overspreading large surfaces, and, forced by the lack of heat, it has been known to make its way up the stems of plants. The limit of heat for this form is 40°C.

The Myxomycetes are peculiar in passing through an Amœboid stage, when they take in solid nutriment and feed like animals, so that in this stage of their existence at least, they resemble animals rather than plants. Their life history too is quite comparable to that of some of the lower animals, as may be seen from the Figures.

Fig. 14 Aethalium septicum (Gr. *aithales,* splendid, from its appearance).
(a.) The Amœboid stage, or Myxopod of the animal series, possess a nucleus.
(b.) The Plasmodium stage is the large, conspicuous, yellowish mass, made up of a protoplasmic network

showing streaming of the contents as indicated by the arrows.
(c.) The Spore possesses a thick cell-wall, which bursts to allow the contents to escape. The rounded mass developes two cilia, which become reduced to one, and thus a body is formed like the Mastigopod of the animal series. Even this single cilium

disappears, and the Amœboid stage is reached, as at the beginning.
Fig. 15 Sporangium of Arcyria—unopened and opened. The elasticity of the fibres composing the Capillitum (Lat. *capillus,* a hair) ultimately ruptures the case and jerks out the spores.

Life History.—In fixing the starting-point for the life history of the Myxomycetes I have been guided by its evident similarity to that of some of the Monera described by Haeckel, and so

24

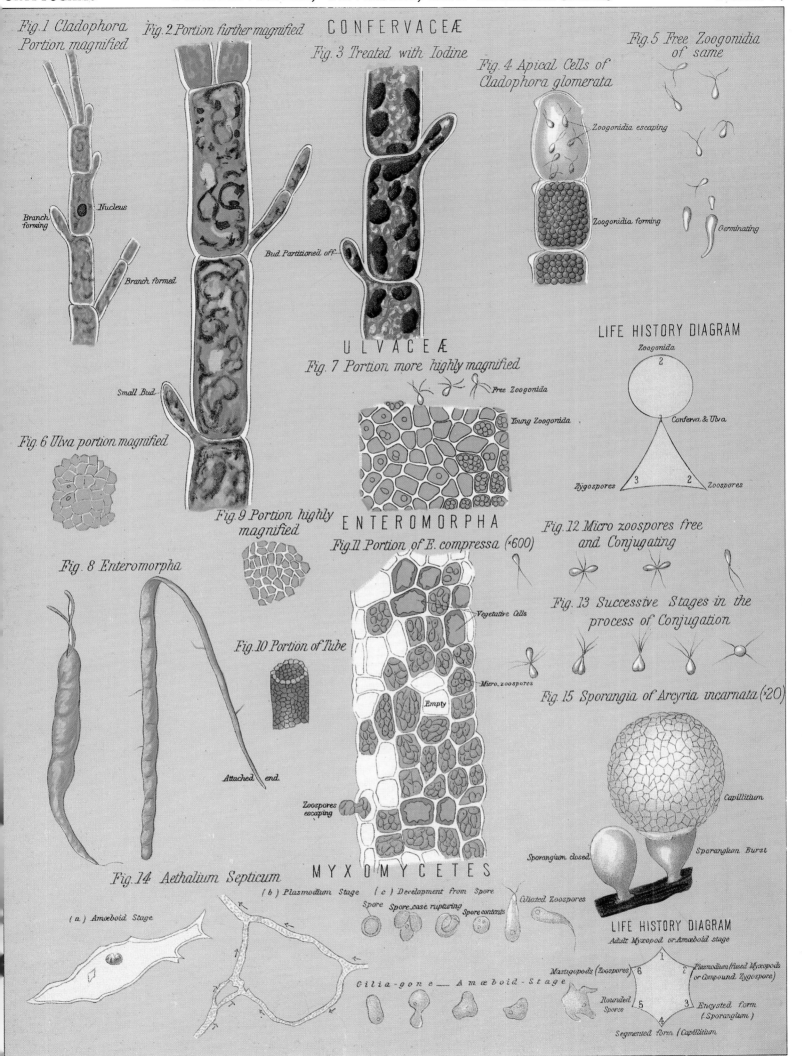

CONFERVACEÆ

Fig. 1 Cladophora Portion magnified

Fig. 2 Portion further magnified

Fig. 3 Treated with Iodine

Fig. 4 Apical Cells of Cladophora glomerata

Fig. 5 Free Zoogonidia of same

Branch forming — Nucleus — Branch formed — Small Bud — Bud Partitioned off — Zoogonidia escaping — Zoogonidia forming — Germinating

ULVACEÆ

Fig. 6 Ulva portion magnified

Fig. 7 Portion more highly magnified

Free Zoogonida — Young Zoogonida

Fig. 8 Enteromorpha

Fig. 9 Portion highly magnified

Fig. 10 Portion of Tube

Attached end.

ENTEROMORPHA

Fig. 11 Portion of E. compressa (×600)

Vegetative Cells — Empty — Micro zoospores — Zoospores escaping

LIFE HISTORY DIAGRAM

Zoogonida — 2 — Conferva & Ulva — Zygospores — 3 — 2 — Zoospores

Fig. 12 Micro zoospores free and Conjugating

Fig. 13 Successive Stages in the process of Conjugation

Fig. 15 Sporangia of Arcyria incarnata (×20)

Sporangium closed — Capillitium — Sporangium Burst

MYXOMYCETES

Fig. 14 Aethalium Septicum

(a) Amœboid Stage — (b) Plasmodium Stage — (c) Development from Spore — Spore — Spore case rupturing — Spore contents — Ciliated Zoospores

LIFE HISTORY DIAGRAM

Adult Myxopod or Amœboid stage

Cilia gone — Amœboid-Stage — Mastigopods (Zoospores) — 6 — 1 — Plasmodium (fused Myxopods or Compound Zygospore) — Rounded Spores — 5 — 3 — Encysted form (Sporangium) — Segmented form (Capillitium) — 4

Engraved, Printed and Published by W. & A.K. Johnston, Edinburgh.

start with the Amœboid form as the first stage in the cycle. If the phases through which it passes are compared with those of Protomyxa—an undoubted animal found in the sea by Haeckel—it will be found that the agreement is striking.

The first, or Amœboid stage, has all the characters of an amœba, possessing a nucleus, throwing out processes in different directions, moving about, and taking in solid particles for food.

The second, or Plasmodium stage, consists of a number of amœboid masses run together to form one large spreading mass capable of a creeping motion, as already observed, along with internal motion of the contents. The nuclei of each originally independent mass remain distinct, so that there is coalescence of cells but not conjugation.

The third, or Encysted stage, is represented by the Sporangium. The irregularly-shaped Plasmodium assumes a more definite shape as its power of throwing out processes becomes weakened, and usually forms a rounded mass of protoplasm invested by a cellulose wall.

The fourth, or Segmented stage, is produced by the internal protoplasm, differentiating in such a way as to form a network of fibres, and the protoplasm still remaining in the meshes becomes the Spores. The hair-like structure, in the meshes of which the Spores are developed, is known as the Capillitium.

The fifth stage, or Rounded Spores. The contents of the liberated Spores escape and become—

The sixth stage, or Zoospores, which have two cilia, then one, and finally pass into the Amœboid form with which we started.

It will be evident from the above description that the Myxomycetes cannot retain their position among the conjugating forms of Fungi ; and even when their animal nature is considered they do not fall into the lowest strata either of Plant or Animal society.

PLATE VI.
SPIROGYRA, DESMIDS, and DIATOMS.

(Spirogyra chiefly after Sachs; Desmid and Diatom after Oersted.)

SPIROGYRA (Gr. *guros,* a ring) is readily recognised under the microscope from the spiral bands of green-coloured protoplasm. It floats in bright green masses near the surface of clear, fresh waters, such as ponds, and slips through the fingers on attempting to handle it.

The bands of coloured protoplasm are variable in their number and arrangement. They contain numerous starch-granules and oil globules, and a nucleus is present in each cell. This condensed portion of the protoplasm is surrounded by a layer of protoplasm, which sends delicate threads towards the cell-wall, giving the nucleus a star-like appearance. There is also a layer of protoplasm lining the cell-wall, to which these threads are attached, and this lining is made very evident by the application of iodine, which causes the protoplasm to contract and withdraw itself from the wall. The protoplasm is broken up into shreds and bands, because, being unable to fill the cell, the cavities are filled with cell-sap, and these, by spreading and increasing, finally leave the protoplasm in this scattered form. Protoplasm thus on the stretch, as it were, displays much of its intimate nature, which is concealed in the more uniform condition.

Multiplication of the cells takes place by Division, and Reproduction by Conjugation.

Fig. 1 Either take a small portion of the water in which odd pieces are floating, or a minute portion of the green mass, and examine under highest power.
Long filaments made up of cells, with distinct walls and green spiral bands, in which numerous granules are visible.
Diagram—Showing arrangement of bands.
Careful focussing is necessary to make out the exact continuity of the bands, and this may be made out better after treatment with reagents than in natural specimens.
In this particular species the bands are arranged in two spirals, which intersect each other. In S. longata (Fig. 4) there is but a single spiral band.
Fig 2 Stain with Iodine.
Iodine makes the nucleus prominent, turns the starch-granules blue, and causes the layer of protoplasm lining the cell-wall to contract about the spiral bands. This layer of protoplasm has received the name of "primordial utricle," but it is simply a portion of the protoplasm which lines the cell-wall.
Fig. 3 As division takes place during night, in order to get cells in the act of division place them in alcohol shortly after mid-night and examine with highest power.
The cellulose is seen to be extending inwards on each side.
Fig. 4a Cell in the living state, with single nucleus and regularly-arranged bands.
b Protoplasm contracted by the alcohol. Infolding of the protoplasm lining the wall, and cellulose formed in the notch.
Two nuclei formed during division, one for each new cell.
c Infolding further advanced, which would ultimately form a complete partition across.
Figs. 5 and 6 Conjugation.
Two filaments lay themselves alongside each other, and adjoining cells of each filament throw out pockets simultaneously towards each other, which eventually meet and form a connecting *tube* between the two cells. The contents of one cell pass over and fuse with that of the other, the nuclei also coalescing, thus producing a Zygospore, as in Fig. 6.
Fig. 7 Germination.
The outer wall of the Zygospore ruptures, and the innermost layer protrudes as a filament, gradually growing and forming transverse partitions until a proper filament is produced.

DESMIDS (Gr. *desmos,* a band) are beautiful, minute, green plants, found in fresh water, and consisting usually of a single cell. The cells are generally divided into two symmetrical halves, and the coloured protoplasm is arranged in bands.

Multiplication by Division is shown in next Plate. Sexual reproduction by Conjugation is shown here.

Fig. 8 Different views of Cosmarium, showing the two halves and the coloured bands.
Fig. 9 Two cells approach one another, the narrow waist ruptures, and the contents of each fuse.
Fig. 10 A single rounded mass is formed, with the empty halves of each Desmid still adhering to it.
Fig. 11 The Zygospore secretes a cellulose wall, which grows out into beautiful spines.
Fig. 12 The Zygospore escapes from its case and begins to germinate.
Fig. 13 Zygospore divides into two new Desmids, which lie across each other.

DIATOMS (Gr. *dia,* through; *temno,* I cut) are so named from the common genus Diatoma, in which the cell-walls, or Frustules (Lat. *frustum,* a fragment), remain connected in a zigzag fashion after each division, looking like a continuous structure cut up into a number of similar fragments. Various forms are sure to be met with while examining fresh-water Algæ, Euglena, and the like.

They are unicellular like the Desmids, but are yellowish in colour, have not the characteristic median constriction, and their cell-walls are silicious, exhibiting on their surface those beautiful markings which are a never-ending source of delight and interest to the microscopist. It is owing to this indestructible character of the cell-wall that Diatoms form geological deposits, and their beautiful structure has been preserved as finely as those living at the present day. The Diatom muds, of a pale straw colour, beneath peat-mosses, have acquired great importance recently from being used in the manufacture of dynamite, which is a combination of the silicious material with nitro-glycerine.

They exhibit slow movement from place to place, and exposed to light in considerable numbers they evolve oxygen.

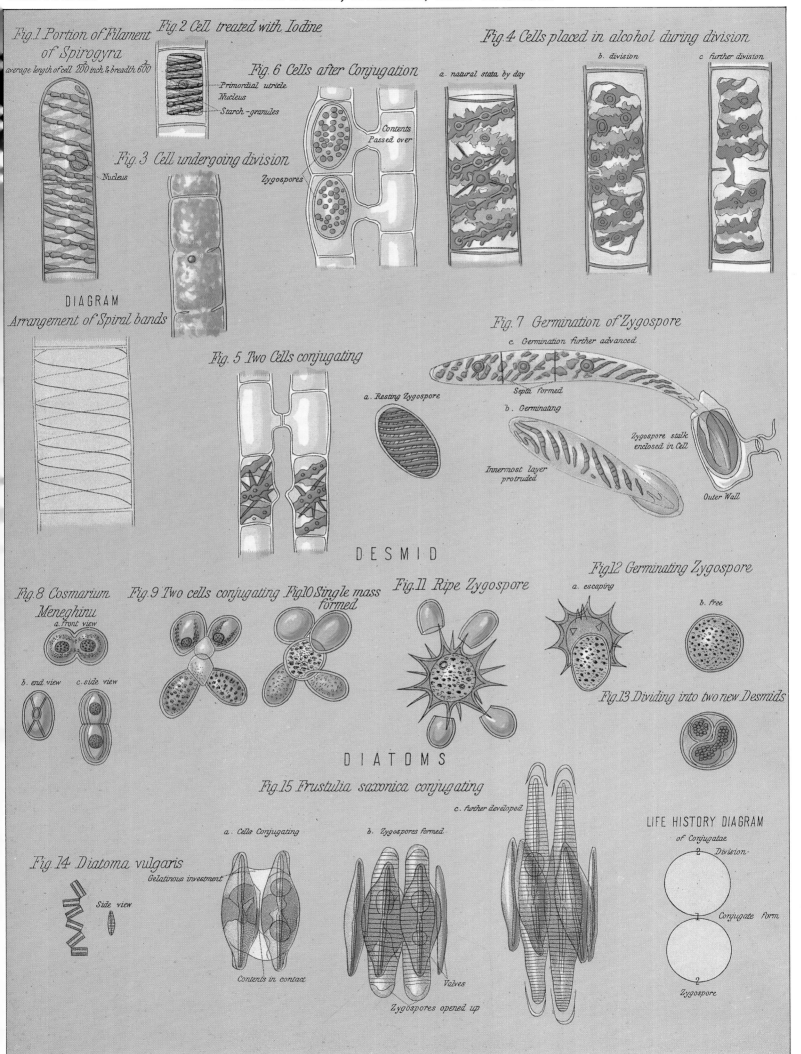

Fig.1 Portion of Filament of Spirogyra
average length of cell 200 inch & breadth 600
Nucleus

Fig.2 Cell treated with Iodine
Primordial utricle
Nucleus
Starch-granules

Fig. 3 Cell undergoing division

DIAGRAM
Arrangement of Spiral bands

Fig. 6 Cells after Conjugation
Contents Passed over
Zygospores

Fig.4 Cells placed in alcohol during division
a. natural state by day
b. division
c further division

Fig. 5 Two Cells conjugating

Fig. 7 Germination of Zygospore
c. Germination further advanced
Septa formed
a. Resting Zygospore
b. Germinating
Innermost layer protruded
Zygospore stalk enclosed in Cell
Outer Wall

DESMID

Fig.8 Cosmarium Meneghinii
a.front view
b. end view
c. side view

Fig.9 Two cells conjugating

Fig.10 Single mass formed

Fig.11 Ripe Zygospore

Fig.12 Germinating Zygospore
a. escaping
b. free

Fig.13 Dividing into two new Desmids

DIATOMS

Fig.15 Frustulia saxonica conjugating
a. Cells Conjugating
Gelatinous investment
Contents in contact
b. Zygospores formed
c. further developed
Valves
Zygospores opened up

Fig.14 Diatoma vulgaris
Side view

LIFE HISTORY DIAGRAM
of Conjugatae
Division
Conjugate form
Zygospore

Engraved, Printed and Published by W. & A.K. Johnston, Edinburgh

Multiplication takes place by Division, Reproduction by Conjugation.

Fig. 14 Diatoma, a very common form. The cells formed by successive divisions remain slightly attached.
Fig. 15 Conjugation of Frustulia saxonica.

(*a.*) Two Diatoms beside each other surround themselves with a gelatinous mass, the valves then fall apart like an opened book, and the contents of each come together, but do not mix.

(*b.*) Next, the two contents clothe themselves with a delicate membrane, elongate, and form two Zygospores.
(*c.*) Each Zygospore now forms two valves, and becomes fully formed.

PLATE VII.

COSMARIUM BOTRYTIS—a Desmid.

(After Dodel-Port and De Bary.)

Desmids (Gr. *desmos,* a bond) are unicellular Algae, of a green colour, found in fresh-waters. They are remarkable for their beauty and symmetry of form, exhibiting division into two symmetrical halves, with a bond or connection between the two—hence the name. They multiply either by *division* or *conjugation.* Multiplication by division is the most common, and is that here shown.

Figures X 1450.

Fig. 1 Adult form in front view. The cell is divided by a deep constriction into two symmetrical halves. Each half looked at from the side is round, inclining to oval. The Cell-wall is marked by tuberosities scattered over it, giving it a remarkably elegant, sculptured appearance. Each half-cell contains protoplasm coloured green, two round starch grains, each with four chlorophyll-bands or green-coloured protoplasm lying over it, and several clear vacuoles containing a number of oscillating granules.

The Protoplasm generally is of a pale-green colour, only it becomes clear in the middle where the nucleus lies. The plates of protoplasm, the so-called "chlorophyll-bands," are of a dark-green colour, and only one-half the number are seen in this view. The Starch-grains are symmetrically disposed, two being on each side of the principal axis. The Vacuoles are filled with fluid, and lie between the starch-grains and the cell-wall. There are also a number of oil-drops scattered throughout the mass.

Figs. 2, 3, and 4 Multiplication by Division—
The central constricted portion lengthens, and a delicate partition forms, dividing the whole into two equal halves, as in Fig. 2.
Next, the daughter-cells thus formed increase in size, and the contents of each original portion begin to pass over, as in Fig. 3.
Finally, the newly-formed portions assume the dimensions of the old, as in Fig. 4, till, in about ten hours, two full-grown individuals appear.

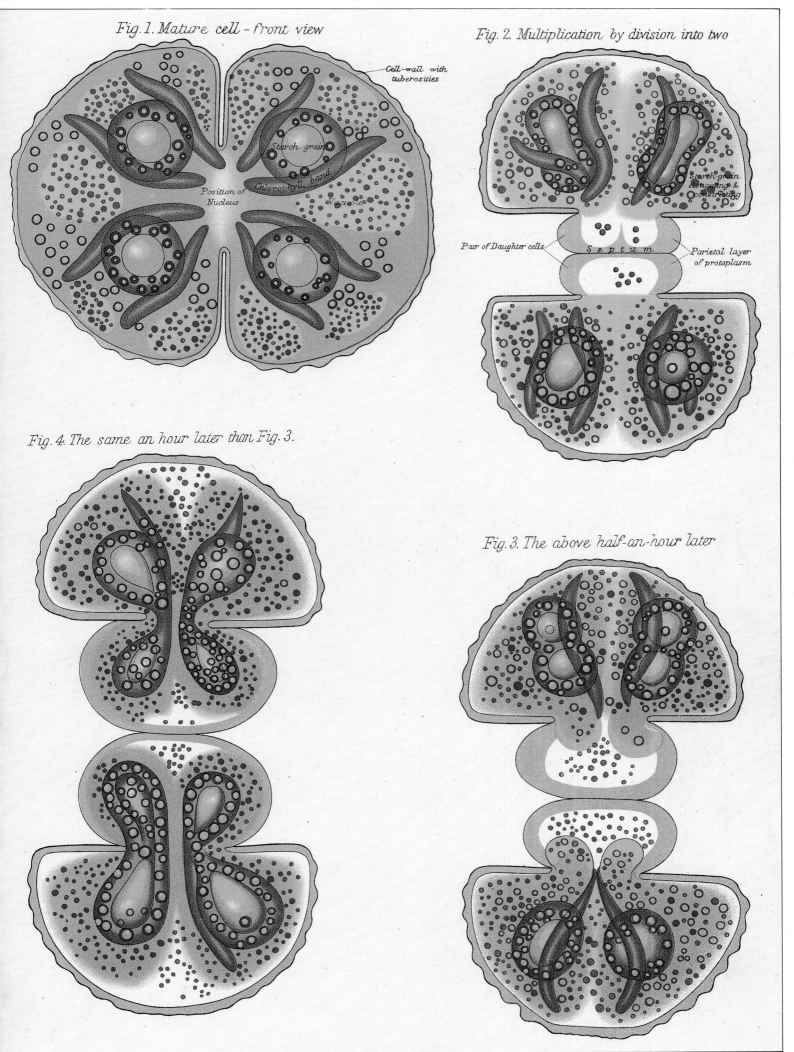

Fig. 1. Mature cell - front view

Cell-wall with tuberosities

Starch grain

Position of Nucleus

Chlorophyll band.

Vacuole

Fig. 2. Multiplication by division into two

Starch grain elongating & constricting

Pair of Daughter cells

Septum

Parietal layer of protoplasm

Fig. 4. The same an hour later than Fig. 3.

Fig. 3. The above half-an-hour later

Engraved, Printed and Published by W. & A.K. Johnston, Edinburgh & London.

PLATE VIII.

COMMON BROWN MOULD (*Mucor mucedo*).

(Conjugation after Brefeld.)

This Mould is to be found in damp, close places growing on a variety of substances. It may be obtained in a form suitable for examination either from bones, or from potatoes which have been pared and boiled. If the latter are allowed to stand for a few days in a covered dish, they produce a luxuriant crop. Mucor affords a good illustration of a simple form of the sexual process, in which two perfectly similar and stationary elements unite or *conjugate*, and produce a body capable of reproducing the plant.

Nuclei have been observed, although not shown in the drawings.

Fig. 1 Full-grown Mycelium developed from the gonidium.
The gonidium sends out various prolongations, which branch in all directions, so that the entire mycelium is formed, consisting of a tubular single cell. But at a further stage *septa* are formed in various parts, so that it becomes multi-cellular.
From a swelling an aerial branch arises, terminating in the young sporangium.
Fig. 2 Sporangium containing spores.
The swollen head of the aerial hypha becomes divided off by a partition, and this bulging up into the interior constitutes the Columella.
The Sporangium-wall becomes coated with needle-like crystals of oxalate of lime.
The Endo-gonidia are formed from the protoplasm in the interior and become coated with a cellulose wall.
The residue of the protoplasm forms an intermediate substance capable of swelling.
Fig. 3 Ruptured Sporangium.
The sporangium having imbibed moisture swells. The outermost layer is brittle but not distensible, so with the swelling of the innermost layer and the intermediate substance, it bursts, setting free the gonidia, and often leaving a remnant in the torn collar.
Figs. 4 and 5 Gonidia germinating.
The outer coat of the spore is inelastic, and the inner protrudes as a filament, growing and branching till it becomes full-grown, as in Fig. 1.
Fig. 6 Gonidia are not only produced by aerial hyphæ, but not unfrequently from old *submerged* hyphæ. Septa arise close to one another, forming distinct joints, and these become rounded off, fall away, and are able, under favourable conditions, to germinate. These bodies are the so-called Mucor-yeast or Chlamydo-spores (Lat. *chlamys,* a cloak).
Fig. 7 The sexual process—Conjugation.
Branches from two adjacent filaments of the Mycelium approach, the double wall between them is absorbed, and on each side of the central portion a partition is formed, thus marking off the Zygospore.
Fig. 8 Ripe Zygospore with thickened granulated outer wall.
Fig. 9 Zygospore germinating.
It produces a single hypha, which sends up an aerial branch forming a Sporangium in which Endo-gonidia are produced in the ordinary way.

Life History of Mucor.—The mycelium of Mucor produces upright branches in the swollen ends of which gonidia are produced. giving rise, on germination, to a new Mucor, or submerged hyphæ produce gonidia with the same result. This mode of multiplication is non-sexual, but sexual reproduction also occurs. Two short branches unite end to end, forming a Zygospore. This Zygospore germinates, producing an upright branch with a sporangium at the end, and the gonidia give rise to the non-sexual generation as at first.

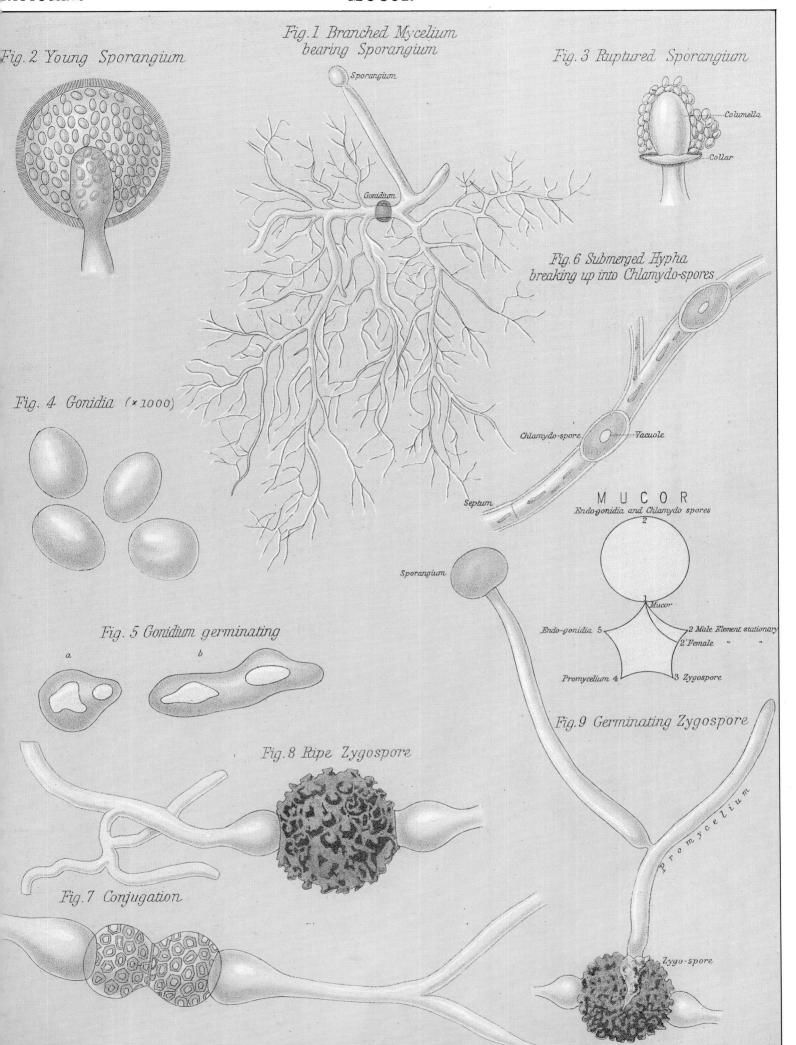

Fig.1 Branched Mycelium bearing Sporangium

Fig.2 Young Sporangium

Fig.3 Ruptured Sporangium

Fig.6 Submerged Hypha breaking up into Chlamydo-spores

Fig. 4 Gonidia (×1000)

Fig. 5 Gonidium germinating

Fig.8 Ripe Zygospore

Fig.7 Conjugation

Fig.9 Germinating Zygospore

MUCOR — Endo-gonidia and Chlamydo spores

Engraved, Printed and Published by W. & A.K. Johnston, Edinburgh

PLATE IX.

THE ROLLING SPHERE (*Volvox globator*).

(From Dodel-Port.)

Volvox, so named from its rolling motion, is found in fresh-water pools, and attains a size sufficient to be distinguished by the naked eye. It is a hollow sphere, and the entire periphery is formed of small cells, each furnished with two cilia. Its slow, stately, rolling motion is due to the harmonious action of these cilia. The sphere consists of vegetative cells and reproductive cells. It is so large that it would be a physical impossibility for every cell to undergo a process of division, and as the organization becomes more complex there arises a necessity for a division of labour. The work, which in a simpler form every portion of the organism was fitted to do, has now to be distributed and assigned to certain cells. Cells are thus set apart for the work of reproduction from a very early period, and are much larger than the vegetative cells. Not only so, but the male and female elements are decidedly different; in the one case being a tapering portion of protoplasm provided with cilia and motile, in the other a stationary rounded ball of protoplasm. Thus the two elements of reproduction are becoming more and more distinct. At first they were undistinguishable, as in Mucor; next distinguishable only in size, as in Pandorina; but now their form as well as their dimensions are different.

When Volvox is kept in a warm room, it has been observed in some cases that the protoplasm strays from the cells and creeps about in the water after the manner of an amoeba. Here the green protoplasm of a plant behaves like the protoplasm of an animal, putting forth processes and progressing by reason of the contractility of the protoplasm. It shows that the fundamental difference between the lower plants and the lower animals consists in the one being free to move and the other not. Plants have their protoplasm inclosed in a rigid cell-wall, which curbs and restrains them, and under such conditions the protoplasm is forced to behave differently.

Fig. 1 Volvox-sphere in the sexual stage.
Reproductive cells.—Female Zoospores are flask-shaped at first, but finally become spherical. This stationary rounded mass of protoplasm is now called the Oosphere, and with its gelatinous cell-wall is called the Oogonium.
Antheridia, containing bundles of Antherozoids, or sperm-cells.
Fig. 2 Portion of periphery much

magnified.
Reproductive cell relatively large, with nucleus and nucleolus. Vegetative cells smaller, often with red "eyespot."
Fig. 3 The Antherozoids have bored through the gelatinous investment of the Oogonium, and now surround the Oosphere.
Fig. 4 The outer investment of the unripe Oospore is a firm and spinous Exosporium, while the inner is a gelatinous Endosporium.

Fig. 5 Antheridium, with its gelatinous investment containing the bundle of Antherozoids.
Fig. 6 Iodine kills the Antherozoids, and makes their cilia distinct.
The Antherozoids are of a whiplash shape, with a pair of cilia towards the rounded end.
Fig. 7 The Antherozoids have a wriggling movement, caused by the expansion and contraction of their bodies, aided by the cilia.

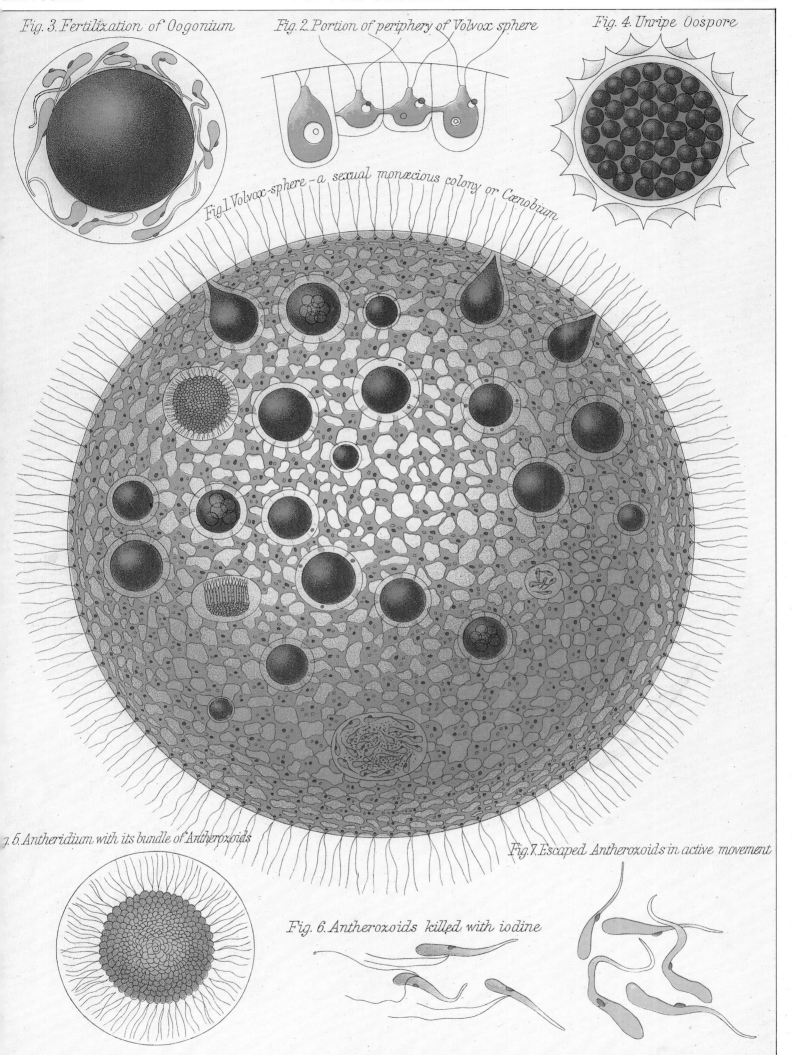

Fig. 3. Fertilization of Oogonium

Fig. 2. Portion of periphery of Volvox sphere

Fig. 4. Unripe Oospore

Fig.1. Volvox-sphere – a sexual monœcious colony or Cœnobium

g. 5. Antheridium with its bundle of Antherozoids

Fig. 7. Escaped Antherozoids in active movement

Fig. 6. Antherozoids killed with iodine

Engraved, Printed and Published by W. & A.K. Johnston, Edinburgh

PLATE X.

VOLVOX MINOR.

(From Dodel-Port, after Dr Kirchner.)

Volvox minor produces both male and female cells in the same colony, but they are ready at different times—the female first, the male afterwards. The germinating Oospore is shown in this Plate, and it is only within the last few years that the process has been traced. The preliminary act in this life drama is shown in the blending of the Antherozoids with the Oosphere. This sets agoing that activity in the cell which finally issues in the formation of a young Volvox-sphere.

Figures X 880.

Fig. 1 Oosphere and Antherozoids in contact.
The floating Antherozoids find their way to an Oosphere, and readily blend with it. This is the process of Fertilisation—and the result is an Oospore.
Fig 2 Ripe Oospore invested by two coats—an outer (Exosporium) and an inner (Endosporium). The investment is unlike that of *V. globator* in being smooth.
Fig. 3 Exosporium ruptured.
The swelling contents cause the rupture of the outer coat, and the Oospore is now free to undergo division.
Fig. 4 First division into two.

Fig. 5 Division at right angles to the first, forming four daughter-cells.
Fig. 6 After division into eight comes division into sixteen. The Exosporium in this instance has remained attached.
Fig. 7 Young Volvox formed, green and motile, after about nine divisions altogether in geometrical progression.

Life History of Volvox.—Volvox multiplies *non-sexually*, a single cell repeatedly dividing and producing a new colony, or there is *sexual reproduction* by Antheridia and Oogonia. The Antheridia or male cells are larger than the vegetative cells, and their contents break up into Antherozoids. The Oogonia or female cells are at first flask-shaped, but latterly become spherical, each containing a rounded mass of protoplasm—the Oosphere. The Antherozoids floating in the water ultimately come into contact with a liberated Oogonium, bore through its gelatinous wall, and being merely protoplasm destitute of any investment, they blend with the Oosphere, and so produce a body ready to germinate, now called the Oospore. The future history of the Oospore is indicated in this Plate, where it is seen by repeated divisions to form a young Volvox.

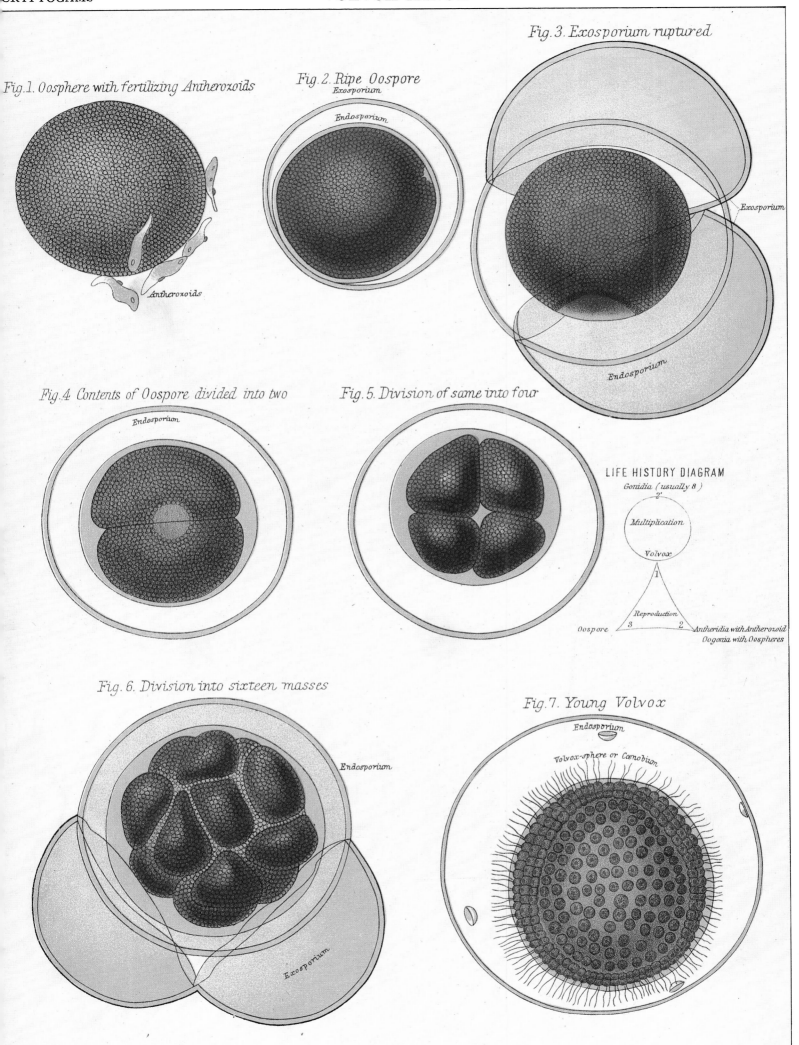

Fig. 1. Oosphere with fertilizing Antherozoids

Antheroxoids

Fig. 2. Ripe Oospore

Exosporium

Endosporium

Fig. 3. Exosporium ruptured

Exosporium

Endosporium

Fig. 4 Contents of Oospore divided into two

Endosporium

Fig. 5. Division of same into four

LIFE HISTORY DIAGRAM

Gonidia (usually 8)

2′

Multiplication

Volvox

1

Reproduction

3   2

Oospore   Antheridia with Antherozoid

Oogonia with Oospheres

Fig. 6. Division into sixteen masses

Endosporium

Exosporium

Fig. 7. Young Volvox

Endosporium

Volvox-sphere or Cœnobium

Engraved, Printed and Published by W & A.K. Johnston, Edinburgh & London.

PLATE XI.

VAUCHERIA and ŒDOGONIUM.

VAUCHERIA.

Vaucheria, named in honour of the Swiss botanist Vaucher, occurs usually on damp soils as a green film, but may readily be obtained from the surface earth of flower-pots kept in green-houses. It is a long filamentous green Alga, consisting of a single tubular cell which branches, and also forms root-like structures.

Fig. 1 Take a small portion of the green film, tease it out in a drop of water, and examine under microscope. Filament showing the granular protoplasm lining interior of tube.

MULTIPLICATION

Fig. 2 End of branches forming Zoogonidia.
These are formed during night, by the protoplasm, towards the end of a tube, collecting itself into an oval mass and becoming separate from the rest by a partition. The end of the tube gives way allowing this oval mass to escape into the surrounding moisture, where it revolves and progresses by means of delicate cilia with which the whole surface is covered. The cilia, however, soon disappear, and the motionless mass then sinks to the bottom.

Fig. 3a, b, c Germinating Zoogonidium—It gives rise to filaments at two or even three points, which branch and grow to the size of the parent. Delicate transparent branches are also formed (as in *c*) which serve to fix the plant to solid bodies, and thus partly serve the purpose of rootlets.

REPRODUCTION

Figs. 4 and 5 Male and Female Organs—Antheridia and Oogonia. Both organs arise as branches, sometimes as in Fig. 4, or as in Fig. 5, where a branch ends in a hooked Antheridium, with an Oogonium on each side below it.

The contents of the Antheridium break up into minute particles of protoplasm, each furnished with two cilia and motile—called Antherozoids. The Oogonium forms a single body in its interior-the Oosphere which is a portion of the protoplasm marked off from the rest by a partition. It is relatively large and motionless, and the antherozoids find access to it through a rupture in the cell-wall, thus converting it into an Oospore.

Fig. 6 Germinating Oospore.
The Oospore is surrounded by a three-layered membrane and, after resting for a few months, the contents protrude to form a branching tube.

Life History.—Vaucheria either multiplies by Zoogonidia, or reproduces itself by means of Antherozoids and Oospheres. The naked protoplasm of the Antherozoids blends with the naked protoplasm of the Oosphere, and the result is a body capable of germination—an Oosphere. This surrounds itself with a membrane, becomes detached along with the Oogonium, and is finally set free by the dissolution of the Oogonium. After a period of rest it germinates and gives rise to the original branched structure.

ŒDOGONIUM

(*After Juranyi.*)

Œdogonium (Gr. *oideo,* to swell; *gone,* seed) derives its name from the fact that the joints of the filament swell out to form the female organs. It may be looked for in waters where Conferva and such organisms are found, and occurs as patches of green filaments, composed of cells attached end to end.

Fig. 7 Young Filament, consisting of a row of cells.
The green-coloured protoplasm is arranged in stars and stripes, and each cell has a distinct nucleus.

MULTIPLICATION

Fig. 8 Zoogonidia produced in the cells.
The protoplasmic contents of each cell form a single rounded mass—the Zoogonidium, which escapes by a fissure in the wall, and revolves and progresses by means of the band of cilia.

Fig. 9 Germination of Zoogonidium.
The zoogonidium loses its cilia and settles down, producing from the colourless ciliated end a root-like structure for fixing the plant, while the opposite end divides and forms a row of cells.

REPRODUCTION

Fig. 10 Male Filament.
The contents of certain cells become orange-yellow and produce the Antherozoids, which resemble the Zoogonidia in form and motion, differing mainly in the colour. In some cases, however, zoogonidia are formed in the cells, which become rudimentary plants, and the sole object of these *Dwarf-males*, as they are called, is to produce Antherozoids. They attach themselves to the Oogonium, as in Fig. I2, and the upper portion separates like a lid to allow the antherozoids to escape.

Figs. 11 and 12 Female Filaments.
The joints here and there are swollen, forming the Oogonia, which contain the Oospheres. The ripe Oosphere consists of a coloured and a small colourless portion, which protrudes through a small opening.

Fig. 13 Process of Fertilisation.
An Antherozoid blends with an Oosphere, and the result is an Oospore.

Fig. 14 Ripe Oospore.
It becomes surrounded with a membrane, and assumes an orange-red colour. The swelling of the Oospore finally ruptures the Oogonium, and the oospore escapes as a naked mass of protoplasm.

Figs 15, 16, and 17 Germinating Oospores. The germinating Oospore does not grow in the usual way, but surrounds itself with a new membrane, and the contents divide into four portions generally. The Zoospores thus formed are set free by the dissolution of the membrane, and produce a young plant, as in Fig. 17.

Life History.—Œdogonium multiplies by Zoogonidia, or is reproduced by Antherozoids and Oospheres. An Antherozoid produced either directly from the joint of a filament or through the intermediate agency of Dwarf-males, blends with the Oosphere and produces an orange-red Oosphere. This Oosphere does not directly produce the Plant, but divides into usually four Zoospores, like the zoogonidia, except in the matter of colour, and each germinates and grows into a filament, as in Fig. 17.

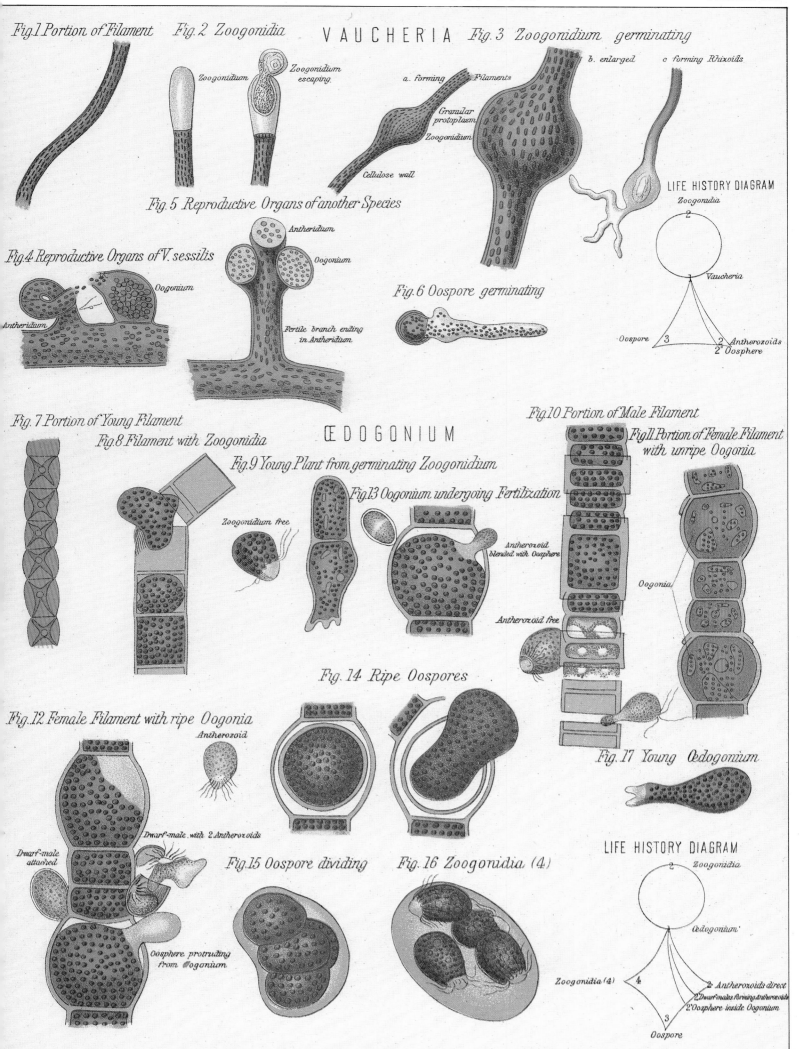

VAUCHERIA

Fig.1 *Portion of Filament*   Fig. 2 *Zoogonidia*   Fig. 3 *Zoogonidium germinating*

Zoogonidium

Zoogonidium escaping.

a. forming   Filaments

Granular protoplasm

Zoogonidium

Cellulose wall

b. enlarged   c forming Rhixoids

LIFE HISTORY DIAGRAM
Zoogonidia
2
Vaucheria
Oospore   3   2 Antherozoids
2 Oosphere

Fig. 5 *Reproductive Organs of another Species*

Antheridium

Oogonium

Fig.4 *Reproductive Organs of V. sessilis*

Oogonium

Antheridium

Fertile branch ending in Antheridium

Fig. 6 *Oospore germinating*

ŒDOGONIUM

Fig. 7 *Portion of Young Filament*

Fig.8 *Filament with Zoogonidia*

Fig.9 *Young Plant from germinating Zoogonidium*

Zoogonidium free

Fig.13 *Oogonium undergoing Fertilization*

Antherozoid blended with Oosphere

Antherozoid free

Fig.10 *Portion of Male Filament*

Fig.11 *Portion of Female Filament with unripe Oogonia*

Oogonia

Fig.14 *Ripe Oospores*

Fig.12 *Female Filament with ripe Oogonia*

Antherozoid

Dwarf-male with 2 Antherozoids

Dwarf-male attached

Oosphere protruding from Oogonium

Fig.17 *Young Œdogonium*

Fig.15 *Oospore dividing*   Fig. 16 *Zoogonidia (4)*

LIFE HISTORY DIAGRAM
Zoogonidia
2
Œdogonium
Zoogonidia (4)   4   2 Antherozoids direct
2 Dwarf males forming Antherozoids
2 Oosphere inside Oogonium
3
Oospore

Engraved, Printed and Published by W. & A.K. Johnston, Edinburgh & London.

PLATE XII.

POTATO-DISEASE FUNGUS (*Phytophthora infestans*).

(Principally after De Bary.)

The Potato-disease Fungus was formerly known as *Peronospora*, but the fuller investigation of its history has caused it to be placed in the genus *Phytopthora*. Although its life-history has been traced to a certain extent, yet, as in the case of Rust of Wheat and other parasitic fungi, a satisfactory mode of dealing with the disease has not yet been found.

It is but fair to add that some consider this fungus-growth as a consequence and not as a cause of the disease. They maintain that a fungus cannot establish itself upon a living plant, until that plant has become enfeebled; and further, that before any appearance of the disease in the potato could be detected by the eye or microscope, it was possible to reveal it by a simple chemical test. This was done by using a minute borer and taking a thread of the potato bored out and placing it in a flask with milk in a warm closet. If the milk curdled in a very short time, the potato was found to be diseased; and if healthy, no curdling took place. The diseased potato soon showed signs of decay and of premature germination, and so the actual disease is supposed to be antecedent to the appearance of the fungus.

Fig. 1 Diseased Leaf of Potato. The infected parts of the leaf turn black.

Figs. 2 and 3 Hypha bearing Stylo-gonidia. The filament bores its way through the tissues of the plant, absorbs and appropriates their nutriment, and gradually traverses the whole plant.

Eventually it puts forth hyphæ through the stomata of the leaf, which branch and bear capsules styled *Stylo-gonidia*.

Figs. 4, 5, and 6 The contents of the Stylo-gonidium break up into separate portions (usually six), which escape by rupturing the wall.

Fig. 7 Each Zoogonidium possess a pair of cilia, and through the medium of rain or dew may find their way from one plant to another and thus infect a whole field.

Fig. 8 Zoogonidium germinating. The inner membrane protrudes as a filament, penetrating the epidermis, and begins to ramify through the underlying tissue.

Life History. — The fungus traversing the potato-plant bears aerial hyphae with Stylo-gonidia, the contents of which break up into Zoogonidia. These motile Zoogonidia, on reaching the epidermis of a potato-plant, germinate to form a unicellular filament which branches among the tissues and becomes like the parent-form. This is the non-sexual mode of multiplication, but a sexual process has not yet been observed.

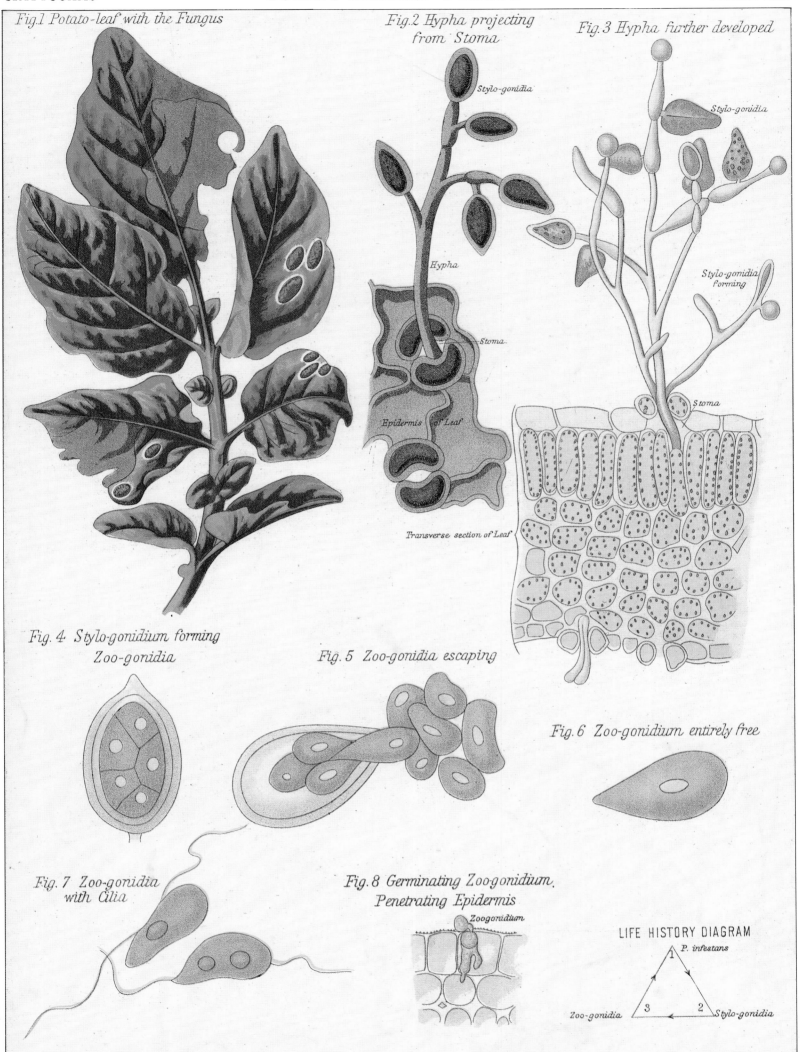

Fig.1 Potato-leaf with the Fungus

Fig.2 Hypha projecting from Stoma

Stylo-gonidia

Hypha

Stoma.

Epidermis of Leaf

Transverse section of Leaf

Fig.3 Hypha further developed

Stylo-gonidia

Stylo-gonidia forming

Stoma

Fig. 4 Stylo-gonidium forming Zoo-gonidia

Fig. 5 Zoo-gonidia escaping

Fig.6 Zoo-gonidium entirely free

Fig. 7 Zoo-gonidia with Cilia

Fig.8 Germinating Zoo-gonidium Penetrating Epidermis

Zoogonidium

LIFE HISTORY DIAGRAM

P. infestans

1

Zoo-gonidia   3   2   Stylo-gonidia

Engraved, Printed and Published by W. & A.K. Johnston, Edinburgh.

PLATE XIII.

COMMON BLADDER WRACK (*Fucus vesiculosus*) and TANGLE (*Laminaria digitata*).

Fucus (G. *phukos,* sea-weed) and Laminaria (Lat. *lamina,* a thin plate) may be taken as representatives of the brown-coloured sea-weeds. They are common objects of the shore wherever rocks abound.

In *Fucus,* the flat expansion or Thallus is dichotomously branched, and attached to the rocks by suckers, so that there is a superficial resemblance to stem, roots, and leaves. But it is only superficial, since the whole plant is bathed with sea-water from which, and not from the soil or air, every part withdraws its appropriate nourishment. The root-like portion consists of delicate hair-like branches with thin cell-walls. It acts like a boy's sucker; it can be pressed very close to the rock, and the pressure of the water, just like the air in the previous case, keeps the two together.

The stem-like narrow portion, as well as the more expanded upper portion, is slimy all over, and this is due to the cell-walls of the outer cells becoming mucilaginous.

The air-bladders serving the purpose of floats contain various gases.

The reproductive organs are borne by the swollen ends of branches and developed in little cavities known as Conceptacles. These are seen by the naked eye as little elevations with openings, and have been formed by a pushing-in or indentation of the exterior. Each dimple or Conceptacle contains Antheridia with Antherozoids or male organs, and Oogonia with Oospheres or female organs.

The most common species are *F. vesiculosis* (Lat. *vesicula,* a little bladder) with a midrib running along each part of the thallus, and air-bladders arranged in a double row; *F. nodosus,* with air-bladders arranged singly and no midrib; and *F. serratus* (Lat. *serra,* a saw) destitute of air-bladders and margins toothed.

Laminaria digitata (Lat. *digitus,* the finger) is so named because the expanded portion is split up like the fingers of the hand. It has a root-like portion consisting of numerous branching stalks expanded at their attached end; a stem-like portion which is perennial, and increases in thickness by concentric layers added year after year; and the split-up leaf-like portion which is renewed every year.

Multiplication takes place by Zoogonidia developed from the expanded portion. Sexual reproduction is as yet unknown.

Fig. 1 Portion of plant, natural size. Thallus branching in a forked manner or dichotomously, with a well-marked midrib.
Air-bladders occurring in a double series.
Fertile branches swollen and studded over with little papillæ.
Fig. 2 Make a transverse section of a fertile branch, so as to get one of these little papillae in section which are called Conceptacles. There is a confused mass of hairs, amongst which may be seen the male and female organs. The close-set cells of the exterior are continued right round the Conceptacle, thus suggesting an infolding of the exterior and not an interior cavity afterwards opening externally.
Antheridia, branching hairs.

Oogonia, swollen hairs.
Figs. 3 and 4 Take some of the yellow colouring matter from Conceptacle and mix with salt-water to see Antheridial hairs and Oogonia clearly, Antheridial hairs repeatedly branched, the ends of the branches swollen and filled with yellow granular matter. When ripe the contents of these cells consist of Antherozoids each provided with two cilia whereby they move rapidly about in the water.
Oogonia are globular bodies, derived from a single cell and producing eight Oospheres. The protoplasm of the surrounding hairs and stalk is broken up into threads, because of the numerous vacuoles formed, owing to the cells getting too large for their contents, as in Spirogyra.
Fig. 5 Oogonium discharging its

contents.
The wall of the Oogonium consists of two layers—an outer, inelastic, which splits, and an inner, extensible, which stretches a deal before giving way.
The Oospheres are discharged into the conceptacle, then into the surrounding water.
Fig. 6 The liberated Oospheres meet with Antherozoids which surround them, blend with them, and convert them into Oospores, ready to germinate.
Fig. 7 Germination of an Oospore. It first becomes pear-shaped, then divides into two, and the tapering end soon develops organs of attachment. The upper end divides further and further in all the dimensions of space until the adult form is attained.

Life History.—Fucus reproduces itself sexually by Antheridia and Oogonia, either produced together or on separate plants. The Antherozoids or the Antheridia fertilise the Oospheres of the Oogonia after being set free, and each Oospore thus produced may develop a new plant.

HISTOLOGY.

Fig. 8 Make a transverse section of the narrow stem-like portion, and examine in alcohol or glycerine under low power.
Cells close-set towards exterior, but arranged loosely in interior.
Fig. 9 Stain transverse section with magenta, and examine under high power.
Cells are round, oval, or elongated,

and cell-walls very gelatinous.
Fig. 10 Cut across Tangle and examine—*first,* with naked eye; *second,* a transverse section under low power.
(*a.*) Outer yellowish-brown portion, and inner colourless portion.
(*b.*) Outer coloured portion, small and close-set cells. In old specimens there is a ring of oval slime-cavities pretty near one another. Inner almost

colourless portion of larger cells.
Fig. 11 Make a longitudinal section, and examine interior cells as in Fucus. The elongated cells are bounded by a firm inner membrane, and between this membrane, of two adjoining cells, there is a gelatinous intercellular substance often arranged in layers. Short Pits occur here and there in the membrane.

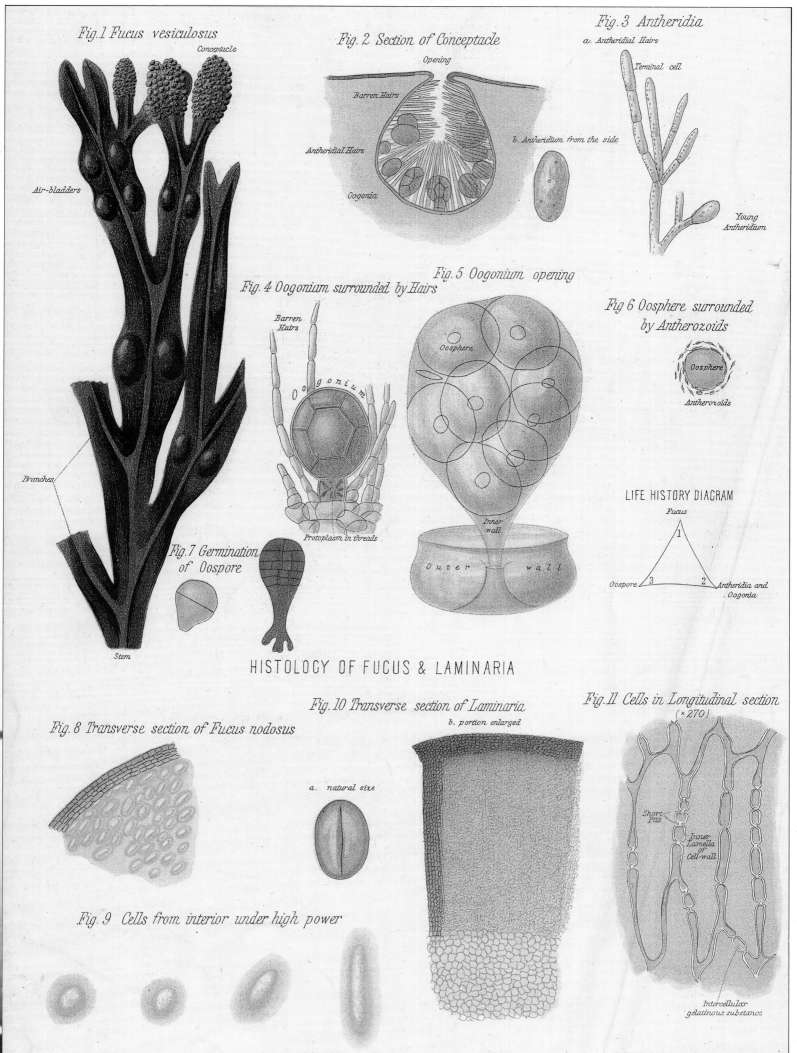

Fig.1 Fucus vesiculosus

Conceptacle

Air-bladders

Branches

Stem

Fig. 2 Section of Conceptacle

Opening

Barren Hairs

Antheridial Hairs

Oogonia

Fig. 3 Antheridia

a. Antheridial Hairs

Terminal cell

b. Antheridium from the side

Young Antheridium

Fig. 4 Oogonium surrounded by Hairs

Barren Hairs

Oogonium

Protoplasm in threads

Fig. 5 Oogonium opening

Oosphere

Inner wall

Outer wall

Fig 6 Oosphere surrounded by Antherozoids

Oosphere

Antherozoids

LIFE HISTORY DIAGRAM

Fucus

1

Oospore 3

2 Antheridia and Oogonia

Fig. 7 Germination of Oospore

HISTOLOGY OF FUCUS & LAMINARIA

Fig. 8 Transverse section of Fucus nodosus

Fig. 9 Cells from interior under high power

Fig. 10 Transverse section of Laminaria

b. portion enlarged

a. natural size

Fig. 11 Cells in Longitudinal section (×270)

Short Pits

Inner Lamella of Cell-wall

Intercellular gelatinous substance

Engraved, Printed and Published by W. & A.K. Johnston, Edinburgh

PLATE XIV.

PEZIZA AND PENICILLIUM.

PEZIZA.

The Pezizæ are usually found on decaying vegetable matter, such as rotten wood, old cow-dung, dunghills, and the like. They also grow among moss, and may occur on growing plants. The Spore-fruit, which results from Fertilisation, is disc-like or cup-shaped, stalked or sessile, and may be black or white, red or yellow, etc. The mycelium ramifies through the substance on which it grows; for instance, the bright green colour often staining as it were decayed wood, is due to these mycelial threads.

Fig. 1 Piece of rotten wood with Spore-fruits of peziza upon it. This specimen is pretty common in such situations, and has a brightly coloured spore-fruit with stiff hairs on its margin.

Fig. 2 Scrape off with a needle a little of the surface of the spore-fruit, tease out in water, and examine with high power.

A number of radiating filaments will be seen, many slender, fewer swollen. The slender filaments are barren, while the swollen filaments contain spores to the number of eight. The barren filaments are called Paraphyses, and the spore-bearing filaments Asci (Gr. *Askos*, a bag), hence the spores are Ascospores.

Fig. 3 Ascus and Ascospore detached.

The eight Spores are usually arranged obliquely, following one another, and in the centre of each is a Nucleus.

Fig. 4 Formation of Spores in the Asci of *P. confluens*.

In the early stage (*a*) the small sac is filled with granular protoplasm and a few vacuoles, but no nucleus.

Next, a nucleus appears with a nucleolus (*b*). By repeated division this original nucleus becomes divided into two, four, and finally eight nuclei (*f*). The protoplasm now begins to aggregate around each as a preliminary operation in the formation of the spores, until finally the ripe spores are produced (*h*). Each spore is now surrounded by a firm membrane, the nucleus disappears, and a small oil-globule appears at each end.

Fig. 5 Reproduction of *P. confluens*. (The Male and Female organs are coloured artificially—male, red; female, blue.) Adjoining branches of the mycelium form respectively the slender Male organ or Antheridium, and the swollen Female organ or Carpogonium. The free end of the Antheridium comes into contact with the hooked end of the Carpogonium (*a*), and, as a result of Fertilisation, a Spore-fruit is formed with innumerable spores. This Spore-fruit consists not only of the fertilised Carpogonium, but of an investment of delicate hyphæ (*b*) which grow and branch till they finally form the coloured cup on the surface of which the Asci lies.

PENICILLIUM.

Common Green Mould or Penicillium (Lat. *penicillium*, a painter's brush) is so named from the brush-like form of the fertile hyphae, bearing innumerable gonidia which give the familiar greyish-green hue to the mould. These minute gonidia on reaching a suitable medium are able to germinate, hence it is that the mould spreads with such wonderful rapidity and appears so constantly where the conditions are favourable. But even under unfavourable conditions, the mould can still survive and reproduce itself. If the supply of Oxygen is checked, so that the ordinary course of life cannot be run, then it resorts to a sexual process, just as a plant might throw itself into flower when food-supplies are limited.

Fig. 6 Remove a small piece of the crust with its green covering and tease out in water. Fertile hyphæ may be met with.

Hypha branching, contents granular with vacuoles, divided here and there by *septa*.

Fertile hypha branching regularly, the terminal branches breaking up into gonidia. The end portion of this small branch rounds itself off and becomes detachable, the new end repeats the same process, and so on till a row is formed.

Fig. 7 Sow some of the gonidia in a clear fluid, such as Pasteur's, to observe germination.

The Gonidium at first is spherical, but when germination begins, one or more protuberances appear which grow in length, divide, and form *septa*. Continued growth produces a mycelium bearing fertile hyphæ, and so the life-history repeats itself.

Fig. 8 The Sexual process has only been lately discovered, and occurs under peculiar conditions, as yet attained only by artificial means. The Male and Female organs are formed by short branches—the Antheridium being simple and the Carpogonium coiled like a cork-screw. These two come together and produce a Spore-fruit which is about the size of a pin-head.

Fig. 9 The Spore-fruit is naturally of a yellowish colour, and consists of a mass of Spore-bearing hyphæ, enclosed by sterile hyphæ.

Fig. 10 Portion of Spore-bearing tissue removed from Spore-fruit.

(*a.*) Asci, containing the Ascospores.

(*b.*) Ascospore, separate.

Fig. 11 Germinating Ascospore producing a mycelium like the Gonidium.

Life History of Penicillium. — Upright hyphæ give off numerous small branches which become rounded off at their ends to form gonidia. These gonidia germinate and give rise to a new plant. This is non-sexual multiplication, but sexual reproduction has recently been discovered by Brefeld.

When the plant is deprived of air and light, the development of gonidia is interfered with, and sexual organs appear. Two short hyphæ lay themselves together—Antheridium and Carpogonium—and the result of their union is a Spore-fruit, in which Spores are afterwards formed, contained in bags or Asci. Each Ascospore may germinate and produce a mycelium bearing aerial hyphæ as before.

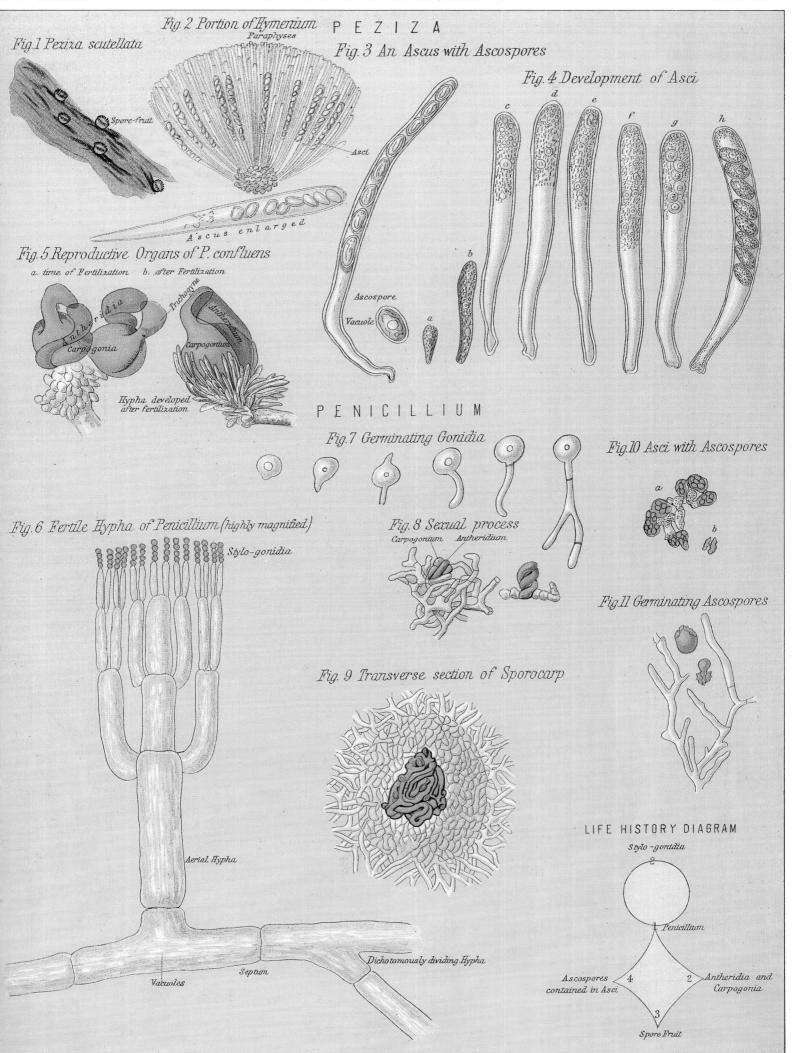

Fig.1 *Peziza scutellata*

Spore-fruit

Fig.2 Portion of Hymenium

Paraphyses

P E Z I Z A

Fig.3 An Ascus with Ascospores

Asci

Fig.4 Development of Asci

Ascus enlarged

Fig.5 *Reproductive Organs of P. confluens*

a. time of Fertilization   b. after Fertilization

Antheridia   Trichogyne

Carpogonia   Carpogonium   Antheridium

Hypha developed after fertilization

Ascospore

Vacuole

P E N I C I L L I U M

Fig.7 Germinating Gonidia

Fig.10 Asci with Ascospores

Fig.6 *Fertile Hypha of Penicillium (highly magnified)*

Stylo-gonidia

Fig.8 Sexual process

Carpogonium   Antheridium

Fig.11 Germinating Ascospores

Aerial Hypha

Fig.9 Transverse section of Sporocarp

LIFE HISTORY DIAGRAM

Stylo-gonidia

Penicillium

Dichotomously dividing Hypha

Ascospores contained in Asci

Antheridia and Carpogonia

Vacuoles   Septum

Spore Fruit

Engraved, Printed and Published by W. & A.K. Johnston, Edinburgh

PLATE XV.

ICELAND MOSS (*Cetraria islandica*).

The *Lichen-thallus* is regarded, according to the most recent investigations, as forming not one individual organism but a kind of composite structure. It is a *commensal* organism, formed by the partnership of different individuals preying upon, and at the same time mutually accommodating, each other. The *hyphae* form one of the plants which is an Ascomycetous Fungus, and the gonidia or green cells form another plant which belongs to the Palmellaceous Algae, in this instance, viz.— *Cystococcus humicola*. These Algae living among the mycelial filaments of the Fungus supply them with nutriment, and receive in return that amount of moisture and protection, which enables them to grow and multiply. The hyphæ in fact are parasites upon the gonidia, abstracting from them the materials they manufacture as green plants. But the gonidia, though thus kept in check are not exterminated, and the survivors go on growing and multiplying, so that there is always an excess over and above the wants of the lichen. As the gonidia multiply so do the hyphæ, and the scale on which the business is carried on necessarily becomes larger. It is a combination for the supply of continually increasing wants, which almost suggests forethought in its striking adaptation.

Fig. 1 The so-called Iceland Moss is a *Lichen*, growing on the ground with its thallus erect. It may be procured in the dry state from the chemist, as it is used medicinally.
The lobes of the thallus are numerous and tufted, and the edges are fringed with short teeth. The so-called "fructification" is rare, and is called an Apothecium, because the surface of the receptacle is very slightly concave (when the receptacle is excessively concave, it is called a Perithecium).

Fig. 2 The Thallus or flat expansion of the Lichen shows in vertical section several distinct layers:—
Cortical or superficial layer of closely applied thick-walled cells.
Gonidial layer, a looser layer of intermingled hyphæ in the meshes of which are entangled green rounded cells—the "gonidia."
Medullary layer of thread-like cells forming the bulk of the thallus.
Cortical layer as above.

Fig. 3 Vertical section of the "Fructification" and underlying Thallus.
Asci containing Ascospores originating from the colourless filaments here called the Sub-hymenial layer.
Paraphyses are barren filaments.
Figs. 4 and 5 The Asci are club-shaped and the Ascospores are elliptical.
Fig. 6 Spermogonia occur on the margin of the thallus and produce Spermatia.

Life History.—The Sub-hymenial layer of the Thallus produces numerous Asci, each containing several Ascospores. The Asci absorb moisture as they ripen, causing their membranes to swell, until finally the tension is so great, at the top of the tube, that it gives way and the sudden collapse jerks out the spores. The moist spores are accompanied by hymenial gonidia and put forth several embryo-tubes, some of which lay hold of the substratum, and the others embrace the gonidia and ramify to form the thallus of the Lichen.

The Spermogonia are considered to be Male Organs; and as they appear before the fructification is formed, it is very probable that a Female Organ lies imbedded in the thallus, to which the Spermatia are conveyed by water. In this case the fructification would be developed as a result of fertilisation.

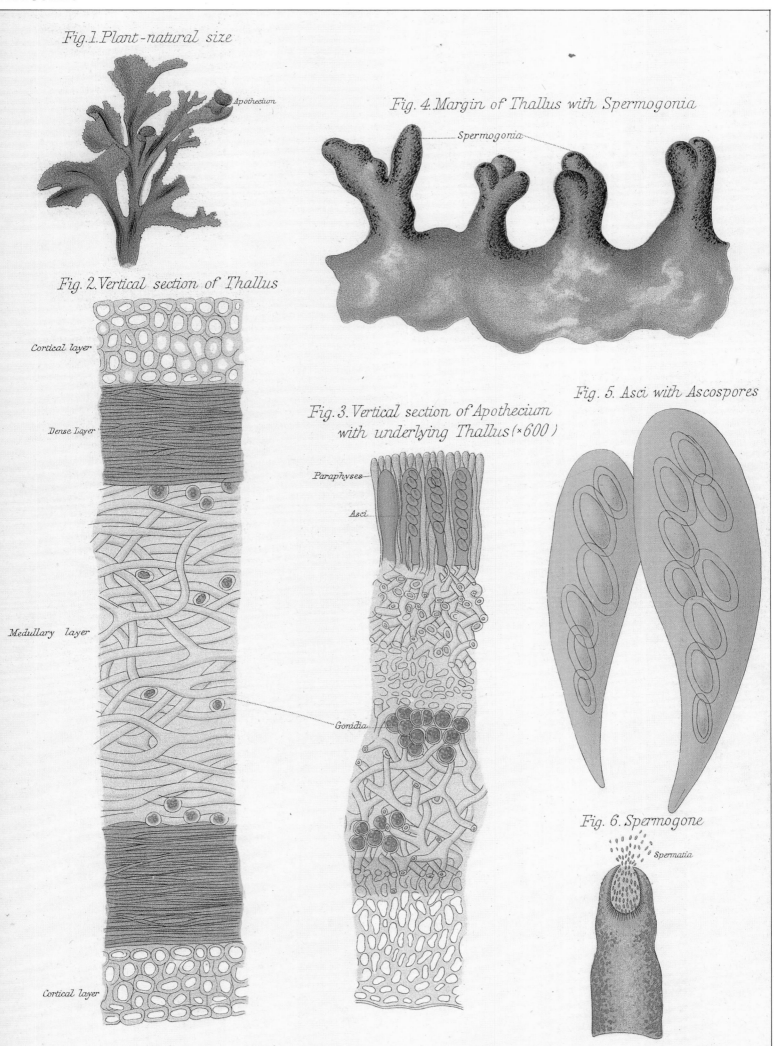

Fig.1. Plant-natural size

Apothecium

Fig. 4. Margin of Thallus with Spermogonia

Spermogonia

Fig. 2. Vertical section of Thallus

Cortical layer

Dense Layer

Medullary layer

Cortical layer

Fig. 5. Asci with Ascospores

Fig. 3. Vertical section of Apothecium with underlying Thallus (×600)

Paraphyses

Asci

Gonidia

Fig. 6. Spermogone

Spermatia

Engraved, Printed and Published by W. & A.K. Johnston, Edinburgh

PLATE XVI.

RUST OF WHEAT.

(After Dodel-Port, De Bary, and Tulasne.)

The Rust of Wheat is interesting on various grounds, for the varied forms it assumes, and the change of quarters it delights in, as well as for the effects produced by it. It has a curious history, owing to the fact that its connection with the Barberry was recognised by farmers in practice long before scientific men had traced or even dreamt of the connection. It was found out that in going its various rounds in order to complete its life history, there existed the same relation between Rust and Barberry as between Lodger and Boarder.

Although so well investigated, no remedy has yet been found for its ravages.

Fig. 1 Leaves of Barberry bearing yellow or orange patches on stalk and blade—the Aecidium-fruit. Towards the end of summer these patches appear, called Barberry rust.

Fig. 2 Transverse section of such a leaf. The mycelium of the fungus has penetrated through the tissue of the leaf, extracting nourishment and draining the leaf by the way. It has also produced a fructification of two kinds; one on the upper side, the other on the under side of the leaf. The Spermogonia are flask-shaped bodies on the upper surface, producing numerous filaments called Spermatia.

The Aecidium-fruit on the under surface is a globular body surrounded by a wall or peridium, which on opening allows the spores to escape.

Fig. 3 Aecidio-spore germinating. It sends out two filaments, which branch and form the Mycelium of the Rust.

Fig. 4 Streaks of a rusty colour appear on the surface of the leaf owing to the Uredo-spores bursting through.

Fig. 5 Transverse section of leaf. The mycelium ramifies through the tissues of the leaf and towards the surface, branches produce the Uredo-spores. These cause a swelling, and the epidermis ruptures, when the spores are easily blown about by the wind.

Fig. 6 Uredo-spores produced late in the summer along with Teleuto-spores. The double coat of the Uredo-spore is relatively thin, and covered with minute projections, while that of the Teleuto-spore is thick and brown.

Fig. 7 Uredo-spore germinating, and giving rise to a branched mycelium in the leaf, which again reproduces Uredo-spores, and so on.

Fig. 8 Teleuto-spore germinating. This spore is two-celled, and was formerly supposed to belong to a different fungus, which was named Puccinia graminis.

It forms a branching pro-mycelium of several cells, from the branches of which Sporidia arise.

Fig. 9 A Sporidium falling on the Barberry, when it is to be found in hedge-rows adjoining corn-fields, germinates on the under surface of the leaf, and produces the form in Fig. 1.

Life History.—The Cluster-cups, or Aecidium-fruits on the Barberry, produce numerous Aecidio-spores, which germinate on the damp leaves of Wheat. There a mycelium is formed, the Uredo, which gives rise to Uredo-spores, forming the rusty powder on the surface of the leaf. The Uredo-spores, or Summer-spores, may in turn germinate on a leaf of Wheat, produce a mycelium giving rise to Spores, and this course may be repeated over and over again, spreading the Rust till the harvest season. Then Teleuto-spores, or Winter-spores, are produced, which germinate next spring, and develop Sporidia at the end of branches of a short filament, which can form the Aecidium-fruits on the young Barberry leaf, as in Fig. I. The Rust of Wheat may appear even before the appearance of Barberry leaves, owing to the Uredo-spores persisting during the winter and directly germinating on the young Wheat.

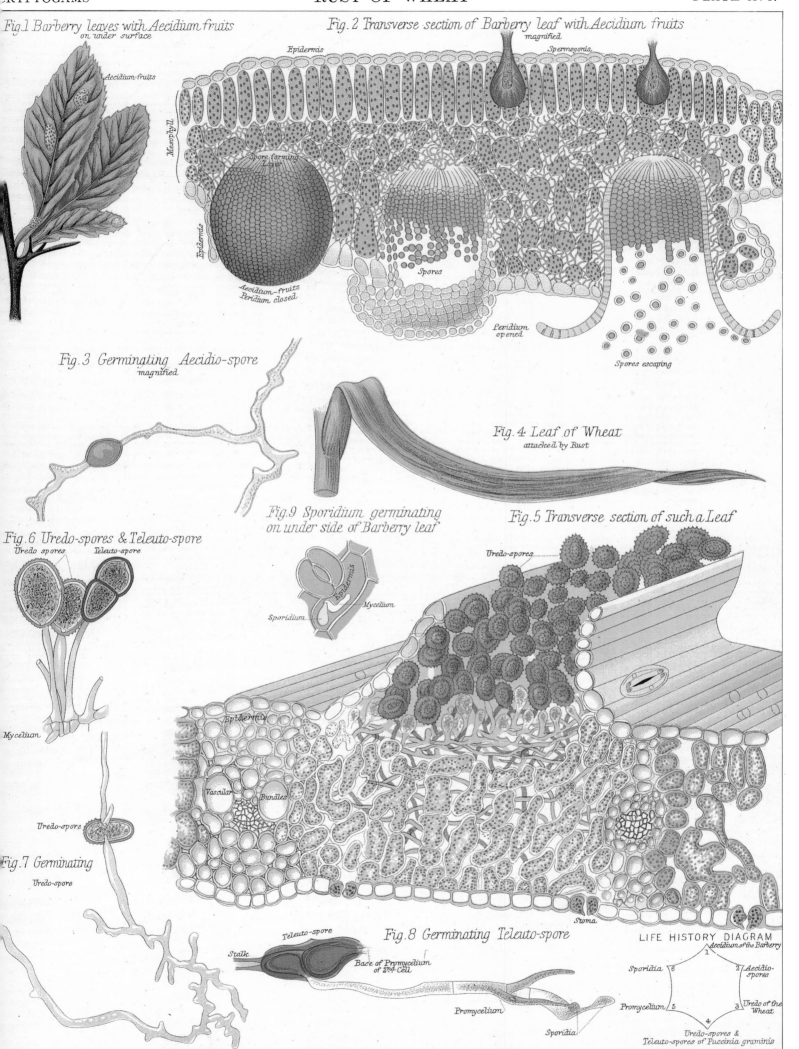

Fig.1 *Barberry leaves with Aecidium fruits* on under surface

Aecidium-fruits

Fig. 2 *Transverse section of Barberry leaf with Aecidium fruits* magnified

Epidermis

Spermogonia

Mesophyll

Epidermis

Spore forming Layer

Spores

Aecidium-fruits Peridium closed

Peridium opened

Spores escaping

Fig. 3 *Germinating Aecidio-spore* magnified

Fig. 4 *Leaf of Wheat* attacked by Rust

Fig.9 *Sporidium germinating on under side of Barberry leaf*

Fig.5 *Transverse section of such a Leaf*

Uredo-spores

Sporidium

Epidermis

Mycelium

Fig.6 *Uredo-spores & Teleuto-spore*

Uredo spores

Teleuto-spore

Mycelium

Epidermis

Vascular   Bundles

Fig.7 *Germinating*

Uredo-spore

Uredo-spore

Stoma

Fig.8 *Germinating Teleuto-spore*

Teleuto-spore

Stalk

Base of Promycelium of 2⁰ᵈ Cell

Promycelium

Sporidia

LIFE HISTORY DIAGRAM

Aecidium of the Barberry

1

Sporidia   6

2 Aecidio-spores

Promycelium   5

3 Uredo of the Wheat

4

Uredo-spores & Teleuto-spores of Puccinia graminis

Engraved. Printed and Published by W. & A.K. Johnston, Edinburgh

PLATE XVII.

COMMON MUSHROOM (*Agaricus campestris*) and RED SEA-WEED (*Polysiphonia*).

MUSHROOM.

The Pezizae are distinguished by producing their spores in the *interior* of cells called Asci, and the Mushroom produces its spores on the *exterior* of enlarged cells called Basidia, hence the name applied to the group—*Basidiomycetes*. The common Mushroom may be found towards the end of summer in open pastures, but it can be raised from spawn at any season of the year. Mushroom spawn simply consists of the mycelium mixed up with decaying organic matter, and under proper treatment, as to moisture and temperature, mushrooms may be produced.

Although the mushroom belongs to the most highly organised group of *Fungi,* just as the Red Sea-weed belongs to the highest group of *Algae,* yet no sexual stage has yet been discovered.

Fig. 1 Mushroom, full grown.
The mycelium consists of interlacing threads spread out in the mould, and what is called the Mushroom is really the Spore-fruit arising from this mycelium.
Spore-fruit composed of—Stalk with a remnant surrounding it near the top, of what once extended to the margin of the Cap.
Cap spread out like an umbrella, and bearing on its under surface the radiating plate-like Gills.
Fig. 2 Young Mushroom, entire and in section.
The cap and stalk are already roughly indicated.
The section shows the commencement of the gill-chamber, which is really a hollow ring in which the gills are formed.
Fig. 3 Mushroom more advanced—in section.

Velum (Lat. *a veil*), forming a floor to the gill-chamber from the roof of which the gills are developed.
Fig. 4 Remove a gill, embed it in paraffin, and make a section of it. The centre is occupied by mycelial filaments closely packed and adhering side by side, and towards each surface this tissue becomes denser on the outside, giving rise to the Basidia.
Fig. 5 Section under high power. Towards the surface the cells get rounded and the superficial layer of cells is enlarged to form Basidia. The Basidium has four slender processes (two only shown), at the end of which the spores are developed and easily detached.
Fig. 6 Germination of Spore of Coprinus.—The spores may be readily obtained by laying the Spore-fruit upon a sheet of paper, then by placing over the spores a glass slide

moistened by the breath, they may be lifted up and examined.
The spore placed in a drop of an appropriate fluid on a slide begins to germinate in a few hours by putting forth a delicate filament. This grows, becomes divided by transverse partitions and branches, thus forming a mycelium. In the course of from nine to twelve days the Spore-fruit arises directly from the older mycelial filaments.
Fig. 7 In some cases however, a Sclerotium is formed first.—This consists originally of an aerial branch, which divides and branches on all sides till it forms a small ball of closely packed and interosculating filaments. One of the surface-cells grows out and becomes the young spore-fruit, which, in this instance, is entirely invested by the velum.

Life History.—It is very tempting to suppose that the Spore-fruit is the result of a sexual process, but as experiments specially directed to that point have failed to show any trace of it, it is now generally believed that in the whole of the Basidio-mycetes the Spore-fruit arises directly from the mycelium or indirectly from a Sclerotium.

The stages through which they pass would be briefly as follows:—the Mycelium (or Spawn) produces a Spore-fruit directly, which bears the numerous spores from which the mycelium is again produced, and so on; or, in some cases, the Spore-fruit is preceded by a Sclerotium.

RED SEA-WEED.

Polysiphonia (Gr. *polus,* many; *siphon,* a tube) is one of the Red Sea-weeds—plants usually of a graceful form and beautiful colour, so that they attract attention. This form is found about low-water mark, attached to rocks, the stalks of the Tangle, etc., and although so finely divided, it may be removed from the water without collapsing. These divisions might be regarded as of the nature of leaves, just as in the next form considered (Chara). There are three distinct forms of this plant, all agreeing in general appearance, but differing in their reproductive habit—the Non-sexual, the Male and the Female; and it is the first of these which will be considered now.

Fig. 8 Plant much divided.
Fig. 9 Plocamium is one of the feathery red sea-weeds, and when simply spread out in water under the microscope, it shows clearly the single growing cell—cells a little further back dividing longitudinally to produce breadth, and a single cell growing laterally and dividing to form one of the numerous branches. The cell-walls

are gelatinous.
Fig. 10 Portion of Non-sexual plant showing Tetragonidia.
They appear as little round balls, but under a high power division is seen. The four gonidia do not lie in one plane, but are arranged like a tetrahedron; hence, either one or three divisions may be seen.

The gonidia escape by a parting between the peripheral cells.
Fig. 11 Germination.The Gonidium elongates, divides transversely, one of the divisions serving for attachment, the other growing and dividing longitudinally and transversely, and branching, till it becomes a parent plant.

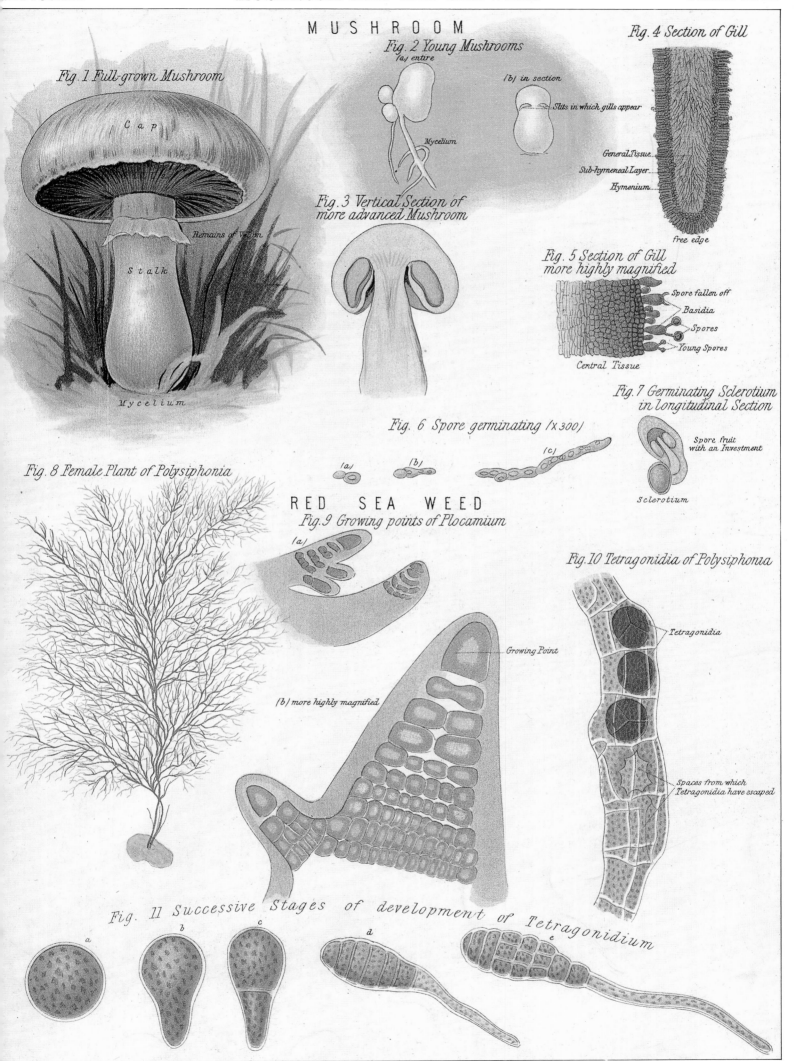

MUSHROOM

Fig. 1 Full-grown Mushroom

Cap

Stalk

Remains of Veil

Mycelium

Fig. 2 Young Mushrooms

(a) entire

(b) in section

Mycelium

Slits in which gills appear

Fig. 3 Vertical Section of more advanced Mushroom

Fig. 4 Section of Gill

General Tissue
Sub-hymeneal Layer
Hymenium

free edge

Fig. 5 Section of Gill more highly magnified

Spore fallen off
Basidia
Spores
Young Spores

Central Tissue

Fig. 6 Spore germinating (x 300)

(a)   (b)   (c)

Fig. 7 Germinating Sclerotium in Longitudinal Section

Spore fruit with an Investment

Sclerotium

Fig. 8 Female Plant of Polysiphonia

RED SEA WEED

Fig. 9 Growing points of Plocamium

(a)

(b) more highly magnified

Growing Point

Fig. 10 Tetragonidia of Polysiphonia

Tetragonidia

Spaces from which Tetragonidia have escaped

Fig. 11 Successive Stages of development of Tetragonidium

a   b   c   d   e

Engraved, Printed and Published by W. & A.K. Johnston, Edinburgh

PLATE XVIII.

RED SEA-WEED (*Polysiphonia Subulata*)—*continued.*

Fig. 1 Male Plant.
Antheridia, or male sexual organs, are cone-like, supported by a short stalk. Forked hair on the outside of each protecting it.
Fig. 1a Ripe Antheridium in optical section (× 430).
There is a basal-cell forming the Stalk, a row of cells in the centre forming an Axis, and the mother-cells of the Antherozoids are grouped around this Axis. The Antherozoids are spherical motionless masses of protoplasm, discharged into the surrounding water by the bursting of the ripe mother-cell.
Figs. 2 and 3 Female Plant.
Carpogonia, or female sexual organs, are obovate, when ready for fertilisation, and consist of three principal parts—
1. Foot or attachment.
2. Fertile spore-forming part. This is the swollen portion, and consists of a central cell surrounded by a number of peripheral cells.

3. Hair apparatus, consisting of the forked hair and the Trichogyne (Gr. *trichos,* hair; *gone,* seed).
Fig. 4 The process of Fertilisation is extremely interesting, because of the part that Infusoria have recently been found to play in it. The antherozoids, discharged into the surrounding sea-water by the bursting of the ripe antheridia, are passively floated about by the waves, since they are motionless in themselves, and they may accidentally come into contact with the trichogyne of a female plant; but their chances are greatly increased by the action of unconscious agents, such as Infusoria, which create currents in the water in the neighbourhood of the female organs. Vorticella, or the Bell Animalcule, is a stalked Infusorian, attached to this red sea-weed. The stalk may either be lengthened out, as in the drawing, or shortened by being coiled into a spiral. The bell is surmounted by a crown of cilia which move in a

definite order, so as to cause currents which will sweep particles of food down the gullet. The Vorticella is at first a free-swimming unstalked bell, but with the stalk it becomes fixed, and it naturally settles down where their is likely to be an abundance of food. The currents set up necessarily send antherozoids down the gullet, but some come in contact with the apex of the trichogyne, and are retained there. The forked hair, too, will serve to break the force of the current, and form a sort of eddy, so that the antherozoids may the more readily settle down where wanted. The antherozoid thus blends with the trichogyne, and its substance passes down the canal of the trichogyne, till it reaches the central cell, and thus fertilisation is effected.
The forked hair and trichogyne both disappear after fertilisation, having served their purpose.

Life History.—The Red Sea-weeds multiply by a simple non-sexual process, or are reproduced sexually in a complicated manner.

The contents of certain cells break up into four portions, which escape by rupturing the cell-wall, and germinating reproduce the parent plant. These are the Tetragonidia produced non-sexually.

In some red sea-weeds the male and female organs are on different parts of the same plant, but in Polysiphonia they are on different plants. The Male plant produces Antheridia, which begin as a single-celled branch, then become a row of cells, and finally a cone-like mass of cells. The forked hair arises from the stalk-cell, and the other cells produce the rounded Antherozoids. The Female plant produces Oogonia, but as they become spore-fruits after fertilisation, they are called Carpogonia. These arise, like the Antheridia, from a single cell, which eventually becomes a basal portion or Foot, consisting of a ring of four cells, and one in the centre; a middle or Fertile portion, consisting of a large central cell, surrounded by a number of cells ; and a top portion, consisting of a long cell or Trichogyne, with a forked hair. An Antherozoid reaching the apex of the trichogyne, in the way already described, is retained there, and strange to say, the fertilising effect is produced at some distance in the central cell and surrounding cells of the Carpogonium. The surrounding cells grow and divide till they form a fruit-like cover, while the central cell forms a number of close.set branches, at the ends of which the Carpospores are developed. There is thus a Spore-fruit formed, which discharges its so-called Carpospores or Endogonidia by a hole at the top; these on germination give rise to young plants.

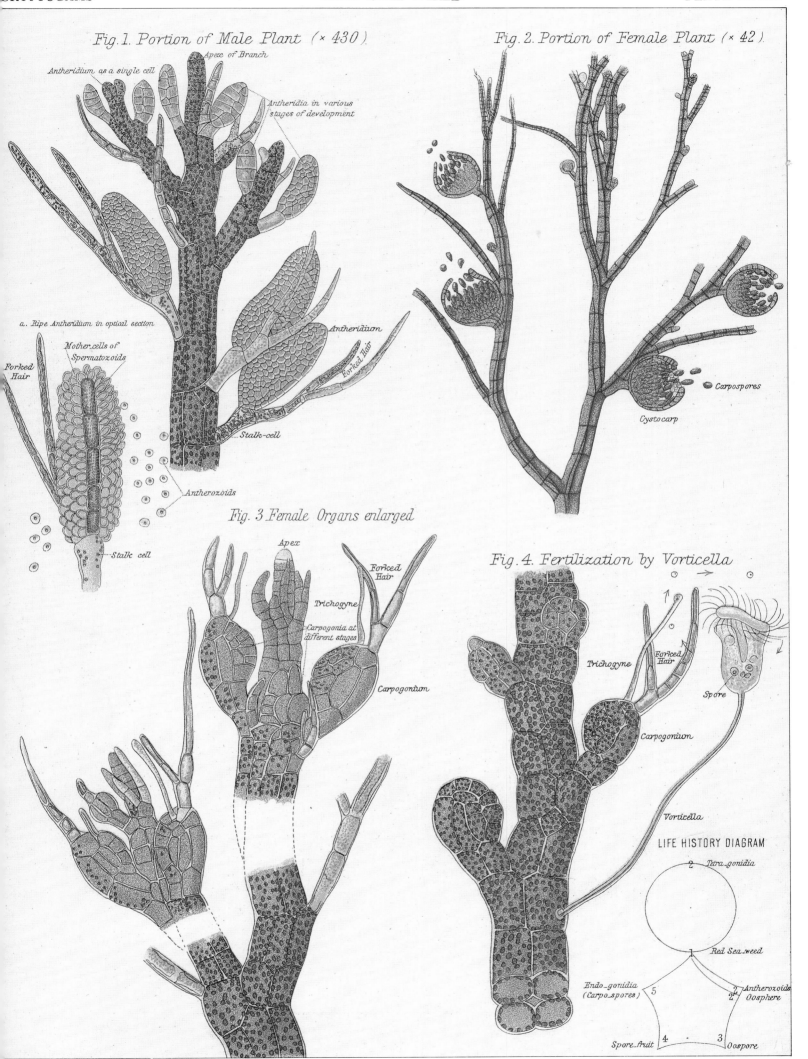

Fig. 1. Portion of Male Plant (× 430)

Apex of Branch

Antheridium as a single cell

Antheridia in various stages of development

a. Ripe Antheridium in optical section

Mother cells of Spermatozoids

Forked Hair

Antheridium

Forked Hair

Stalk-cell

Antherozoids

Stalk cell

Fig. 2. Portion of Female Plant (× 42)

Carpospores

Cystocarp

Fig. 3 Female Organs enlarged

Apex

Forked Hair

Trichogyne

Carpogonia at different stages

Carpogonium

Fig. 4. Fertilization by Vorticella

Trichogyne

Forked Hair

Spore

Carpogonium

Vorticella

LIFE HISTORY DIAGRAM

2 Tetra-gonidia

1 Red Sea-weed

Endo-gonidia (Carpo-spores)   5

2 Antherozoids
2 Oosphere

Spore-fruit   4

3 Oospore

Engraved, Printed and Published by W. & A.K. Johnston, Edinburgh & London.

PLATE XIX.

STONEWORT (*Chara*).

(Development after Pringsheim.)

Chara may be found growing in ponds and streams, varying in height from a few inches to several feet. It is entirely submerged and the stem is often encrusted with calcareous matter derived from the water, which makes it exceedingly brittle. In bog-pools however, where the water is soft they may be found free from this, and so more useful for purposes of study.

This plant differs from those hitherto considered in possessing an Axis and Appendages. The Axis grows in the direction of its length and is furnished with an apical cell, by the division of which growth is continued. Certain cells of the stem have also different functions assigned to them. The Lateral Appendages arise from one kind of cell while another kind are much longer and form the main part of the axis.

Fig. 1 Portion of Chara in Fruit. It is composed of a long thread-like stem, giving off at intervals appendages arranged in whorls, and ending in a terminal bud. The place where each whorl of appendages comes off is called a Node, and the space between two nodes is called an Internode. An internode and node with its appendages forms a Segment, and the whole axis is thus a repetition of similar segments. Branches or secondary axes repeating the structure of the primary axis, arise from the angle between the leaves and the stem. *Fig. 2* Harden specimens in a weak solution of chromic acid, which also dissolves any limy incrustation, then get as small a portion as possible of the terminal bud and press it out, without destroying it, in glycerine. The apical cell or growing point is a nucleated hemispherical cell. It is hemispherical, for its free rounded surface is not influenced by pressure, while the under surface is flat, being pressed against its neighbour. Below the second cell, which is flat on both surfaces, comes three cells formed from a single cell by vertical divisions. Next is an undivided cell, followed by a divided cell. *Fig. 3* Fertile leaf detached. Antheridia or Male Organs, globular. Carpogonia or Female Organs, more elongated. *Fig. 4* Portion of same enlarged.

The Antheridia and Carpogonia arise from a node, and the leaflets or bracteoles protect them. *Fig. 5* Tease out a ripe Antheridium and examine portions under highest power of microscope. The essential parts are the filaments divided into numerous cells, each containing an Antherozoid. *Fig. 6* The liberated antherozoid is seen to have two long cilia at the tapering end and granular contents at the blunt end. *Figs. 7, 8, and 9* The spores on germination gives rise to a Primary Rootlet and a Pro-embryo, one of the cells of which buds forth and produces a Chara.

Life History of Chara.—Chara produces Antheridia with Antherozoids and Carpogonia with their central cells. The antherozoids fertilise the central cell of the Carpogonium thus converting it into an Oospore. This germinates and produces a Pro-embryo, from a bud of which Chara is developed.

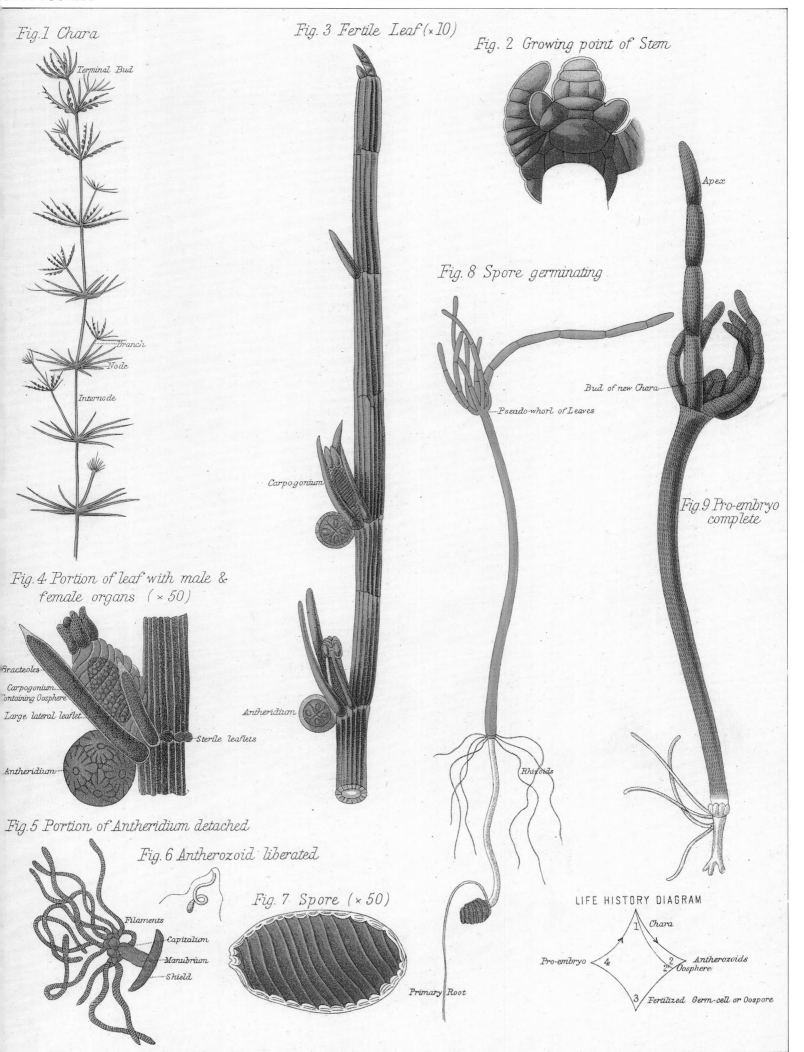

Fig.1 Chara

Terminal Bud

Branch
Node
Internode

Fig. 3 Fertile Leaf (×10)

Carpogonium

Antheridium

Fig. 2 Growing point of Stem

Fig. 8 Spore germinating

Pseudo-whorl of Leaves

Bud of new Chara

Apex

Fig.9 Pro-embryo complete

Fig. 4 Portion of leaf with male & female organs (×50)

Bracteoles
Carpogonium containing Oosphere
Large lateral leaflet
Antheridium
Sterile leaflets

Rhizoids

Fig.5 Portion of Antheridium detached

Fig. 6 Antherozoid liberated

Filaments
Capitalum
Manubrium
Shield

Fig. 7 Spore (×50)

Primary Root

LIFE HISTORY DIAGRAM

1 Chara
2 Antherozoids
2' Oosphere
Pro-embryo 4
3 Fertilized Germ-cell or Oospore

Engraved, Printed and Published by W. & A.K. Johnston, Edinburgh & London.

PLATE XX.

MOONWORT (*Lunalara vulgaris*) and
VARIABLE LIVERWORT (*Marchantia polymorpha*).

LUNULARIA.

Lunularia, so named from its crescent-shaped receptacles, is found on neglected flower-pots left in a damp and shady place, and such like. It only produces buds in this country and is very convenient for seeing the Gemmæ at different stages, while the Marchantia may serve for tracing the sexual process. It forms a small, bright-green bifurcating Thallus.

Fig. 1a Female plant with fertile branch, forming a cross-shaped apex bearing Archegonia.

Figs. b and c The gemmæ-bearing plant, with a forked growing apex, and withering away behind. The upper surface has gemmæ-cups and the under surface a tangled line of root-hairs.

Fig. 2 Upper surface of *Thallus* under simple microscope shows irregularly shaped tracts with Respiratory-pore in centre of each.

Fig. 3 Peel off a very thin slice of epidermis and examine under high power.

Opening of Respiratory-pore (seen in section, in Fig. 7).

Fig. 4 Embed small portion of Thallus in paraffin and make transverse section.

Upper Epidermis of close-fitting cells. Respiratory-cavity containing green cells.

Colourless cells.

Lower Epidermis, giving rise to Root-hairs each composed of a single cell and with walls strengthened by incomplete spiral thickenings.

Fig. 5 Embed a young Receptacle in paraffin and make transverse section. The Gemmæ are seen at all stages of development, from little pear-shaped bodies (1) till they reach maturity (8), ready to be detached and shed.

MARCHANTIA.

Marchantia is very common in moist or damp places, spreading over damp rocks or soil, or on the mould of flower-pots. It is a leathery flat expansion and grows by repeated bifurcation at one end, so that it gradually forms a fan-shaped mass. The upper surface is dark-green, while the under surface, in contact with the soil or rock, is pale in colour. There are not only root-hairs on the under surface to fasten it, but a double row of membranous appendages which are apparently comparable to leaves.

Fig. 6a Male plant with fertile branch spread out at the top in umbrella fashion. The upper surface of this fertile branch is studded with little openings which are the mouths of sacs containing Antheridia

Fig. 6b Female plant with fertile branch expanded at the top into a star-like disc bearing Archegonia on its under surface.

The cup-shaped receptacle with toothed margin contains gemmæ.

Fig. 7 Embed piece of cup in paraffin and make section—or a piece of the Thallus may be used.

On the inner surface of cup (lower surface in drawing) the cells are relatively large and colourless, and the outer surface has its epidermal cells close together. Beneath the epidermis there are Respiratory cavities containing branched rows of chlorophyll-containing cells, to which air has admission through the little openings seen on the surface of the Thallus (Fig. 2) called Respiratory-pores.

The object of this arrangement is only to admit the air where most wanted. The general arrangement of the tissues is impermeable to air, and the plant does not readily dry up, from its tough and leathery texture; but by means of these little lung-like chambers the air plays freely among the spread-out green cells and enables them to decompose carbonic acid in the presence of sunlight.

Fig. 8 Embed portion of male plant containing Antheridia and make sections. Examine first under low power, then add a drop of spirit, afterwards glycerine, and examine under high power.

Antheridium with stalk, an outer wall, and inner mass of cells developing antherozoids.

The ripe antheridium bursts irregularly on one side to discharge its contents. The cell-walls swell up with water and burst, then the gelatinous contents poured out are gradually dissolved by the water, and the freed antherozoids may be seen moving about with two cilia.

Fig. 9 Ripe Archegonium, showing the margins of the lobes of the disc growing down to form a sort of investment or perianth.

Fig. 10 Sporogonia or Spore-fruits on under surface of disc, consisting of rounded bodies.

The interior mass of cellular tissue is converted into alternating rows of spores and spiral filaments. As water is absorbed the spore-capsule bursts and, under the same influence, the spiral filaments, coiled up like a spring, spread out and scatter the accompanying spores with considerable force.

Fig. 11 Spores and Elaters. The Elaters are doubly coiled filaments enclosed by a wall.

Life History of Marchantia.—Marchantia multiplies by asexual buds or Gemmæ, which are little green bodies enclosed in cup-shaped receptacles, and on becoming detached may develop into new individuals.

Marchantia also reproduces itself sexually. The male organs (or Antheridia) and the female organs (or Archegonia) are borne by different individuals. The Antherozoids fertilise the central cell of the Archegonium, converting it into an Oospore which swells up and grows into a Sporogonium full of spores. The spore germinates, producing the green, flat expansion, as at the beginning.

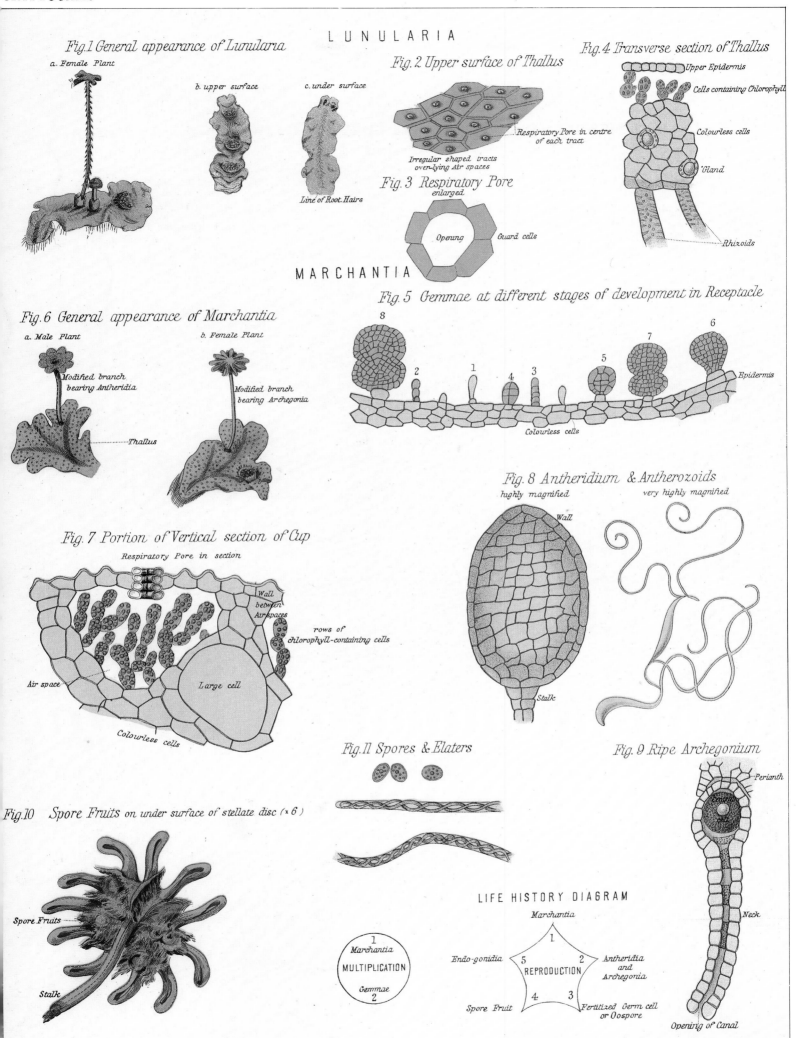

LUNULARIA

Fig.1 General appearance of Lunularia

a. Female Plant

b. upper surface

c. under surface

Line of Root Hairs

Fig. 2 Upper surface of Thallus

Respiratory Pore in centre of each tract

Irregular shaped tracts over-lying Air spaces

Fig. 3 Respiratory Pore enlarged

Opening   Guard cells

Fig. 4 Transverse section of Thallus

Upper Epidermis

Cells containing Chlorophyll

Colourless cells

Gland

Rhizoids

MARCHANTIA

Fig. 5 Gemmae at different stages of development in Receptacle

Epidermis

Colourless cells

Fig. 6 General appearance of Marchantia

a. Male Plant

Modified branch bearing Antheridia

Thallus

b. Female Plant

Modified branch bearing Archegonia

Fig. 8 Antheridium & Antherozoids

highly magnified

very highly magnified

Wall

Stalk

Fig. 7 Portion of Vertical section of Cup

Respiratory Pore in section

Wall between Airspaces

rows of Chlorophyll-containing cells

Air space

Large cell

Colourless cells

Fig.11 Spores & Elaters

Fig. 9 Ripe Archegonium

Perianth

Central cell

Neck

Fig.10 Spore Fruits on under surface of stellate disc (× 6)

Spore Fruits

Stalk

Opening of Canal

LIFE HISTORY DIAGRAM

Marchantia

1

Marchantia   MULTIPLICATION   Gemmae

2

Endo-gonidia   5   REPRODUCTION   2   Antheridia and Archegonia

Spore Fruit   4   3   Fertilized Germ cell or Oospore

Engraved, Printed and Published by W. & A.K. Johnston, Edinburgh.

PLATE XXI.

COMMON HAIR-MOSS (*Polytrichum*) and FUNARIA HYGROMETRICA.

Mosses are common everywhere, on wall-tops, roofs, and trees, decking the banks with a mantle of green, or carpeting the forests with their luxuriance. Mosses, however, like other plants, have also their favourite haunts and their favourite seasons, but Funaria has this advantage, that it may be found in fruit at almost any season of the year.

The Hair-Moss (*Polytrichum*) is common on waste-ground and heaths where it forms tufted masses. The male and female organs are borne by distinct plants, and the hairy cap of the moss-fruit may be readily recognised. The stem may be several inches in height.

Funaria occurs on walls, roofs, and waste-places pretty common. The leafy plant is small, but the stalk bearing the pear-shaped capsule is an inch or two in length. This stalk has the peculiarity of contracting to a spiral on drying after being moistened.

Fig. 1 Male Plant of Polytrichum, with numerous brown root-hairs and slender stem.
The apex of the stem forms a leafy expansion bearing the male organs.
Fig. 2 Female plant of Funaria.
In the young condition the Capsule is sessile, but it is borne on a long stalk later.
The Leafy plant has a very short stem, with bright green leaves overlapping each other.
Fig. 3 The flattened apex is bounded by leaves, and bears stalked bodies of considerable size intermixed with barren filaments.
The stalked bodies are the male organs or Antheridia, consisting of a wall formed of a single layer of cells, and the interior cells developing Antherozoids.
Tease out portions of the apex, and examine under high power for

Antheridia with Antherozoids, and Archegonia.
Fig. 4 Antherozoid, a coiled body with two cilia. Stain with iodine to kill them and make cilia visible.
Fig. 5 Archegonium a flask shaped body with long neck and a lower swollen portion containing the central cell.
Fig. 6 Sporocarp of Polytrichum.
The unripe Capsule is still green and covered by its brown hairy cap.
The lid beneath the cap is peaked.
The ripe Capsule is of a brownish-yellow and the cap yellowish.
Fig. 7 Ripe Spore-capsule of Polytrichum (June).
The lid is cast off and the spores escape.
The mouth of the capsule is surrounded by sixty-four teeth forming the Peristome.

The Epiphragm is the expanded end of the Columella.
Fig. 8 Peristome of Funaria consisting of sixteen teeth converging to a centre.
Fig. 9 Embed Capsules of Funaria in paraffin, and make longitudinal and transverse sections.
Outer wall or peripheral layer of cells.
Columella or central cylinder of colourless cells.
Spore-sac surrounding columella.
Air-cavity with strings of green cells permeating through it.
Fig. 10 Ripe spore consisting of inner and outer wall, protoplasm and oil-globules.
Fig. 11 Sow spores on blotting-paper kept moist under a glass shade.
Fig. 12 The germinating spore gives rise to a thread-like branching body the Protonema, and a bud forms which grows up into the leafy Moss.

Life History of a Moss.—The leafy Moss-plant forms at its apex either Antheridia producing Antherozoids or Archegonia with their Central-cells. The antherozoids fertilise the central cell, converting it into an Oospore. This oospore divides and produces directly the Sporogonium with its contained Spores. The top of the ripe capsule detaches itself, and the spores come out : and on a suitable .situation begin to germinate. The thick outer coat is ruptured, and the inner coat protrudes as a filament which grows, divides and branches, till a mass of branched filaments is formed called the Protonema. The Protonema gives rise to a bud by the bulging out of a side branch, and this produces the leafy Moss as at the beginning.

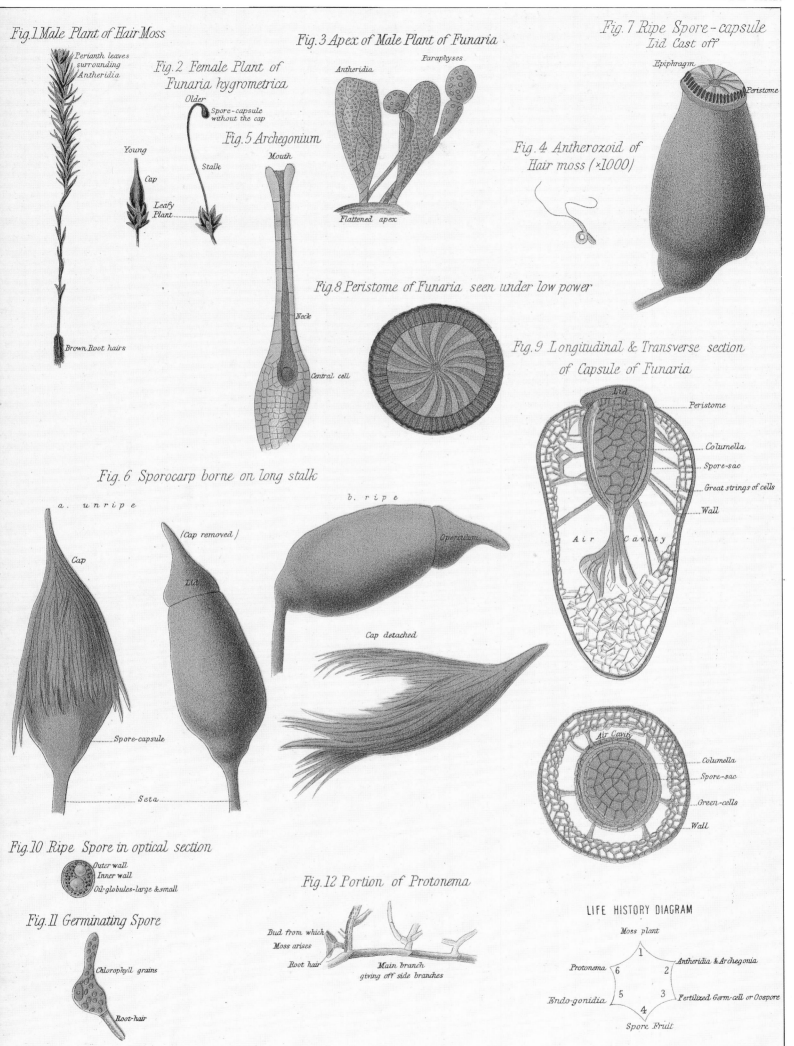

Fig. 1 Male Plant of Hair Moss

Perianth leaves surrounding Antheridia

Fig. 2 Female Plant of Funaria hygrometrica

Young

Cap

Leafy Plant

Older

Spore-capsule without the cap

Stalk

Fig. 5 Archegonium

Mouth

Neck

Central cell

Brown Root hairs

Fig. 3 Apex of Male Plant of Funaria

Antheridia

Paraphyses

Flattened apex

Fig. 4 Antherozoid of Hair moss (×1000)

Fig. 7 Ripe Spore-capsule Lid Cast off

Epiphragm

Peristome

Fig. 8 Peristome of Funaria seen under low power

Fig. 9 Longitudinal & Transverse section of Capsule of Funaria

Lid

Peristome

Columella

Spore-sac

Great strings of cells

Wall

Air Cavity

Air Cavity

Columella

Spore-sac

Green-cells

Wall

Fig. 6 Sporocarp borne on long stalk

a. unripe

b. ripe

Cap

(Cap removed)

Lid

Operculum

Cap detached

Spore-capsule

Seta

Fig. 10 Ripe Spore in optical section

Outer wall

Inner wall

Oil-globules-large & small

Fig. 12 Portion of Protonema

Bud from which Moss arises

Root hair

Main branch giving off side branches

Fig. 11 Germinating Spore

Chlorophyll grains

Root-hair

LIFE HISTORY DIAGRAM

Moss plant

Protonema

Endo-gonidia

Spore Fruit

Antheridia & Archegonia

Fertilized Germ-cell or Oospore

1
2
3
4
5
6

Engraved, Printed, and Published by W. & A.K. Johnston, Edinburgh.

PLATE XXII.

MALE SHIELD FERN (*Aspidium filix-mas*).

Ferns have always attracted notice from their graceful outlines and their varied forms, still it is only comparatively recently that the complete course of their life history has been made out. The frond of the Fern is the most conspicuous, the underground portion being generally overlooked. Having so much leaf about them, they generally inhabit moist and shady situations. Their prevailing colour is green, but towards the autumn a brown hue appears on the under surface of the frond, in streaks or patches, and this is due to the formation of spore-cases containing the spores.

The Male Shield Fern is so named by way of contrast to an allied form—the Lady Fern, with its graceful habit, its elegant form, and its delicate hue. It bears its fronds in tufts, arranged in shuttle-cock fashion, and rising to a height of two or three feet. The young fronds are rolled up like a shepherd's crook, and gradually unfold themselves. The veining of the leaflets is distinctly seen, and that constant forking of the veins so characteristic of Ferns. The spore-cases are arranged in patches, each patch being indicated by its kidney-shaped cover. The amount of spores produced is enormous, and readily accounts for its extensive distribution. Professor Dodel-Port has reckoned the number of spores scattered by a single fern, in a single summer, to be no less than one thousand millions.

Fig. 1 Underground Stem ascends obliquely, and is completely covered with the stumps of leaves, from the base of which the numerous roots arise.

Fig. 2 Fertile leaf or frond bearing Sporangia on under surface.
The leaf is bi-pinnate; the pinnae are long, narrow, tapering, and the pinnules are obtuse.
On the under surface of the leaf, usually at the forking of two veins, kidney-shaped structures appear called Indusia. Each Indusium covers a cluster of stalked capsules, such a cluster being called a Sorus, and each stalked capsule a Sporangium.

Fig. 3 Pinna or leaflet on upper surface.

The pinnules towards the top run into each other.
The forked Venation is evident.

Fig. 4 Pinnule from base of Pinna.
The Indusium may be found *closed* over the cluster of Sporangia, or *raised* on one side to allow the ripe spores to escape, or in some cases *burst*.

Fig. 5 Section of Pinnule through Ripe Sorus in Fig. 4. Indusium arising from central swelling of vascular bundle, arching completely over clusters of Sporangia, and consisting of a single layer of nucleated cells in its expanded portions.
Sporangia in different stages of development, opened and unopened, full and empty of Spores. Some have longer or shorter stalks, with a stalked gland which is peculiar to the species, and there are several hair-like undeveloped Sporangia known as Paraphyses.

Fig. 6 The Sporangia may be rubbed off on a slide and examined in water. They can afterwards be burst by pressure on the cover-glass.
The Sporangium is an oval body borne by a short stalk. There is a ring of thick projecting cells extending from the cleft overhead, and backwards to the top of the stalk. The cells forming the slightly convex wall on either side are thin and easily ruptured.

Fig. 7 Spores.
The Spore has a thick, outer brown coat or Exosporium with irregular markings, and a thin, inner delicate coat or Endosporium.

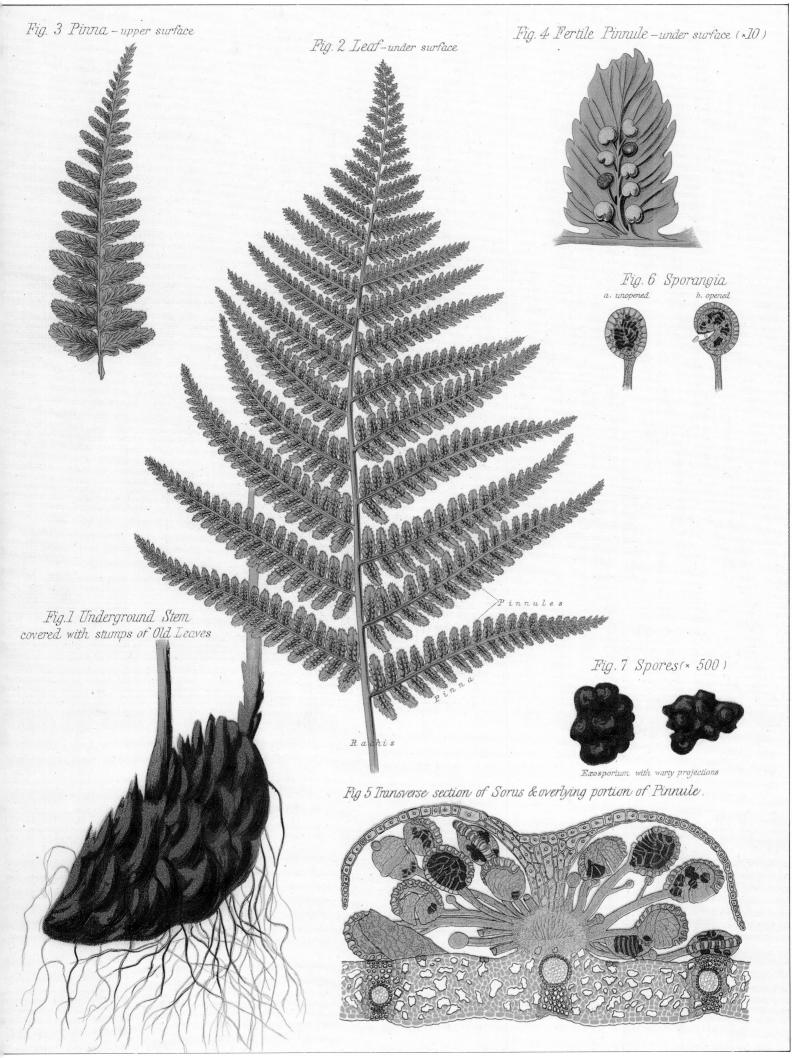

Fig. 3 Pinna – upper surface

Fig. 2 Leaf – under surface

Fig. 4 Fertile Pinnule – under surface (×10)

Fig. 6 Sporangia

a. unopened   b. opened

Pinnules

Fig.1 Underground Stem covered with stumps of Old Leaves

Pinna

Fig. 7 Spores (× 500)

Rachis

Exosporium with warty projections

Fig 5 Transverse section of Sorus & overlying portion of Pinnule.

Engraved, Printed and Published by W. & A.K. Johnston, Edinburgh

PLATE XXIII.

MALE SHIELD FERN.—*continued.*

Fig. 1 Development of Spores.
In each Sporangium a single central cell gives rise to sixteen mother-cells by successive division into 2, 4, 8, and 16.
Each mother-cell divides into four Spores, as shown. The cell-wall of each spore is differentiated into an inner and outer coat, as seen in Fig. 2, and chlorophyll is developed in the contents.
Fig. 2 Spore germinating.
With moisture the Spore swells, and the outer, firm Exosporium ruptures, while the inner, delicate Endosporium protrudes. As this grows a transverse septum is formed, and about the same time the lower cell gives forth the first rootlet.
Fig. 3 Prothallium.
The germinating Spore first produces a row of cells, then, by oblique division, a surface of cells, and finally the flat expansion of the Prothallium. Male and female reproductive organs next arise on the under surface of the Prothallus.
Antheridia, or male organs, arise among the bases of the root-hairs, and Archegonia, or female organs, near to the notch.

Fig, 4 Antheridium.
The Antheridia are rounded projections, the contents of which break up in to mother-cells, in each of which an Antherozoid is developed.
Fig. 5 The coiled-up Antherozoid is seen in the mother-cell.
Fig. 6 Antherozoid free.
Fig. 7 Archegonium.
The central or germ cell is the point which the Antherozoids must reach in order to produce fertilization. For this purpose there is a central canal open at the top, and bounded by four longitudinal rows of cells.

Life History Diagram.—The conspicuous Fern (1) develops Spores or Gonidia (2) on its under surface; and one of these germinating produces a Prothallium (3), afterwards producing male and female organs—Antheridia and Archegonia (4)—on its under surface; the central cell of the Archegonium becomes fertilized by the access of Antherozoids, and the Fertilized Germ-cell (5) develops into the Fern (1).

CLASSIFICATION.

Sub-kingdom. Vascular Cryptogams.
True Roots.
Fibro-vascular bundles.
Prothallus bearing reproductive organs comparatively inconspicuous.

Class. Filicinæ.

Stem usually unbranched. Leaves large and compound.
Sporangia in clusters, and each sporangium developed from a single epidermal cell.
Spores of one or two kinds.

Order. Filices.
Leaves without stipules.
Spores of one kind.
Prothallus independent and monœcious.

Genus. Aspidium.

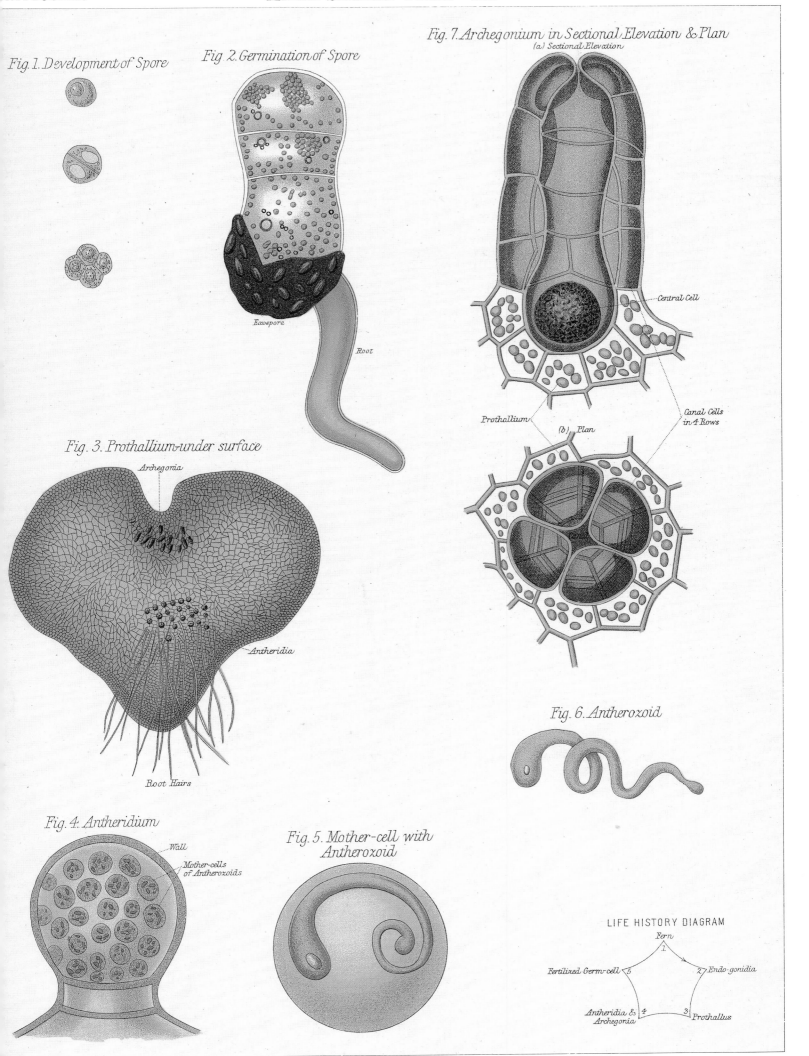

Fig. 1. Development of Spore

Fig 2. Germination of Spore

Ecospore

Root

Fig. 7. Archegonium in Sectional Elevation & Plan

(a) Sectional Elevation

Central Cell

Prothallium

Canal Cells in 4 Rows

(b) Plan

Fig. 3. Prothallium-under surface

Archegonia

Antheridia

Root Hairs

Fig. 6. Antheroxoid

Fig. 4. Antheridium

Wall

Mother-cells of Antheroxoids

Fig. 5. Mother-cell with Antheroxoid

LIFE HISTORY DIAGRAM

Fern
1

Fertilized Germ-cell 5   2 Endo-gonidia

Antheridia & Archegonia 4   3 Prothallus

Engraved. Printed and Published by W. & A.K. Johnston, Edinburgh

PLATE XXIV.

COMMON HORSE-TAIL (*Equisetum arvense*),
GREAT HORSE-TAIL (*E. maximum*),
and PILLWORT (*Pilularia globulifera*).

Horse-tails belong to the smallest natural order among Vascular Cryptogams, there being but a single living genus and representative—*Equisetum*. They all inhabit marshy and damp places.

Gigantic forms existed during the Carboniferous period, such as the Calamites.

The Vegetative structures which these plants produce are extremely dissimilar—according as they are fertile or barren. The fertile shoots are formed in the spring, bear spores, have no chlorophyll, and usually do not branch. The barren shoots, on the other hand, which are relatively large, are formed later in the year, have abundance of chlorophyll, and branch freely, the numerous whorls of branches giving that peculiar appearance suggestive of a horse's tail. The business of the barren shoot is to nourish the plant; so during summer it manufactures and stores up nutriment in the underground stem, to enable it to send up a fertile shoot early next year.

The Underground Stem or Rhizome develops Roots at each of the nodes, and produces Buds which give rise to upright shoots. These buds are sometimes curiously shaped and swollen, being distended, particularly with starch, for the rapid early growth of the young shoot.

The Upright Shoot is a hollow cylinder, interrupted at the regularly recurring nodes by a transverse plate. This is a form of great mechanical strength, combined with lightness and economy of material. The outer surface is usually marked with ridges and furrows; and this roughness, along with the silica contained in the stem, sometimes renders them available for polishing purposes. The presence of silica may easily be shown by fusing a piece of the stem in the hottest part of the gas flame, when little beads of glass are produced.

The Branches are slender green filaments, given off at the nodes, and arranged in whorls. They repeat the structure of the stem in being jointed and possessing leaf-sheaths. They have this peculiarity, that although formed in the axils of leaves just like ordinary buds, yet instead of growing up between the leaf and the stem they burst through the base of the leaf-sheath.

The Leaves are the funnel-shaped sheaths investing the stem, inconspicuous in the barren shoot, more prominent and swollen in the fertile one. They are produced into longer or shorter teeth; the teeth of successive whorls not being placed above one another, but alternating.

The Modified Leaves of the fertile shoot form the shield-like structures of the spike. These little shield-like leaves are *homologous* with the leaf-sheaths, each appearing as a ring of tissue round the axis; the margins, in the one case, growing out into teeth or points, in the other, expanding into plates or shields.

Figs. 1 and 2 The Fertile shoot is clothed at regular intervals with leaf-sheaths, and at the apex is expanded into a club-shaped head covered with little stalked discs, arranged in whorls. Immediately beneath the spike is a wavy ring, representing a rudimentary leaf-sheath, just like bracts or modified leaves in the neighborhood of a flower.

Fig. 3 The Barren shoot is seen to have leaf-sheaths closely embracing the stem, and whorls of branches bursting through their base.

Fig. 4 Make a longitudinal and transverse section of the Spike. The modified fertile leaves of the spike are placed at right angles to it and arranged in whorls, each whorl supposed to correspond to a leaf-sheath, but instead of growing applied to the stem it grows at right angles to it.

Successive whorls of leaves are closely pressed against each other, so that the discs assume a polygonal outline.

Fig. 5 Fertile leaf detached and examined. It has a short stalk bearing its shield, from the under or inner surface of which sporangia containing spores are produced. The sporangia open towards the stalk by a longitudinal slit, and the greenish powdery spores readily escape.

Fig. 6 Embed young spike in paraffin, and cut transverse sections. Mount in glycerine, and examine under low power. Each stalk contains a fibro-vascular bundle, which passes from the axis of the spike, and in the shield branches towards the insertion of each sporangium. Sporangium wall formed of a single layer of cells.

Fig. 7 Examine portion of wall under high power. Cells next to stalk with ring-like thickenings. These ringed cells burst longitudinally when the spores are ripe. Other cells of sporangium with spiral thickenings.

Fig. 8 Shake out some of the green spores on a slide and gently breathe upon them. The Spores are round or somewhat egg-shaped bodies, averaging $\frac{1}{400}$ to $\frac{1}{500}$ inch in diameter, with bright green contents and spirally coiled Elaters. Each spore is furnished with three membranes instead of two, and the outer membrane, as the spore ripens, splits up into ribbon-like strips which are the Elaters.

These Elaters uncoil as the moisture of the breath evaporates; and, by drying and moistening in this way, a perpetual motion can be kept up, which is so lively and jerky that it looks more like vital than purely physical action.

Fig. 9 The germinating spore produces a Prothallus, which may either bear Antheridia or Archegonia. The Prothallus is irregularly lobed, and bears the Antheridia at the end of these lobes; while in the female Prothallus, the Archegonia are developed between the lobes.

Fig. 10 The Antherozoids are not much coiled, but very stout, and have a brush of cilia at the tapering end. They are the largest in the whole vegetable kingdom.

Fig. 11 Early development of the Embryo. There is first division into two cells, the upper half representing the primary axis, the lower half representing the root portion. Each half is again divided into two cells, the upper two representing stem and leaf, the lower two forming root and

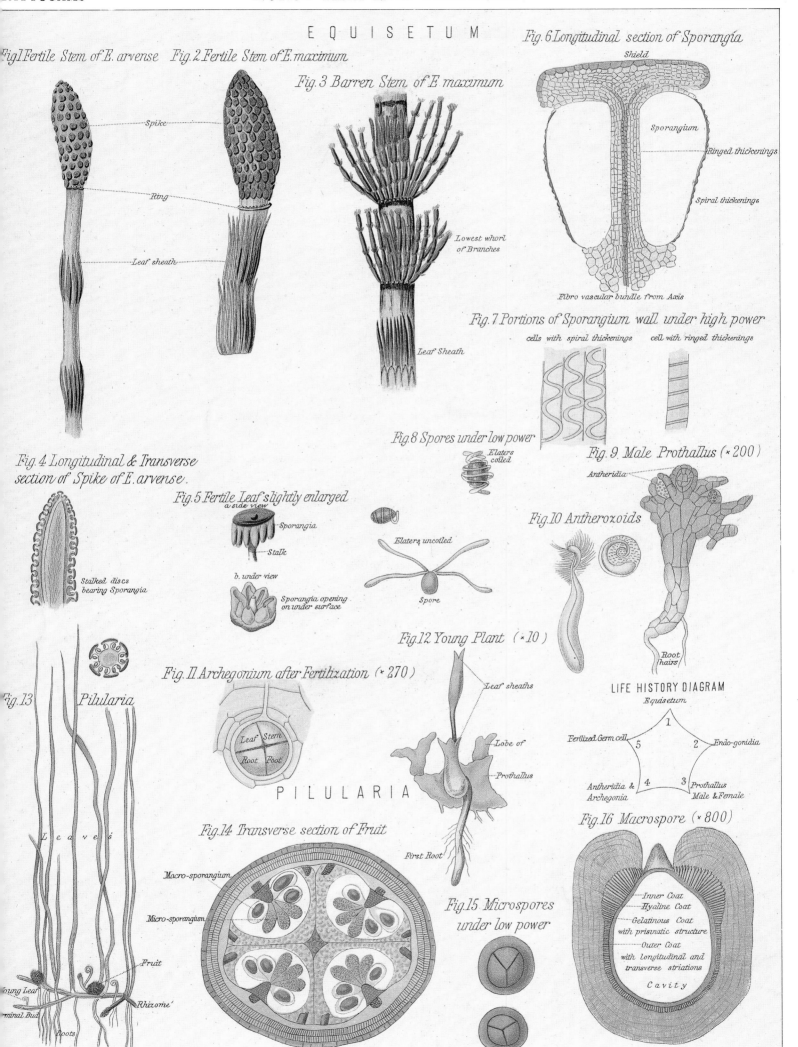

EQUISETUM

Fig.1 Fertile Stem of E. arvense   Fig.2 Fertile Stem of E. maximum

Fig.6 Longitudinal section of Sporangia

Fig.3 Barren Stem of E. maximum

Spike

Ring

Leaf sheath

Shield

Sporangium

Ringed thickenings

Spiral thickenings

Lowest whorl of Branches

Leaf Sheath

Fibro vascular bundle from Axis

Fig.7 Portions of Sporangium wall under high power

cells with spiral thickenings   cell with ringed thickenings

Fig.4 Longitudinal & Transverse section of Spike of E. arvense.

Fig.8 Spores under low power

Fig.9 Male Prothallus (× 200)

Elaters coiled

Antheridia

Fig.5 Fertile Leaf slightly enlarged

a side view

Sporangia

Stalk

b. under view

Sporangia opening on under surface

Stalked discs bearing Sporangia

Elaters uncoiled

Spore

Fig.10 Antherozoids

Root hairs

Fig.12 Young Plant (× 10)

Fig.11 Archegonium after Fertilization (× 270)

Leaf sheaths

Lobe of

Prothallus

Leaf   Stem

Root   Foot

LIFE HISTORY DIAGRAM

Equisetum

Fig.13   Pilularia

PILULARIA

Ferilized Germ cell

1

5   2

Endo-gonidia

Antheridia & Archegonia

4   3

Prothallus Male & Female

Fig.16 Macrospore (× 800)

Leaves

Fig.14 Transverse section of Fruit

Macro-sporangium

Micro-sporangium

Fruit

Young Leaf

minal Bud

Roots

Rhizome

First Root

Fig.15 Microspores under low power

Inner Coat

Hyaline Coat

Gelatinous Coat with prismatic structure

Outer Coat with longitudinal and transverse striations

Cavity

Engraved, Printed and Published by W. & A.K. Johnston, Edinburgh

foot. This foot is functionally the root of the young embryo, and is temporary, while the root proper is for the growing plant.

Fig. 12 Vertical section of lobe of Prothallus, with young plant. The young plant at this stage has its first root formed, and its leaf-bearing axis developing leaf-sheaths.

Life History Diagram.—The fertile branch of Equisetum produces its spike with the sporangia containing the spores. The spores, carried by their outspread elaters to a damp and shady spot, begin to germinate, producing either a Male Prothallus with Antheridia, or a Female Prothallus with Archegonia. The Antherozoids set free, fertilise the central cell of the Archegonium, thus producing an Embryo which grows up into the mature plant.

CLASSIFICATION OF EQUISETUM

Sub-kingdom. Vascular Cryptogams.

Order. Equisetaceæ.
Upright stems, hollow and jointed.
Leaves, small, forming sheaths.
Fertile leaves, in whorls, forming a spike and bearing sporangia on inner surface.
Spores, of one kind, and furnished with Elaters.
Prothallus generally diœcious.
Genus. Equisetum—the only genus.

Species. Arvense— Leaf-sheaths of fertile stem, loose, and distant. Maximum—Leaf-sheaths of fertile stem, large, loose, and close together.

Difference from Ferns. In Ferns, the fertile leaves bearing the sporangia are not usually confined to any particular part, and they act both as ordinary green leaves and as spore-carriers. In Equisetum, different stems are produced at different seasons of the year for these two purposes. The Barren stems are green, and their sole work is to store up nutriment in the underground stem. The Fertile stems do nothing towards their own support, but use up the accumulated nourishment, in order to produce the spores.
The majority of Ferns, too, produce Antheridia and Archegonia on the same prothallus; whereas in Equisetum the two are kept separate, the male prothallus being smaller than the female.

PILULARIA—FRUCTIFICATION.

Pillwort occurs by the margins of lakes or ponds, or in badly drained places. It has a wiry, creeping rhizome, which gives off roots on the under surface, narrow stiff leaves on the upper surface, and terminates in a growing bud. Little pill-like bodies occur towards the autumn, at the base of several of the leaves, either at or beneath the surface, and these are the Fruits. These fruits contain spores of two kinds—Micro-spores or Male spores, and Macro-spores or Female spores. No male prothallus is formed, and only a small female pro-thallus with a single Archegonium.

Fig. 13 Rhizome, slender and creeping, ending in a terminal bud.
Roots, from under surface.
Leaves, in two rows, youngest always nearest the growing point.
Fruits, at the base of the leaves.
Fig. 14 Embed Fruit in paraffin and make sections.
Fruit consisting of four segments, supposed to be modified leaves joined edge to edge, the midrib represented by central fibro-vascular bundle in each.
Each segment with three fibro-vascullar bundles, the middle one forming the core of a projecting cushion on which the spore-cases are produced.
Sporangia borne on the inner surface of modified leaves arranged in a whorl, containing Microspores and Macrospores.
Fig. 15 Microspores examined under low power—average size about $\frac{1}{600}$ inch in diameter.
The Microspore forms no male prothallus, but its contents break up directly into Antherozoids. The tri-radiate markings show the lines along which the spore splits to allow the escape of the Antherozoids.
Fig. 16 Macrospore examined under high power.
Contents.—Cavity filled with nutritious substances, such as starch and oil globules.
Investments.—Four coats of varying quality, formed in succession from within outwards.
Inner coat, compact, the first formed coat.
Hyaline coat, forming papilla at apex.
Third coat, with radiating structure.
Outer gelatinous coat, with concentric and radiating structure. This outer coat swells up with water.

PLATE XXV.

COMMON CLUB-MOSS (*Lycopodium clavatum*)
and *Selaginella*.

(Chiefly from Luerssen's "Medicinisch Pharmaceutische Botanik.")

LYCOPODIUM.

Club-mosses, as the common name denotes are moss-like plants, having slender herbaceous stems, clothed with delicate small leaves, and found in mountainous situations or stony, wet places.

The fossil forms of the Carboniferous period, of which Lepidodendron is the most characteristic, instead of being herbaceous, were large trees.

The prostrate creeping Stem is very leafy, and much branched. From the under surface arise the roots, and from the upper surface the upright fertile shoots, ending generally in two fertile spikes.

The Leaves are hair-pointed, and arranged in a close spiral round the stem.

The Modified Leaves bearing the sporangia are shorter and broader than the ordinary leaves, though sometimes they are quite the same.

The numerous minute spores (Fig. 4) are applied to various uses. They contain a quantity of resinous matter, and their wall is of a greasy nature. This resinous quality renders them readily combustible, hence they are used as "vegetable sulphur" for producing an artificial and sudden flame to represent lightning at theatres, and their greasy coat has caused them to be used for dusting over pills, thus preventing the contained pill from touching the tongue.

Fig. 1 Creeping Stem branches dichotomously, and also the Roots. Leaves thickly set round the stem. Spikes usually in pairs, mounted on a stalk.
Fig. 2 Leaf one-nerved and irregularly toothed, with a long hair-point variable in length.
Fig. 3 Fertile leaf bearing Sporangium at its base on the upper surface. Sporangium kidney-shaped, splitting into two valves, and producing only one kind of spore.
Fig. 4 Spore with netted markings fading away towards apex. Three converging ridges, along which exospore ruptures.
Fig. 5 Prothallus of Lycopodium, discovered by Fankhauser in the autumn of 1872. It is an underground solid structure, without chlorophyll, pretty smooth on the under surface, but deeply grooved on the upper. Antheridia and Archegonia are developed in the grooves.

Life History Diagram.—The discovery of the Prothallus shows that the Lycopod, in its reproductive processes, is more nearly allied to Ferns, such as Adder's tongue (*Ophioglossum*), than to Selaginella, beside which its vegetative characters seemed to place it.

The fertile leaves of the spike bear sporangia on their inner base, the spores of which are of one kind. The spore on germination produces a prothallus, underground, solid, without chlorophyll, independent of the spore, and with Antheridia and Archegonia. The embryo resulting from fertilization forms a foot embedded in the tissue of the prothallus, and grows up into the young plant.

CLASSIFICATION OF LYCOPODIUM.

Sub-kingdom. Vascular Cryptogams.

Class. Dichotomæ.
Stem and Roots branching dichotomously.
Leaves small and simple.

Sporangia solitary.
Spores of one or two kinds.
Order. Lycopodiaceæ.
Leaves without a ligule.
Spores of one kind.
Prothallus large and independent.

Genus. Lycopodium, only British genus.

Species. Clavatum.
Spikes usually in pairs, long-stalked.

SELAGINELLA.

Selaginella, with only one British species, the lesser Club-moss, has a special interest from the fact that it not only belongs to the highest group of Cryptogams, but that it shows a gradual passage from the reproductive processes characteristic of Cryptogams to those of Phanerogams. It is this phase of its character which will receive special attention now.

The Reproductive Structures are of two kinds, and, generally speaking, the Macrosporangia are only produced on the lower leaves, and Microsporangia on the upper. In Pilularia, Sporangia of two kinds were produced, springing in tufts from the inner (or upper) surface of four modified leaves arranged in a whorl, but here they spring singly and separately from the upper surface of leaves arranged spirally. In the one case the leaves were all at one level, united at their edges, and *enclosing* the Sporangia, here the leaves are drawn out into a spiral, and bear the Sporangia without enclosing them.

The developing Embryo (as in Fig. 14) will show the points of contact with higher plants. For the first time there appears in the spore, along with the female prothallus, yet distinct from it, a mass of cells which supply nutriment to the young and growing embryo. This is the *Endosperm* of higher plants. Further, the embryo as soon as it forms the rudiments

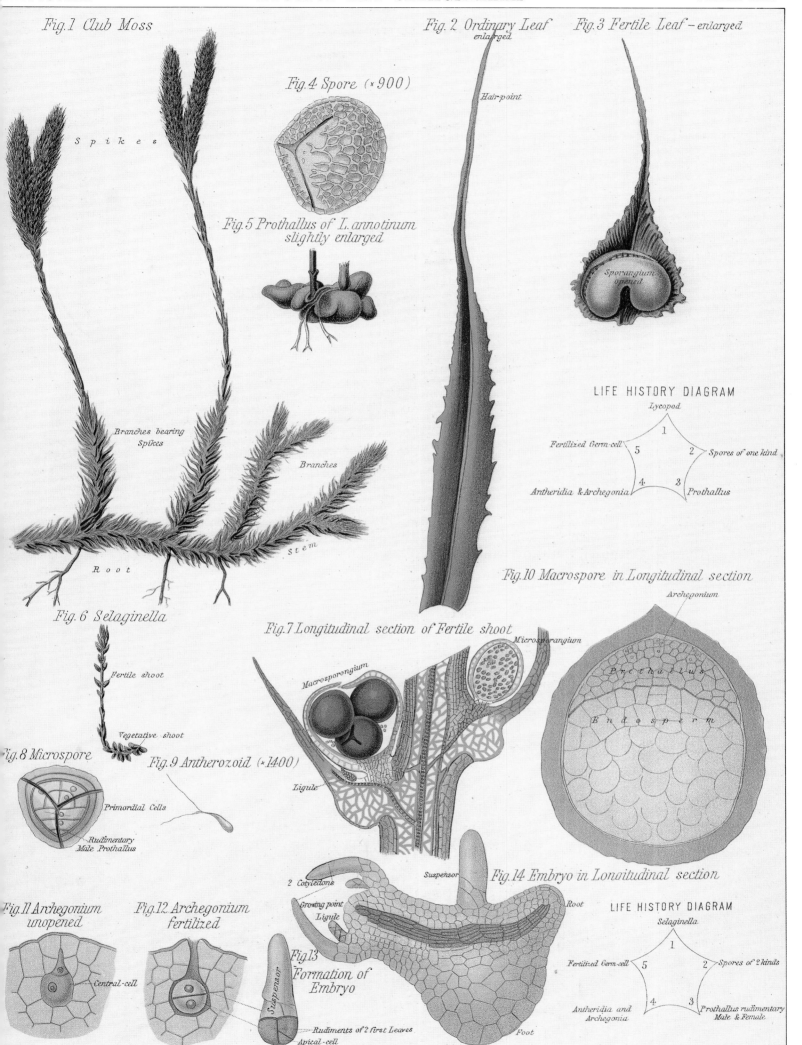

Fig.1 Club Moss

Fig.2 Ordinary Leaf — enlarged

Fig.3 Fertile Leaf — enlarged

Fig.4 Spore (×900)

Spikes

Hair-point

Sporangium opened

Fig.5 Prothallus of L. annotinum slightly enlarged

Branches bearing Spikes

Branches

Stem

Root

LIFE HISTORY DIAGRAM

Lycopod

1

Fertilized Germ-cell   5   2   Spores of one kind

4   3

Antheridia & Archegonia   Prothallus

Fig.6 Selaginella

Fig.10 Macrospore in Longitudinal section

Fertile shoot

Vegetative shoot

Fig.7 Longitudinal section of Fertile shoot

Archegonium

Microsporangium

Prothallus

Macrosporangium

Endosperm

Fig.8 Microspore

Fig.9 Antherozoid (×1400)

Primordial Cells

Ligule

Rudimentary Male Prothallus

2 Cotyledons

Suspensor

Fig.14 Embryo in Longitudinal section

Growing point

Ligule

Root

Fig.11 Archegonium unopened

Fig.12 Archegonium fertilized

Fig.13 Formation of Embryo

LIFE HISTORY DIAGRAM

Selaginella

1

Central-cell

Fertilized Germ-cell   5   2   Spores of 2 kinds

Suspensor

4   3

Antheridia and Archegonia   Prothallus rudimentary Male & Female

Rudiments of 2 first Leaves

Apical-cell

Foot

Engraved, Printed and Published by W. & A.K. Johnston, Edinburgh.

of the stem bearing its two first leaves, or *Cotyledons*, gives rise to a *Suspensor*, as in higher plants.

Fig. 6 Specimens may readily be obtained from hothouses, where they are grown on damp spots for their beautiful and delicate foliage.

Leaves on creeping stem in two lateral rows and two dorsal rows. Those of the upper surface, or dorsal row, are relatively smaller than those of the lateral row.

Upright Fertile Spike, with similar leaves arranged spirally, and bearing sporangia in their axils.

Fig. 7 Embed portion of fertile spike in paraffin and make longitudinal section. Fibro-vascular bundle in centre of axis, united with those going to leaves.

Air-spaces surrounding fibro-vascular bundles, the interspaces composed of numerous green, branching cell filaments.

Outer cells colourless.

Leaf with membraneous Ligule at its base, and bearing a Macrosporangium in its axil.

Leaf on opposite side bearing Microsporangium in its axil.

Microsporangium containing numerous small spores—the Microspores. macrosporangium, the largest, containing four Macrospores arranged like a tetrahedron, and several aborted mother-cells of spores.

Fig. 8 Microspore rendered transparent to show internal division. The contents break up into cells, one of which does not form Antherozoids, and may therefore be regarded as a rudimentary Male Prothallus.

Fig. 9 Macrospore six weeks after escaping from sporangium, and before rupture of the exospore. Prothallus rudimentary, within the spore, bearing Archegonia. Endosperm, loose cellular tissue formed by free cell-formation, *i.e.* a grouping of masses of protoplasm around small internal centres, and forming cell-walls about them, independent of prothallus, but supplying nourishment to it.

Figs. 10 and 11 Archegonium before and after fertilization.

The neck of the Archegonium is at first closed, but afterwards opens to give access to the Antherozoids. The central cell after fertilization divides first into two—one half further dividing and giving rise to stem and leaves, the other half also dividing and forming Suspensor.

Fig. 12 Embryo still within the spore. The Suspensor is a temporary structure, and there are no indications of the root so long as it lasts, but when it withers away the end of the embryo in connection with it forms the root.

The Foot is always embedded in the Endosperm, serving as a means of connection between the embryo and its early food-supplies.

Life History Diagram.—The upright fertile shoot bears the sporangia in the axils of its leaves—either Micro- or Macro-sporangia. The Microspore divides internally into antheridial cells, all but one barren basal cell, which represents a Male Prothallus. The Macrospore forms an internal Prothallus bearing Archegonia, and the rest of the spore is filled with Endosperm for food-supplies. The Archegonia are exposed by the rupturing of the wall of the spore, and the Antherozoids liberated from the Microspore fertilize the central cell. The Embryo thus formed is at first provided with a Suspensor, and grows right down into the Endosperm living at its expense; but by and by the Suspensor withers, the root appears, the growing point begins to turn round, and the line of growth becomes horizontal, as in Fig. 12. Finally, the stem and root structures assume their upright and downright positions, and the young plant emerges from the spore near the point where its development began.

CLASSIFICATION OF SELAGINELLA

Sub-kingdom. Vascular Cryptogams.

Class. Dichotomæ.

Order. Ligulatæ. Leaves ligulate. Spores of two kinds—Microspores and Macrospores.

Family. Selaginelleæ. Stem long and leaves short. Prothallus small, male and female, confined to the spore.

Genus. Selaginella—the only genus.

Advance in Organization. There are two distinct kinds of Sporangia—the Micro sporangia, producing Microspores and the Macrosporangia, producing Macrospores. The Microspore produces the smallest possible Male Prothallus in the interior of the spore, and not outside, as usual.

The Macrospore also developes an internal Female Prothallus, only protruding slightly when the exospore ruptures.

Endosperm is present, as in the seed of higher plants.

Embryo provided with Suspensor and two Cotyledons, as in higher plants.

PLATE XXVI.

SEXUAL PROCESS TRACED FROM MOULD TO FLOWERING PLANT.

In dealing with the life histories of organisms, it has already been shown that the simplest form of the sexual process obtains in Mucor. A bud from one hypha grows out to meet a bud from another hypha, and some mysterious attraction brings them together. The ends of the two blend and become parted off to form a single body, which is thus the result of a process of Conjugation. In Ulothrix, likewise, the sexual process is, if possible simpler. The contents of a cell, instead of growing out, breaks up into small particles, which round themselves off and acquire two cilia, by means of which they move about. When free in the water two moving particles from different cells meet and blend to form one body, as in Mucor.

These two forms may be taken as starting-points for tracing the sexual process in plants; the one representing the condition where the conjugating elements are passive and the plant is without chlorophyll, the other where the conjugating elements are active and the plant possesses chlorophyll.

It will not be necessary to go over each life history in detail for that has been done to a certain extent already, but simply to point out the changes taking place, both in the sexual elements themselves and in their mode of blending, in passing from the lowest to the highest term of the series. It will be convenient to distinguish two principal stages in the life history of each plant—a stage with sexual organs called the *Sexual Generation* and a stage with no sexual organs called the *Non-sexual Generation*. The Sexual Generation opens the chapter, and a return to that ends it. On glancing over the Diagrams it will be seen that the Sexual Generation is gradually suppressed, until in the Flowering plant it is microscopic in its dimensions and reduced to a few cells, while the Non-sexual Generation grows in importance, becoming the stately tree or the conspicuous flowering plant.

Note.—In this comparative view the term *Spore* is used in a different sense from that in the body of the work. In the lower forms it is a cell resulting from a sexual process, viz. Zygospore or Oospore and it is restricted to that throughout the series. Other cells which multiply the plant are *Gonidia*, although from Liverwort onwards they are usually called Spores.

MUCOR.—The *Sexual Generation* is the conspicuous mould, producing the similar and stationary male and female elements, which blend to form a Zygospore.

The *Non-sexual Generation* is the inconspicuous Pro-mycelium, consisting of a single hypha, which produces Endo-gonidia, from the germination of which Mucor is reproduced.

ULOTHRIX.—*The Sexual Generation* is the filamentous Alga, producing similar and motile male and female elements, which blend to form a Zygospore.

The *Non-sexual Generation* is the Zoogonidia, derived directly from the internal division of the Zygospore, and reproducing the filament.

OEDOGONIUM.—The *Sexual Generation* is the filamentous Alga, producing no longer sexual elements which are alike or nearly so, but now clearly distinguishable—Antherozoids and Oospheres—the Oosphere becoming converted into an Oospore by the impregnation of the Antherozoids.

The *Non-sexual Generation* is similar to that of Ulothrix.

CHARA.—The *Sexual Generation* is the plant with whorled appendages, producing Antherozoids and Oospheres, from which result Oospores.

The *Non-sexual Generation* is the Pro-embryo, which gives rise to a bud producing the plant.

MARCHANTIA.—The *Sexual Generation* is the conspicuous green expansion, producing Antherozoids on the male plant, and Oospheres on the female plant. The Oosphere, or central cell of the Archegonium, is impregnated by Antherozoids, and converted into an Oospore.

The *Non-sexual Generation* is the Spore-fruit, producing Endo-gonidia, from the germination of which Marchantia is produced.

MOSS.—Similar to Marchantia, only in the Non-sexual Generation the germinating Endogonidium does not directly produce the Moss, but a Protonema is formed, from

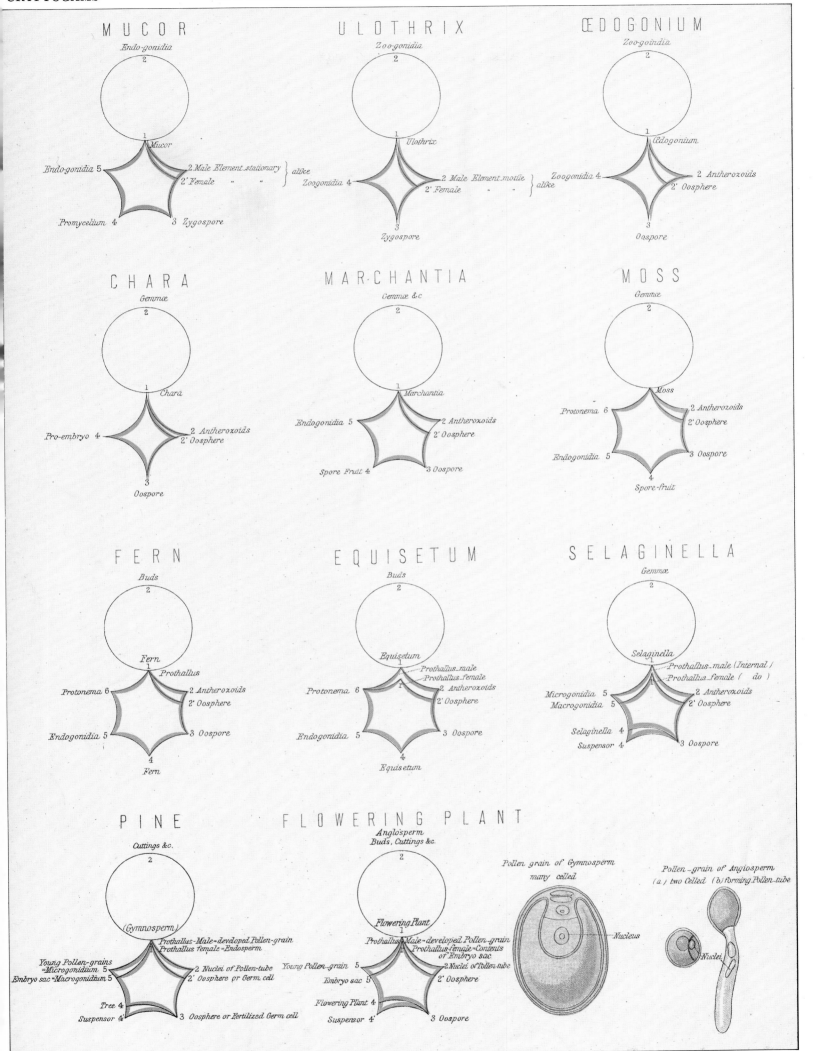

Engraved, Printed, and Published by W. & A.K. Johnston, Edinburgh

which a lateral bud arises and grows into the plant.

FERN.—The *Sexual Generation* is the Prothallus, a minute, green, heart-shaped expansion, corresponding to the leafy Moss. This produces Antherozoids and Oospheres, which latterly become Oospores.

The *Non-sexual generation* is the Fern, corresponding to the Spore-fruit of the Moss. This develops Endo-gonidia, each of which produces on germination a Protonema. The Protonema is a row of green cells, often branched like that of the Moss, and afterwards developing into the Prothallus.

EQUISETUM.—The *Sexual Generation* is the Prothallus, male and female distinct.

The *Non-sexual Generation* is the Equisetum, the fertile shoots of which repeat the history of the Fern.

SELAGINELLA.—The *Sexual Generation* is the Prothallus, male and female distinct and internal.

The *Non-sexual Generation* is the Selaginella, which has in its embryonic condition a special structure called the Suspensor.

PINE.—The *Sexual Generation* is represented by the Male Prothallus, or cells forming the full-grown Pollen-grain, and the Female Prothallus, or Endosperm.

The Male Prothallus is exceedingly simplified. There is only one or a few cells to represent the vegetative part, and a single large cell to represent the antheridial part, or the part which formerly produced Antherozoids. The production of Antherozoids was suitable for plants living in moist situations; but as Conifers live in dry situations, Antherozoids would fail of their purpose, and the nuclei do not develop cilia for locomotion. So the representative of the antheridial cell puts forth a pollen-tube, along which the nuclei are conveyed to their destination, viz. the germ-cell.

The Female Prothallus is represented by the Endosperm, in which the germ-cells are developed.

The *Non-sexual Generation* is the tree quite comparable with Selaginella, the Embryo-sac corresponding to the Macrogonidium, and the young Pollen-grain to the Microgonidium.

FLOWERING PLANT.—The *Sexual Generation* is the Male Prothallus, or cells forming the mature Pollen-grain, and the Female Prothallus, or contents of Embryo-sac.

The *Non-sexual Generation* is the conspicuous Flowering Plant, producing Pollen-grains and Embryo-sac. The modified leaves of the Flower—Stamens and Carpels—which produce Pollen-grains and Embryo-sacs are usually called Sexual Organs; but they are really equivalent to the fertile leaves of Selaginella, the Pollen-grains being Microgonidia in Pollen-sacs, and the Embryo-sacs being Macrogonidia in Ovules. Cells are afterwards developed in the interior of Pollen-grain and Embryo-sac, which represent the Sexual Generation.

MULTIPLICATION takes place in each case by a smaller or larger portion of the plant detaching itself and growing to the size and form of the parent. The directness and simplicity of this process are evident in the highest as well as in the lowest forms.

Fig. 1 Pollen-grain of Larch consisting of several cells.

Fig. 2 Pollen-grain of Monotropa (Dicotyledon).

(*a.*) Young Pollen-grain consisting of two nucleated cells.

(*b.*) Pollen-tube formed containing the two nuclei.

PHANEROGAMS

PLATE I.

CYCADEÆ.

(Cycas and Zamia from Dodel-Port and Luerssen.)

Cycads belong to the warmer parts of the world, their chief centres being Tropical America, South Africa, Eastern Asia, and Australia. Although there are no living representatives in this country, still as they form the base of the lowest class of Phanerogams, or seed-bearing plants, they naturally come in first for consideration.

They show the nakedness of the seeds or Gymnospermy, and the leafy nature of the ovule-bearing organs so clearly, that they are referred to in the most elementary text-books of Botany, and this also must be taken as some sort of justification for introducing them here.

The practical examination of the Coniferæ, with which they are closely allied, will enable the student to understand the various drawings, where he cannot hope to obtain specimens. Cycads may be seen growing in the "Palm-houses" of our Botanic Gardens, where their resemblance to Tree-ferns or Palms, is strikingly manifest.

The genus *Cycas* shows, in a very elementary form, the essential characteristic of the Phanerogams, *viz.* the structure of a Flower producing Seed. The terminal *bud* of the stem becomes a *flower* of the simplest kind—a number of modified leaves arranged spirally on an axis, and these modified or *carpellary leaves* assume the simplest form—their lobes being converted into naked *ovules*. The central bud of the flower again grows out and produces ordinary leaves, thus showing the flower to be a *modified bud*, and the carpels or ovule-bearing organs to be *modified leaves*.

Fossil forms are found in this country, particularly in the Upper Oolite. In the Island of Portland there are the remains of an old land surface, known as the "Dirt Bed," and in it are embedded the roots and woody stumps of Cycads.

GENERAL CHARACTERS

Fig. 1 In Cycas the male and female flowers are produced by distinct individuals, but both plants have the same general aspect.

Stem, woody, fifteen to twenty feet in height, surface covered with the scars of fallen leaves, and summit bearing a terminal crown of leaves, in the centre of which is the terminal bud.

Leaves, of three kinds—scale-like leaves foliage leaves, and carpellary leaves.

Scale-leaves envelope the bud, while a new crown of foliage-leaves is being prepared, and thus alternate regularly with them.

Foliage-leaves are pinnate, and form a palm-like crown.

Carpellary leaves produced by the terminal bud, and bearing ovules.

FLOWER

Figs. 2 and 3 The leafy nature of the carpel shown.

The Carpellary leaf in Cycas bears a general resemblance to the ordinary foliage-leaf, but is smaller, and may be either lobed (Fig. 2) or pinnate (Fig. 3). The lower portion of the leaf is fertile, bearing ovules instead of lobes or pinnæ.

Fig. 4 Mature Ovule about the size of a plum and like it, with a soft outer and a hard inner portion.

Fig. 5 Male Flower of Zamia a cone, consisting of an elongated axis, covered with a number of scales, bearing pollen-sacs.

Fig. 6 Transverse and longitudinal section of flower of Cerato-zamia. Scales arranged radially on a central axis, and bearing pollen-sacs on their under surface.
Fibro-vascular bundles pass out to each scale from the axis.

Fig. 7 Stamen of Zamia shield-shaped.

Fig. 8 Female flower of Zamia a cone, consisting of an elongated axis with scales closely packed, and their thickened ends hexagonal in shape.

Fig. 9 Carpel in the form of a scale, bearing two ovules on the under surface.

SEED

Fig. 10 Mature Ovule, before pollination.
(*a*) Outer succulent coat removed. End of shell perforated where the fibro-vascular bundles passed through.
(*b*) Vertical section.
Outer shell.
Fibrous sheath representing remains of Nucellus.
Primary Embryo-sac.
Secondary Embryo-sacs.

Fig. 11 Seed of *C. circinalis* in vertical section.
Outer succulent layer.
Inner hard layer.
Endosperm.
Embryo with two Cotyledons.
In addition to the perfect Embryo there are several rudimentary Embryos.

CLASSIFICATION.

Sub-kingdom. Phanerogams, so-called because the reproductive organs are generally more conspicuous than in Cryptogams.
Reproductive organs condensed into conspicuous structures known as Flowers.
Seed produced from the flower, and containing an embryo *before* it is detached from the parent plant.
Group. Gymnosperms.
Ovules not enclosed in an ovary.
Embryo-sac with endosperm before fertilisation.
Pollen-grain divided into two or more cells.
Order. Cycadeæ.
Stem, seldom branched.
Foliage-leaves, large and usually pinnate.
Flowers, in the form of cones, or as a rosette of leaves.
Male and Female Flowers produced on different individuals.
Ovules on the margins of carpellary leaves or scales.

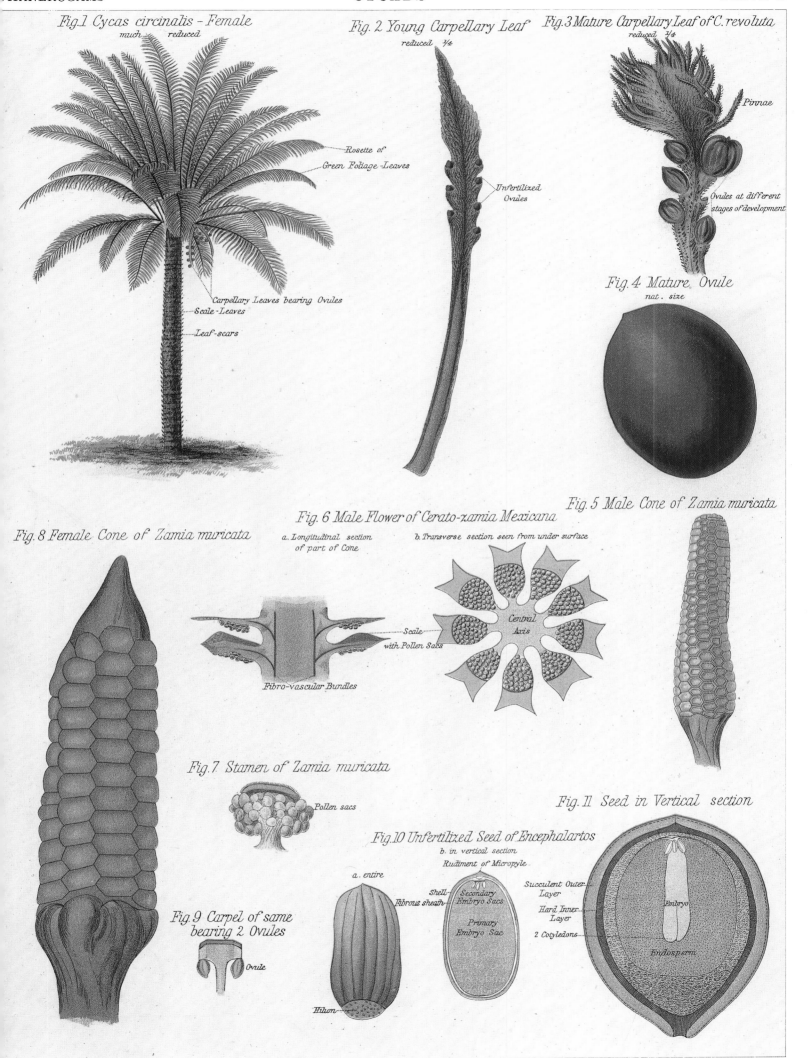

Fig.1 Cycas circinalis - Female
much reduced

Rosette of
Green Foliage-Leaves

Carpellary Leaves bearing Ovules
Scale-Leaves
Leaf-scars

Fig.2 Young Carpellary Leaf
reduced ¼

Unfertilized Ovules

Fig.3 Mature Carpellary Leaf of C. revoluta
reduced ¼

Pinnae

Ovules at different stages of development

Fig.4 Mature Ovule
nat. size

Fig.5 Male Cone of Zamia muricata

Fig.6 Male Flower of Cerato-zamia Mexicana

a. Longitudinal section of part of Cone

b.Transverse section seen from under surface

Central Axis

Scale with Pollen Sacs

Fibro-vascular Bundles

Fig.8 Female Cone of Zamia muricata

Fig.7 Stamen of Zamia muricata

Pollen sacs

Fig.9 Carpel of same bearing 2 Ovules

Ovule

Fig.10 Unfertilized Seed of Encephalartos

a. entire

b. in vertical section
Rudiment of Micropyle

Shell
Fibrous sheath

Secondary Embryo Sacs

Primary Embryo Sac

Hilum

Fig.11 Seed in Vertical section

Succulent Outer Layer

Hard Inner Layer

2 Cotyledons

Embryo

Endosperm

Engraved, Printed and Published by W. & A.K. Johnston, Edinburgh

PLATE II.

CONIFERÆ—*Male organs*

(Figs. 2 and 10 after Dodel-Port; Fig. 9 after Luerssen.)

The Coniferæ are usually trees, with needle-shaped leaves, and fructification in the form of a cone, hence the name cone-bearers. This structure has been already met with in the higher Cryptogams. The cone of a Lycopod or Selaginella has an upright axis, clothed with modified leaves or bracts, bearing sporangia in their axils.

The Stem of Pines and Larches, for instance, bears merely brown scales to represent leaves, and in their axils arise a tuft or a pair of the green foliage-leaves. These pairs or tufts of green leaves are really branches with their axis undeveloped; indeed, if a young Larch is examined, some of the tufts will be met with elongated and developed into branches.

The Flower and Fruit will only be considered now—the Male Flower in this plate and the Female Flower and Fruit in the next. The male flowers are much simpler in their construction than the female flowers. They are little cones developed in the axils of scales. They discharge their pollen about May, and in such enormous quantities as to give rise to the so-called showers of sulphur—the pollen being powdery and of a sulphur-yellow colour.

Fossil forms occur in the Carboniferous formation, the wood exhibiting the bordered pits characteristic of the wood-cells of Conifers.

Fig. 1 Shoot, bearing Inflorescence of nine Male Flowers.
Primary shoot with leaves reduced to mere brown scales.
Rudimentary shoots arising from the axils of the brown scales, each with needle-shaped leaves in pairs.
Terminal bud which develops into new shoot.
Male Flowers arranged at the base of the young shoot.

Fig. 2 Single Male Flower.
Each male flower is situated—like an ordinary bud—in the axil of a bract.
It is a modified shoot, the lateral appendages of which become Stamens.

Fig. 3 Embed Male Flower in paraffin, and make longitudinal section.
Examine first under low power to make out general arrangement, then under high power to make out details of structure.
Axis of cone with fibro-vascular bundles running through it, branching to each stamen.
Pollen-sacs borne on the under surface of modified leaves, one on each side of midrib, which here forms a Connective between the two. When the inner cells of a leaf give rise to pollen-grains, such a leaf is called a Staminal leaf, or simply a stamen; and the particular part of the leaf where this formation of pollen takes place is called an Anther. the Male cone is therefore a single flower, because it consists of a single axis bearing Stamens, which are here arranged spirally.

Fig. 4 Detached Stamen with two pollen-sacs upon its under surface, and provided with a very short stalk or filament.
The pollen-sacs open by a longitudinal slit on the under surface.

Fig. 5 Male Flower of Yew, consisting of an axis bearing a number of shield-shaped bodies. These are the Stamens.
Fig. 6 Embed Male Flower in paraffin, and make transverse section (compare with transverse section of cone of *Equisetum*).
Central axis giving off fibro-vascular bundle to each Stamen.

Fig. 7 Detached Stamen—the pollen-sacs are developed radially, and not bi-laterally, as in Fig. 4.

Fig. 8 Pollen-sacs opening on their under surface.

Figs. 9 and 10 Examine pollen-grains, first under low power, then under high power. Stain with iodine to bring out the division between the two cells.
Pollen-grain with a double coat.
Outer coat or Extine is yellowish, and sculptured all over. It comes off in water, being ruptured by the swelling of the inner. It expands into two wing-like swellings.
Inner coat or Intine is colourless and expansible. Contents divided into two cells—a small
Vegetative cell, representing the last rudiment of a prothallus, and a larger *Antheridial* cell, so-called, because it forms the pollen-tube, which corresponds to an antheridium not developing antherozoids.

Fig. 11 Treat some pollen of Larch with caustic potash, and crush, to rupture outer coat, which is somewhat opaque. Examine under high power. The small vegetative cell is seen to be divided into several cells.

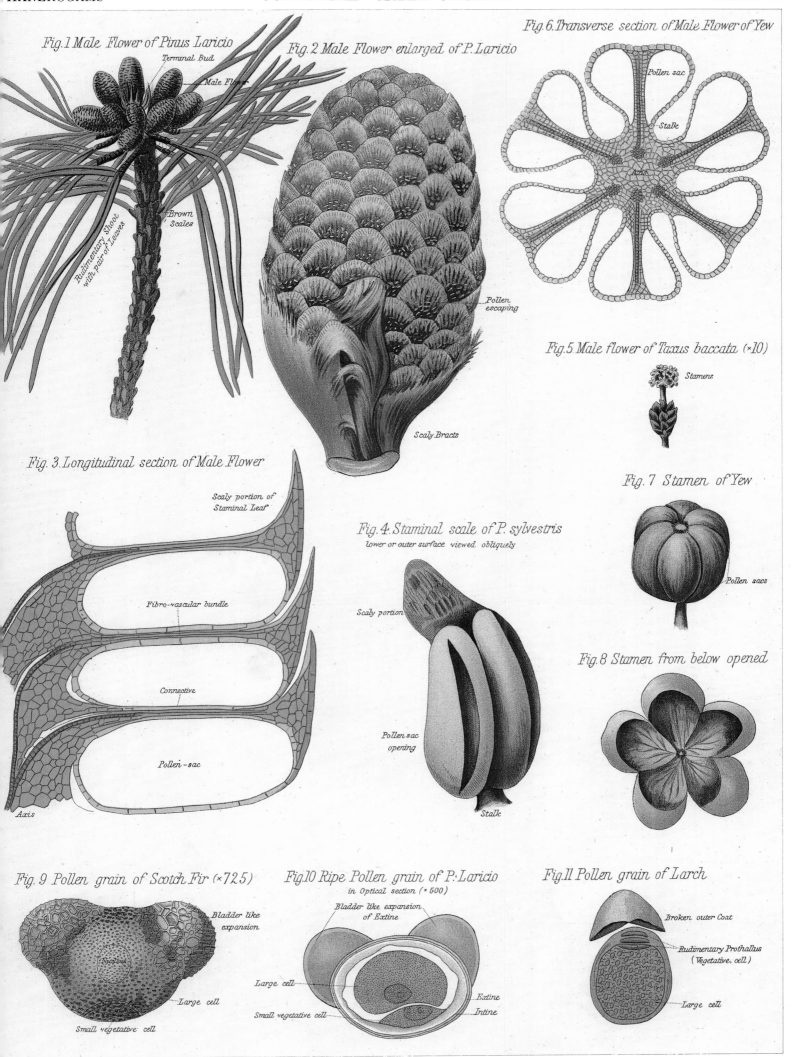

Fig. 1 Male Flower of Pinus Laricio

  Terminal Bud

  Male Flower

  Brown Scales

Rudimentary Shoot with pair of Leaves

Fig. 2 Male Flower enlarged of P. Laricio

Pollen escaping

Scaly Bracts

Fig. 6. Transverse section of Male Flower of Yew

Pollen sac

Stalk

Axis

Fig. 5 Male flower of Taxus baccata (×10)

Stamens

Fig. 3. Longitudinal section of Male Flower

Scaly portion of Staminal Leaf

Fibro-vascular bundle

Connective

Pollen-sac

Axis

Fig. 4. Staminal scale of P. sylvestris
lower or outer surface viewed obliquely

Scaly portion

Pollen sac opening

Stalk

Fig. 7 Stamen of Yew

Pollen sacs

Fig. 8 Stamen from below opened

Fig. 9 Pollen grain of Scotch Fir (×725)

Bladder like expansion

Nucleus

Large cell

Small vegetative cell

Fig. 10 Ripe Pollen grain of P. Laricio
in Optical section (×500)

Bladder like expansion of Extine

Large cell

Small vegetative cell

Extine

Intine

Fig. 11 Pollen grain of Larch

Broken outer Coat

Rudimentary Prothallus (Vegetative cell)

Large cell

Engraved, Printed and Published by W. & A.K. Johnston, Edinburgh.

PLATE III.
CONIFERÆ—*Female Organs.*

(Figs. 2, 8, and 9 from Dodel-Port.)

The Female Organs are the well-known Fir-cones. Fertilisation takes place by the pollen being carried by the wind to a naked ovule; and to assist in this action various expedients are resorted to. The pollen is produced in large quantities, thus allowing for a deal of waste, each pollen-grain has two wing-like expansions to expose a greater surface to the wind, and the needle-shaped foliage-leaves permit ready access of the pollen to the cones. The opening of the micropyle is also filled with a fluid secretion which holds the pollen-grain alighting on it, and as this dries up the pollen-grain gradually slips down till it reaches the spot where the work of fertilisation begins.

The ripening of the cone in *Pinus* is slow. During the first summer the pollen-tube has grown but a short distance into the nucellus. The scales of the cone close together, as in Fig. I, *b*, and there is no further progress, till next summer, when the pollen-tube reaches the embryo-sac and fertilises the central cells of the archegonia. Then, at the beginning of the third summer, the dry woody scales separate as in Fig. 5, and the winged seeds are ready to be scattered, to build up in future the same structures as those from which they were derived.

FLOWER

Fig. 1 (a.) Young Female Cone, as in May, upright and situated in the axil of a bract like one of the rudimentary branches.
(b.) Previous year's cone hanging, with scales firmly closed to protect the ovules.
Ripe cone in Fig. 5.
Fig. 2 Young Female Cone enlarged, showing the beaked, open scales.
Diagram I.—The Ovule-bearing scale in *Pinus* is situated in the axil of a Bract (too small to be seen in Fig. 2), and the arrangement of the fibro-vascular bundles in each shows that the two have their corresponding faces turned towards each other.
Ovule consisting of a central Nucellus enclosed in a Coat which leaves a small opening called the Micropyle leading into the Nucellus.
The Female Cone is variously regarded as equivalent to a single flower—like the male cone—or to an aggregation of flowers forming an Inflorescence. Taking a Flower in its simplest expression to be a modified axis bearing modified lateral appendages for reproductive purposes, then if the bract be regarded as a Carpellary leaf (as is sometimes done), and the scale as the placenta to which the ovules are attached, the whole cone will constitute a *Flower*; but, if on the other hand, as many suppose, the ovule-bearing scale represents a reduced branch, then the primary axis of the cone bears secondary axes, and such an assemblage must be considered as an *Inflorescence*. So

instead of the violent supposition of one leaf in the axil of another, there is a single leaf representing a reduced branch, and the first leaf of the branch is as it should be, opposite to the bract from which it arises.
Diagram II.—The Ovule-bearing scale and Bract are united in *Cupressus*, as shown by the double fibro-vascular bundle, and the inner portions of each bundle being contiguous, shows that the two corresponding faces are opposite to each other. The Ovule is thus borne upon the dorsal surface of the leaf, *i.e.*, the surface originally turned away from the axis bearing it. Ovules may occur singly, as in Yew and Araucaria; in pairs, as in Pines and Firs, Larches and Spruces; or in groups, as in Cypress.
Fig. 3 Embed Female Flower of Yew in paraffin, and make longitudinal section.
Integument, single.
Arillus, supposed to represent outer Integument.
Nucellus, a mass of cellular tissue, at first without any integument.
Embryo-sac, at first a single cell (May), then cellular tissue formed in it by free cell-formation, and from that Endosperm the Secondary Embryo-sacs are gradually derived (June).
The Yew bears male and female flowers on different trees, and the male plants are apparently the more numerous, thus ensuring an abundant supply of pollen.
The growing point of the primary axis is thrust aside, and the flower is apparently terminal. The flower is of the simplest possible description,

consisting merely of a naked Ovule.

FRUIT AND SEED

Fig. 4 Ripe fruit cone, with dry woody scales, opened to allow the escape of the seed.
Fig. 5 The seed-bearing scale of *Pinus* has apparently no bract. In the ripe cone, owing to the excessive crowding of the parts, the bract has become welded to the scale, forming a dense, woody mass; whereas in the Larch, the compression of the membranous scales is not so great, and the bracts remain distinct.
Fig. 6 Detach a seed from the wing, make a vertical section, and examine under low power in glycerine.
Seed-cover or Testa.
Endosperm.
Embryo with several cotyledons arranged spirally.
Suspensor embedded in endosperm.
Fig. 7 The ripe Fruit of the Yew has a crimson cup known as the Arillus. It is fleshy and sweet to the taste, and grows from the base of the seed, surrounding it and finally rising above it. The hard-shelled Seed is attached to the bottom of the cup and is poisonous.

GERMINATION

Fig. 8 Germinating Yew with two Cotyledons, which are *green.*
Fig. 9 Young plant showing the two green Cotyledons opposite and persistent, and succeeding leaves arranged spirally.

CLASSIFICATION.

Sub-kingdom. Phanerogams.

Group. Gymnosperms.

Order. Coniferæ.
Trees or shrubs, extensively branched.
Leaves, small, and often needle-shaped.
Flowers, usually produced in the form of cones.
Male Flowers, in the form of small cones, or reduced scales bearing pollen-sacs.
Female Flowers, in the form of cones, or a single Ovule.
Fruit, woody or scaly cones, or succulent like a berry.
Family or Sub-Order. Taxineæ, represented by Yew.

Abietineæ, represented by Scotch Fir.
Cupressineæ, represented by Cypress.

Genus. Pinus with woody cone.

Species. P. *sylvestris*, or Scotch Fir, with leaves in pairs, and winged seeds.

Advance in Organization. Instead of being herbaceous, like Selaginella, they are usually trees, and this heavier growth is met by the growing point consisting of a *group of cells,* and not of a single apical cell.
Stem increases in circumference, and the vascular bundles possess the power of continuous growth, and are not closed.
Pollen-grain, representing Microspore,

no longer produces antherozoids, but only a pollen-tube. The Antheridial cell producing a tube instead of antherozoids is a beautiful adaptation to changed conditions.
Antherozoids require moisture to move about in, and are adapted for plants living in moist situations; but with the Coniferæ, inhabiting dry mountain slopes, such an arrangement would be evidently unsuitable, and only a single drop of moisture is provided at the entrance gate of the ovule.
Embryo-sac, representing Macrospore, develops Endosperm while connected with the parent plant.

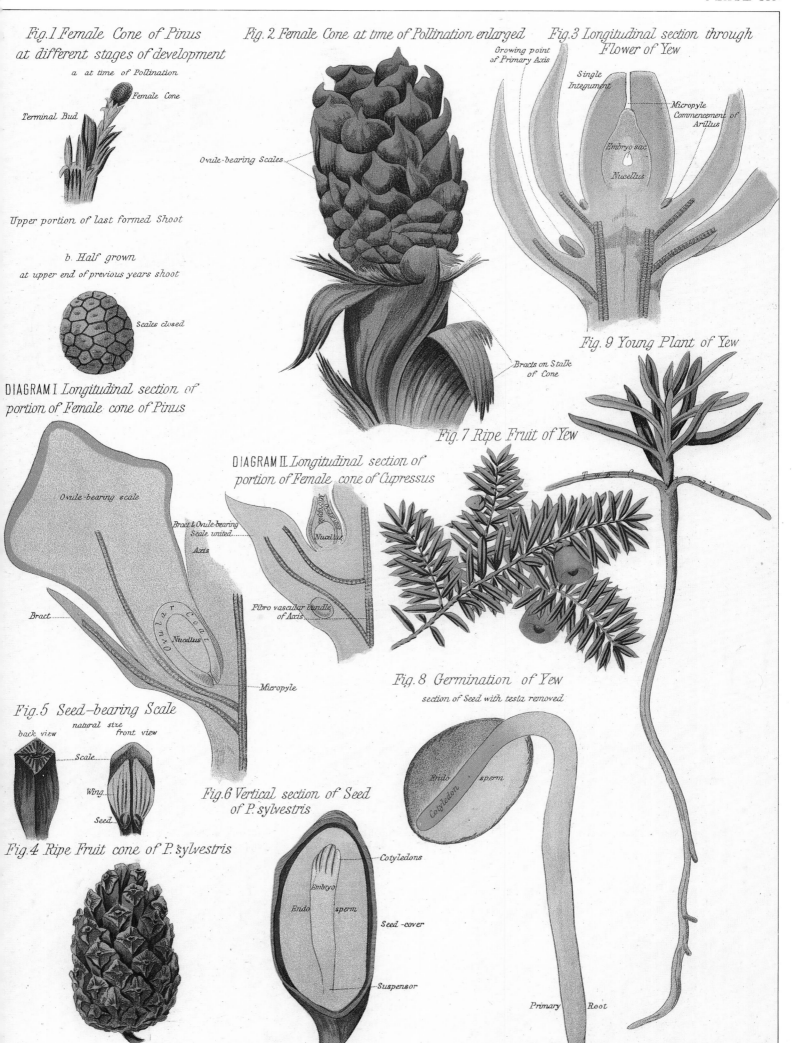

Fig.1 Female Cone of Pinus at different stages of development

a at time of Pollination

Female Cone

Terminal Bud

Upper portion of last formed Shoot

b. Half grown
at upper end of previous years shoot

Scales closed

DIAGRAM I Longitudinal section of portion of Female cone of Pinus

Ovule-bearing scale

Bract

Ovular Cavity

Nucellus

Fig.5 Seed-bearing Scale

natural size

back view   front view

Scale

Wing

Seed

Fig.4 Ripe Fruit cone of P. sylvestris

Fig.2 Female Cone at time of Pollination enlarged

Ovule-bearing Scales

Bracts on Stalk of Cone

DIAGRAM II Longitudinal section of portion of Female cone of Cupressus

Bract & Ovule-bearing Scale united

Axis

Endocarp

Nucellus

Fibro vascular bundle of Axis

Micropyle

Fig.6 Vertical section of Seed of P. sylvestris

Cotyledons

Embryo

Endosperm

Seed-cover

Suspensor

Fig.3 Longitudinal section through Flower of Yew

Growing point of Primary Axis

Single Integument

Micropyle

Commencement of Arillus

Embryo sac

Nucellus

Fig. 9 Young Plant of Yew

Two Cotyledons

Fig. 7 Ripe Fruit of Yew

Fig.8 Germination of Yew
section of Seed with testa removed

Endosperm

Cotyledon

Primary   Root

Engraved, Printed and Published by W. & A.K. Johnston, Edinburgh.

PLATE IV.

ANNUAL MEADOW GRASS (*Poa annua*) and
SAND CAREX (*Carex arenaria*).

GRASS.

The Grass chosen is common everywhere by the road-side, and may be had in flower at almost any season of the year. The flower is exceedingly small, and when the season permits the flower of Wheat might be examined instead.

Grasses are usually wind-fertilised—the pollen is wafted from flower, to flower, and thus there is an interchange of pollen. In accordance with this arrangement, the flower is inconspicuous and without gaudy colours, the anthers hang out on long filaments and turn about with every breath of wind, and the stigma is a branching tree, in miniature, to entangle the pollen as it passes.

Some, however, are self-fertilised—and the Annual Meadow Grass is an example.

Fig. 1 General characters.
Root, fibrous.
Stem, hollow and jointed. In the quickly growing stem, the outer parts grow faster than the inner, so that the interior is ruptured and a hollow produced. The fibro-vascular bundles form a horizontal partition at the nodes, and thus strengthen the stem.
Leaves, linear and alternate, with pointed membranous Ligule at junction of sheath and blade.
Inflorescence consisting of an axis with branches bearing stalked flowers.
Spikelet composed of several flowers.
Fig. 2 Spikelet detached.
There are two bracts at the base, imbricating with each other, and the axis of the spikelet bears the flowers.
Fig. 3 Floret detached.
The Stigma in the centre is seen to be branched and hairy in order to intercept and retain the pollen.
The Anthers are placed on slender filaments.
The Flowering glume and Pale are simply bracts overlapping each other.
Fig. 4 Under the dissecting microscope detach the different parts

of the flower, by steadying it with needle in left hand and removing parts with cutting needle in right. Remove the flowering glume and two little scales will be seen side by side, embracing ovary opposite to pale, and one stamen coming out between them. Great care and steadiness of hand are required in removing these entire, so that they may be laid out and examined.
The Flower is extremely simple, consisting of two little scales, three Stamens, and two Carpels, as indicated by the two Stigmas—
Little scales or Lodicules probably representing a Perianth.
Stamens three, alternating with lodicules. The anthers hang down because the filaments are weak.
Carpels consisting of swollen Ovary, crowned by two diverging feathery Stigmas.
Diagram I.—Plan of flower, showing the parts at one level and in their proper relations.
Perianth of two free segments.
Androecium of three Stamens.

Gynœcium of two united Carpels.
Diagram II.—By comparing a number of flowers it is possible to construct a theoretical diagram, showing the flower of which grass may be a reduced form. In the Rice flower, for instance, there are two rows of stamens of three each.
This diagram will be seen to agree with that of the Lily in the following Plate.
Fig. 5 Ovary with spreading Stigmas.
Figs. 6 and 7 Grains of wheat soaked in water and sections made.
Embryo is at base of seed, and the rest filled up with mealy Endosperm.
Fig. 8 Place a few grains of wheat in flannel, keep moist and at a moderate temperature, and germination will soon begin.
Fig. 9 Root-hairs.
On young roots, the cells of the epidermis are drawn out into delicate root-hairs. These root-hairs being so thin are extremely permeable to fluids, and it is through them the root withdraws from the soil the necessary plant-food.

SEDGE (from *Luerssen*).

Sedges may be contrasted in their general structure with Grasses. The Stem is solid and usually triangular. The Leaves are arranged in three rows on the stem and the sheath is not split. The Flowers are developed in scale-like bracts called glumes, as in grasses, but are usually male and female, and not bi-sexual like the flower of Grass. Sedges are mostly found in damp places.

Fig. 10 Triangular Stem.
Fig. 11 Spike bearing Female spikelets at bottom, female and male spikelets about middle, and entirely Male spikelets at top.
Fig. 12 and *Diagram* III.—Male Flower consisting simply of three Stamens enclosed by a bract.
Fig. 13 and *Diagram* IV.—Female

Flower consisting of two united Carpels, and the bracteole has grown completely round, enclosing it as in a bottle.
Fig. 14 Fruit is of a chestnut colour, and invested by the enlarged bracteole.
Diagram V.—In *Carex* the flower is seen to be really borne on an aborted

axis, which arises in the axil of the outer bract.
In *Elyna* this axis is seen to develop further, producing not only a Female but also a Male Flower.
The apparently single flower in the case of Carex would thus seem to be a reduced Inflorescence.

CLASSIFICATION.

Group. Angiosperms.
Ovules enclosed in an Ovary.
Endosperm, not formed in Embryo-sac before fertilisation.

Class. Monocotyledon.
Leaves with parallel veins.
Parts of Flower in threes.
Embryo with one Seed-leaf or Cotyledon.

Order. Graminaceæ.
Stem, hollow.
Leaves, alternate, with split sheaths, and ligules at junction of blade and sheath.
Flowers, in scaly bracts.
Stamens, three, and anthers versatile.
Stigmas, two, and feathery.
Fruit, dry, and one-seeded.

Seed with Endosperm.
Order. Cyperaceæ.
Stem, solid and triangular.
Leaves, with unsplit sheaths and no ligule.
Flowers, in scaly bracts.
Stamens, one to three.
Stigmas, two or three.
Fruit, dry, and one-seeded.
Seed with Endosperm.

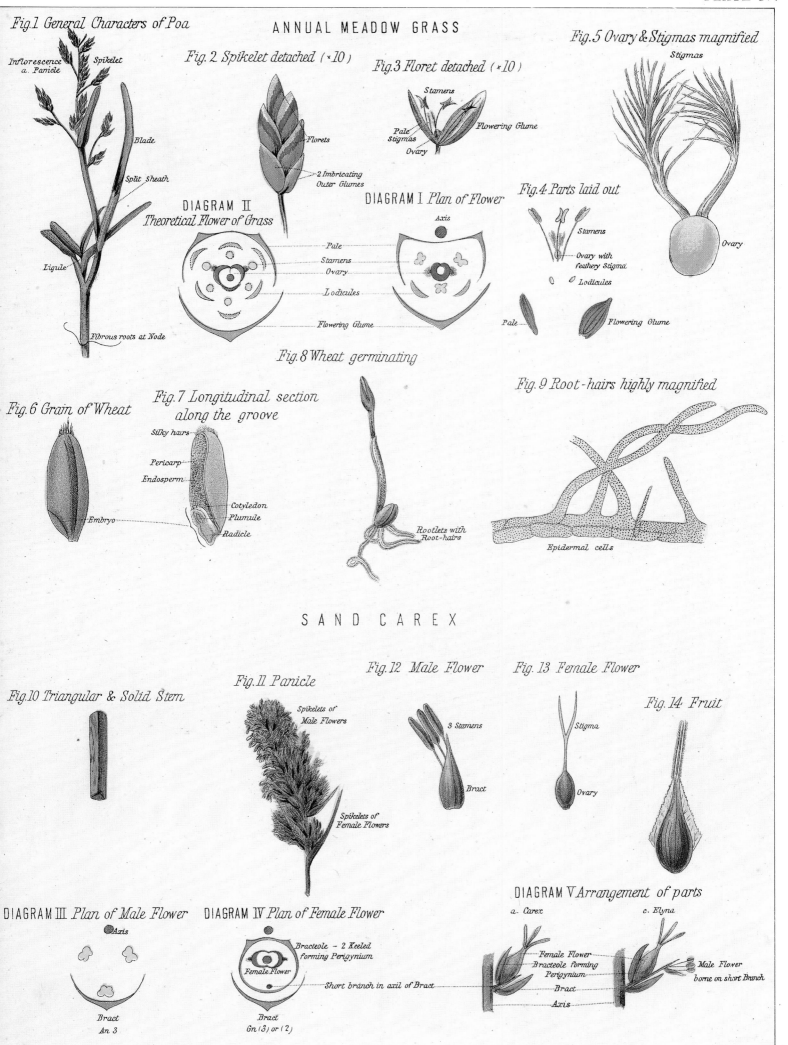

ANNUAL MEADOW GRASS

Fig.1 General Characters of Poa

Inflorescence a. Panicle — Spikelet — Blade — Split Sheath — Ligule — Fibrous roots at Node

Fig.2 Spikelet detached (×10)

Florets — 2 Imbricating Outer Glumes

DIAGRAM II Theoretical Flower of Grass

Pale — Stamens — Ovary — Lodicules — Flowering Glume

Fig.3 Floret detached (×10)

Stamens — Pale — Stigmas — Ovary — Flowering Glume

DIAGRAM I Plan of Flower

Axis

Fig.4 Parts laid out

Stamens — Ovary with feathery Stigma — Lodicules — Pale — Flowering Glume

Fig.5 Ovary & Stigmas magnified

Stigmas — Ovary

Fig.6 Grain of Wheat

Fig.7 Longitudinal section along the groove

Silky hairs — Pericarp — Endosperm — Embryo — Cotyledon — Plumule — Radicle

Fig.8 Wheat germinating

Rootlets with Root-hairs

Fig.9 Root-hairs highly magnified

Epidermal cells

SAND CAREX

Fig.10 Triangular & Solid Stem

Fig.11 Panicle

Spikelets of Male Flowers — Spikelets of Female Flowers

Fig.12 Male Flower

3 Stamens — Bract

Fig.13 Female Flower

Stigma — Ovary

Fig.14 Fruit

DIAGRAM III Plan of Male Flower

Axis — Bract — An 3

DIAGRAM IV Plan of Female Flower

Bracteole – 2 Keeled forming Perigynium — Female Flower — Short branch in axil of Bract — Bract — Gn (3) or (2)

DIAGRAM V Arrangement of parts

a. Carex — c. Elyna

Female Flower — Bracteole forming Perigynium — Bract — Axis — Male Flower borne on short Branch

Engraved, Printed and Published by W. & A.K. Johnston, Edinburgh.

PLATE V.

MARTAGON LILY (*Lilium Martagon*) and
CROWN IMPERIAL (*Fritillaria imperialis*).

(Figs. 1, 8 and 9 after Dodel-Port.)

The flowers hitherto considered have all been rather sombre in their tints. In the case of the Coniferæ there were no brilliant or gaudy colours, but the flowers were hidden, as it were, out of sight with a covering of scales. The Grasses and Sedges, too, had their minute flowers of a greenish or brownish tint, and everything betokened business, but no attempt at decoration.

But when we come to Lilies and such like, the beauty of their flowers form the most striking feature, often with further attractions in the shape of perfume and honey. This change from grave to gay, to sweetness and scent, has probably reference to the visits of insects; and now, instead of the pollen being scattered by the wind with extravagant wastefulness, a more economical method has been found in the agency of insects. Insects are attracted first of all by the colour and scent, then honey is provided, so that in obtaining it they may carry the pollen of one flower to the stigma of another, and thus unconsciously, while pursuing their own selfish ends, effect cross-fertilisation, which enables the plant to produce a stronger and healthier progeny than otherwise.

The Nectary consists of a tissue, formed of small, thin-walled cells, from which sweet juices exude and keep it constantly moist. They are generally placed in the recesses of the flower, and in the present instance occupy the base of the perianth-leaves.

The Martagon Lily is an instance of a *regular* Monocotyledon flower adapted for cross-fertilisation by insects, although in the absence of insects it may be self-fertilised.

Fig. 1 Flower of Martagon Lily fully developed.
The flower in the bud condition has its various parts arranged, as in Fritillaria (Fig. 2). The coloured leaves are directed downwards, enclosing the straight stamens and style; but as the flower expands these different parts diverge, until finally the coloured leaves curl upwards and meet around the stalk; the stamens spread out like a fan, and the style curves in the direction of most light. The nectaries, at the base of the coloured leaves, secrete drops of honey, and the anthers open to discharge their pollen. If, now, an insect visits the flower, alighting on the spread-out stamens, as a convenient resting-place, while sipping the honey with its long proboscis, it will carry away pollen on various parts of its body, and likely leave some of it on the stigma of the next flower it visits.

Figs. 2 and 3 Fritillaria has been halved lengthwise in its natural pendent position, and the six nectaries are seen at the base of the perianth-leaves in Fig. 3.
Diagram I.—Plan of Flower, representing typical Monocotyledon.
Calyx or outer whorl of three free Sepals.
Corolla or inner whorl of three free Petals, alternating with the Sepals.

When the parts of the Calyx and Corolla are similar in size, shape, and colour, it is usual to call them collectively the Perianth. The Nectaries are at the base of each perianth-leaf.

Andrœcium of two whorls of three Stamens each.
Gynœcium of three united Carpels.

Figs. 4 and 5 The Foliage-leaves get smaller on ascending the stem, till you pass by regular gradations into the bracts at the base of the flower-stalks.
Fig. 6 Stamen.
The Anther appears at first to be quite in line with the Filament, but as the stamen curves outwards, the anther comes to swing on the very top of the filament, so as readily to discharge its contents (as in Fig. I).
Figs. 7 and 8 Each Anther-lobe consists of two pollen-sacs, and opens by a longitudinal slit down the side.
Fig. 9 The Pollen-grain of Mantagon Lily is a striking example of beauty and utility combined. It is beautifully netted on the outer surface, and each mesh of the net usually contains a globule of oil. This oil is to keep it moist until it reaches the stigma with its secretion, and the netted arrangement distributes the oil more evenly and generally over the surface.

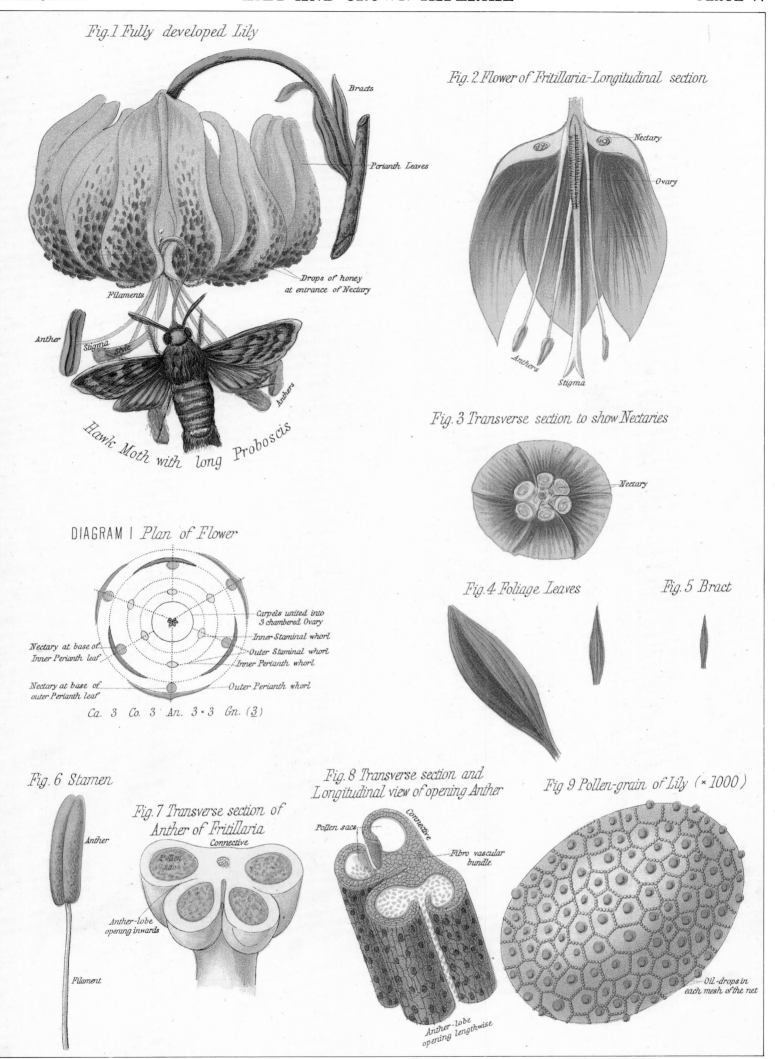

Fig.1 Fully developed Lily

Bracts

Perianth Leaves

Drops of honey at entrance of Nectary

Filaments

Anther

Stigma Style

Anthers

Hawk Moth with long Proboscis

Fig.2 Flower of Fritillaria-Longitudinal section

Nectary

Ovary

Anthers

Stigma

Fig.3 Transverse section to show Nectaries

Nectary

DIAGRAM I Plan of Flower

Carpels united into 3 chambered Ovary
Inner Staminal whorl
Outer Staminal whorl
Inner Perianth whorl
Nectary at base of Inner Perianth leaf
Nectary at base of outer Perianth leaf
Outer Perianth whorl

Ca. 3 Co. 3 An. 3 × 3 Gn. (3)

Fig.4 Foliage Leaves

Fig.5 Bract

Fig.6 Stamen

Anther

Filament

Fig.7 Transverse section of Anther of Fritillaria

Connective

Pollen sacs

Anther-lobe opening inwards

Fig.8 Transverse section and Longitudinal view of opening Anther

Pollen sacs

Connective

Fibro vascular bundle

Anther-lobe opening lengthwise

Fig 9 Pollen-grain of Lily (× 1000)

Oil-drops in each mesh of the net

Engraved, Printed and Published by W. & A.K. Johnston, Edinburgh

PLATE VI.

CROWN IMPERIAL and MARTAGON LILY.

(Figs. 3 and 4 after Dodel-Port.)

FLOWER—*contd.*

Fig. 1 Gynœcium of Crown Imperial.
Ovary is elongated.
Style with three grooves.
Stigmas, three, distinct.
Fig. 2 Gynœcium of Martagon Lily.
Ovary with six grooves.
Style smooth.
Stigma, indistinctly lobed, three narrow clefts marking off lobes.
Fig. 3 Transverse section about the middle of Ovary, and Longitudinal section through its lower portion.
Three Carpels evidently united together, forming a three-chambered Ovary.
Ovules in two vertical rows in each chamber of ovary.
Placentation is axile, because the ovules arise from a central axis which is attached to walls of ovary.
Fig. 4 Longitudinal section of Stigma with pollen, showing two stigmatic lobes—highly magnified.
The *Stigmatic* surface is seen to consist of an epidermis, the cells of which have either grown out into papillae or hairs. Such a surface evidently entangles pollen-grains falling upon it, and the *secretion of the stigma* not

only retains the pollen, owing to its viscid nature, but supplies nourishment for the growth of the pollen-tube.
The Pollen-tube is seen to grow down the *canal* of the style, the walls of which are furrowed, so as to guide the pollen-tube to the ovules.
In order to see Pollen-tubes distinctly, take a drop of the secretion from the stigma on a slide, by simply bringing it into contact with the moist stigma, then apply this to the tip of the mature anther, and a few pollen-grains will stick. In a short time (about half-an-hour) the pollen-grains will begin to put forth their tubes, if the secretion is kept moist, and the tubes with their contents appear beautifully transparent.
Fig. 5 Embed Style of Crown Imperial in paraffin, and make longitudinal section to show pollen-tubes passing down to fertilise the ovules.
The Style consists of loose tissue through which the pollen-tubes make their way. The secretion of the stigma will give the pollen-tube a start, then it passes down the centre of the style, where the cells are largest and loosest,

and thus follows the line where the ovules are attached.
The growth of the pollen-tube is thus seen to be different in the two cases. In the Lily, the pollen-tube depends entirely on its own resources and the secretion of the stigma, whereas in the Crown Imperial, it bores into the tissue of the style, just like the hypha of a fungus, absorbing it, and dying off in its hinder parts as it proceeds.

FRUIT AND SEED

Fig. 6 Fruit of Lily consisting of a Capsule, which splits lengthways along the middle of each carpel to allow the seed to escape.
Figs. 7 and 8a The Seeds are flattened out and lie one above another in two rows in each chamber.
There is a margin to each, and the Embryo is seen embedded in the endosperm.
Figs. 8b and 9 Take the flattened seed between finger and thumb and cut it in two, parallel with its flattened surface.
Embryo occupies the axis of the seed, and is slightly curved.

CLASSIFICATION.

Class. Monocotyledon.

Order. Liliaceæ.
Perianth, inferior, petaloid, usually in two whorls of three leaves each.
Stamens, in two whorls of three each.

Gynœcium, superior, of three united carpels.
Ovules, numerous, and Placentation axile.
Fruit, a capsule usually.

Seeds, with endosperm.

Genera. Fritillaria, flowers surmounted by a crown of leaves.
Lilium.

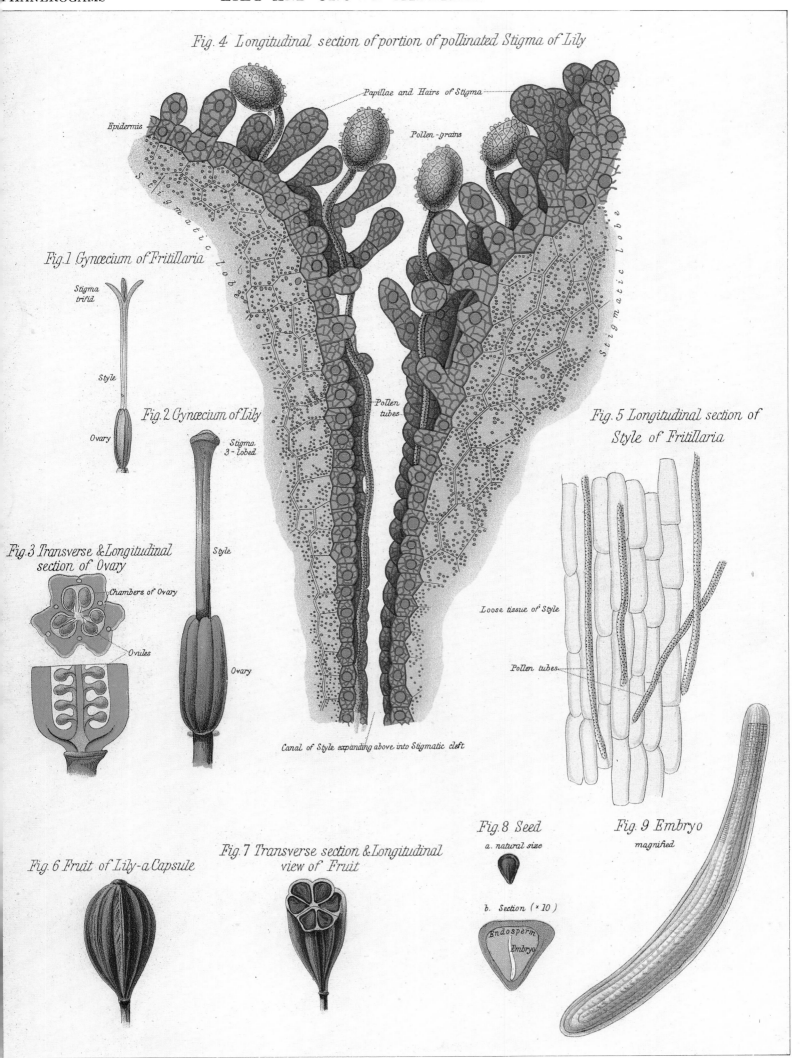

Fig. 4 *Longitudinal section of portion of pollinated Stigma of Lily*

Papillae and Hairs of Stigma

Epidermis

Pollen-grains

Stigmatic lobe

Stigmatic lobe

Fig. 1 *Gynœcium of Fritillaria*

Stigma trifid

Style

Ovary

Fig. 2 *Gynœcium of Lily*

Stigma 3-lobed

Style

Ovary

Pollen tubes

Fig. 3 *Transverse & Longitudinal section of Ovary*

Chambers of Ovary

Ovules

Fig. 5 *Longitudinal section of Style of Fritillaria*

Loose tissue of Style

Pollen tubes

Canal of Style expanding above into Stigmatic cleft

Fig. 8 *Seed*

a. *natural size*

b. *Section (×10)*

Endosperm

Embryo

Fig. 9 *Embryo*

magnified

Fig. 6 *Fruit of Lily-a Capsule*

Fig. 7 *Transverse section & Longitudinal view of Fruit*

Engraved, Printed and Published by W. & A.K. Johnston, Edinburgh

PLATE VII.

NARCISSUS.

The Daffodil is a favourite garden-flower appearing in the early spring. It occurs in woods, in moist and shady situations, sometimes in great profusion. The flower is solitary, on a long stalk; but in the *Polyanthus Narcissus* there are a number of flowers forming an umbel.

In the Daffodil the most striking part of the flower is the Corona, which forms the central tube. In *Polyanthus Narcissus* it is simply like a little cup; and in the Snowdrop, belonging to the same Natural Order, it disappears altogether. This structure is merely an appendage of the perianth, resembling the ligule of grasses, and the processes we shall meet with in Pinks, at the throat of the corolla.

Fig. 1 Daffodil.
Bract, membranous.
Perianth of six spreading segments with a large tubular Corona. The corona or crown is an outgrowth from the perianth-leaves, and is to be regarded as composed of ligules, which have united by their edges so as to form a tube.
Stamens concealed by the corona.
Ovary, inferior.
Fig. 2 The umbellate arrangement of the flowers in *Polyanthus Narcissus* is here shown, and the single bract at their base.

Figs. 3 and 4 Vertical section of *Polyanthus Narcissus*.
Perianth with long tube.
Corona, short, relative to perianth-segments.
Stamens, six, inserted in the tube.
Ovary with slender style and blunt stigma.
Diagram I.—Calyx of three Sepals.
Corolla of three Petals alternating with the Sepals. } Perianth
Andrœcium, of six Stamens, in two alternating whorls.

Gynœcium of three united Carpels.
Diagram II.—Showing imbricate arrangement of perianth-leaves in bud.
Fig. 5 Anther capable of turning on short filament, and opening inwards.
Fig. 6 Ovary three-angled, and three-chambered.
Ovules, in two vertical rows in each chamber of Ovary.
Placentation, axile.
Fig. 7 Ovule of *Narcissus poeticus* in section.
Make horizontal sections of Ovary and you also get sections of Ovules.

In the previous Plate the pollen-grain was traced from the stigmatic surface, where it formed a tube through the style, till it reached the place where the ovules are attached. Here the pollen-tube will be traced into the ovule, and the ovule itself considered.

The ovule may be perfectly erect, as in the Yew, or it may be curved, but in the vast majority of cases it is inverted. The opening of the ovule is thus turned towards its attachment, and the line of attachment is the course followed by the pollen-tube, so that, as the pollen-tubes go on growing, they can hardly help making their way into this entrance, and coming in contact with the surface of the nucellus. Then they pass through and reach the embryo-sac when the process of Fertilisation takes place.

(*a.*) Three principal parts of Ovule.
Stalk or Funicle, attaching it to ovary-wall.
Outer and Inner Coat, leaving a narrow passage for the entrance of pollen-tube.

Nucellus or central mass of tissue.
(*b.*) Embryo-sac in detail—
Embryo-sac, originally a single cell of the Nucellus, growing fast and enlarging.
Embryo-cell with two other cells called Synergidæ or Co-operative cells.

These three cells are without a cell-wall.
Three Antipodal cells, each with a cellulose-wall.
Nucleus of Embryo-sac, surrounded by a vacuole.

CLASSIFICATION.

Class. Monocotyledon.

Order. Amaryllideæ.
Perianth, superior and petaloid.
Stamens, six, with anthers opening inwards.
Gynœcium, inferior, of three

united carpels.
Ovules, numerous, and
Placentation, axile.
Fruit, a capsule.
Seeds, endospermous.
Genera. Narcissus with a

corona.
Galanthus (Snowdrop) without corona, and outer perianth-segments largest.
Leucojum (Snow-flake) without corona, and perianth-segments equal.

90

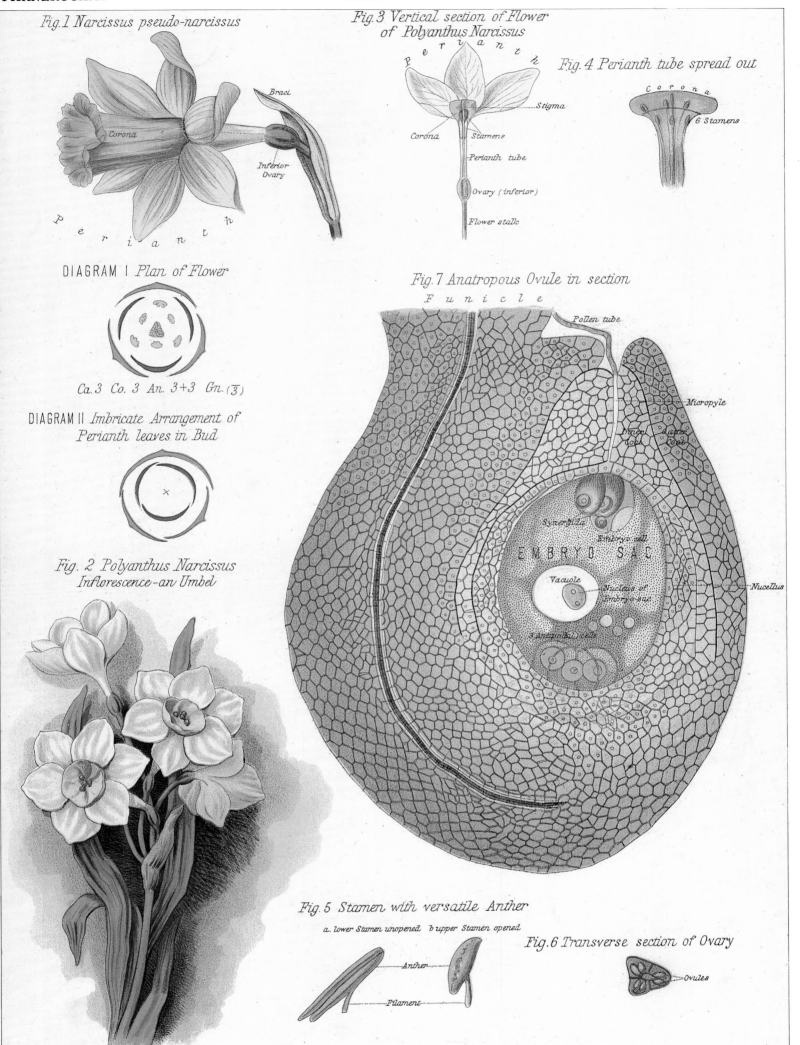

Fig.1 Narcissus pseudo-narcissus

Corona

Perianth

Bract

Inferior Ovary

DIAGRAM I Plan of Flower

Ca.3 Co.3 An.3+3 Gn.($\overline{3}$)

DIAGRAM II Imbricate Arrangement of Perianth leaves in Bud

Fig.2 Polyanthus Narcissus Inflorescence-an Umbel

Fig.3 Vertical section of Flower of Polyanthus Narcissus

Perianth

Stigma

Corona

Stamens

Perianth tube

Ovary (inferior)

Flower stalk

Fig.4 Perianth tube spread out

Corona

6 Stamens

Fig.7 Anatropous Ovule in section

Funicle

Pollen tube

Micropyle

Inner Coat

Outer Coat

Synergidæ

Embryo cell

EMBRYO SAC

Vacuole

Nucleus of Embryo sac

Nucellus

3 antipodal cells

Fig.5 Stamen with versatile Anther

a. lower Stamen unopened   b upper Stamen opened

Anther

Filament

Fig.6 Transverse section of Ovary

Ovules

Engraved, Printed and Published by W. & A.K. Johnston, Edinburgh.

PLATE VIII.

CROCUS.

The Crocus, the Gladiolus, and the Iris are well-known members of a family, prized for their large and showy flowers, which vie with the rainbow in their hues. Yellow, blue, purple, and crimson are the prevailing colours.

The Crocus comes to us as the harbinger of spring, and forms a very good introduction to that wealth of floral display which is continued onwards almost to the close of the year. But it has not merely beauty to recommend it, for the Saffron or *Crocus sativus*, which has been cultivated for centuries yields that beautiful yellow colouring matter which is used for dyeing, for flavouring soups, and also in medicine. It is from the stigmas, which are of a deep orange-red colour passing into yellow, that the dye is obtained. This order is characterised by having three stamens, the anthers of which open outwards, and the stigmas usually petaloid.

Figs. 1 and 2 Two different flowers are represented to show the relative position of Stigma and Anther in each case.
Fig. 1 shows the expanded stigmas projecting above the Anthers, while Fig. 2 shows the mature Anthers at the mouth of the perianth-tube, the stigmas being lower down.
Fig 3 Perianth of six Segments uniting below to form a long slender tube.
Fig. 4 Detach flower from underground stem, and slit it up from below.

Flower-stalk, relatively short. Perianth-tube, expanding into the showy Segments. The Segments are usually equal, but in this particular instance they were as indicated. Ovary, underground, and Ovules arranged around a central axis. The Ovary is *apparently* inferior and the Perianth superior, but as the ovary ripens the Perianth-tube is clearly seen to arise from the base of the ovary, as in Fig. 9.

The ovules are fertilised while still underground, but the flower stalk afterwards lengthens, thus raising the Ovary above ground where the ripening of the seeds is completed. Style, long and filamentous, usually projecting from the tube and ending in the three-lobed Stigma.
Diagrams I. and II.—Examine young Crocus, and make out spiral arrangement of Perianth-leaves as in Diag. II.

PLAN OF FLOWER

Calyx of three coloured Sepals, united at base to form a tube.
Corolla of three coloured Petals,
Androecium of three Stamens inserted at the base of the three outer segments of the Perianth.
Gynoecium of three united Carpels.

Fig. 5 The underground Stem is distinguished as a Corm (Lat. *cormus*, a solid bulb), because the swollen portion is chiefly composed of stem, whereas in the Bulb it is composed largely of the swollen bases of leaves as well.
Fig. 6 Foliage-leaves, long, narrow and pointed, with a *furrow* running along

the middle, and a corresponding *ridge* on the opposite side.
This is well seen in a transverse section of the leaf.
Fig. 7 Stamen—the Filament is flattened, and the Anther is arrow-shaped.
Fig. 8 The Stigmatic surface is a lobed expansion, and when fully expanded, as in *c*, there are three distinct stigmas.

Fig. 9 Fruit, a Capsule which opens by three valves, and has an elongated slender stalk. Each carpel splits along the middle of its length, so that each valve of the fruit is composed of the halves of two adjacent carpels.
Fig. 10 Seed, somewhat globular, and containing Endosperm in addition to the Embryo.

CLASSIFICATION.

Class. Monocotyledon.

Order. Iridaceæ.
Leaves, long and narrow.
Perianth, petaloid, of six segments.

Stamens, three, with anthers opening outwards.
Carpels, three, united.
Ovules, numerous; Placentation,

axile.
Fruit, capsular, opening by valves.
Seed with endosperm.

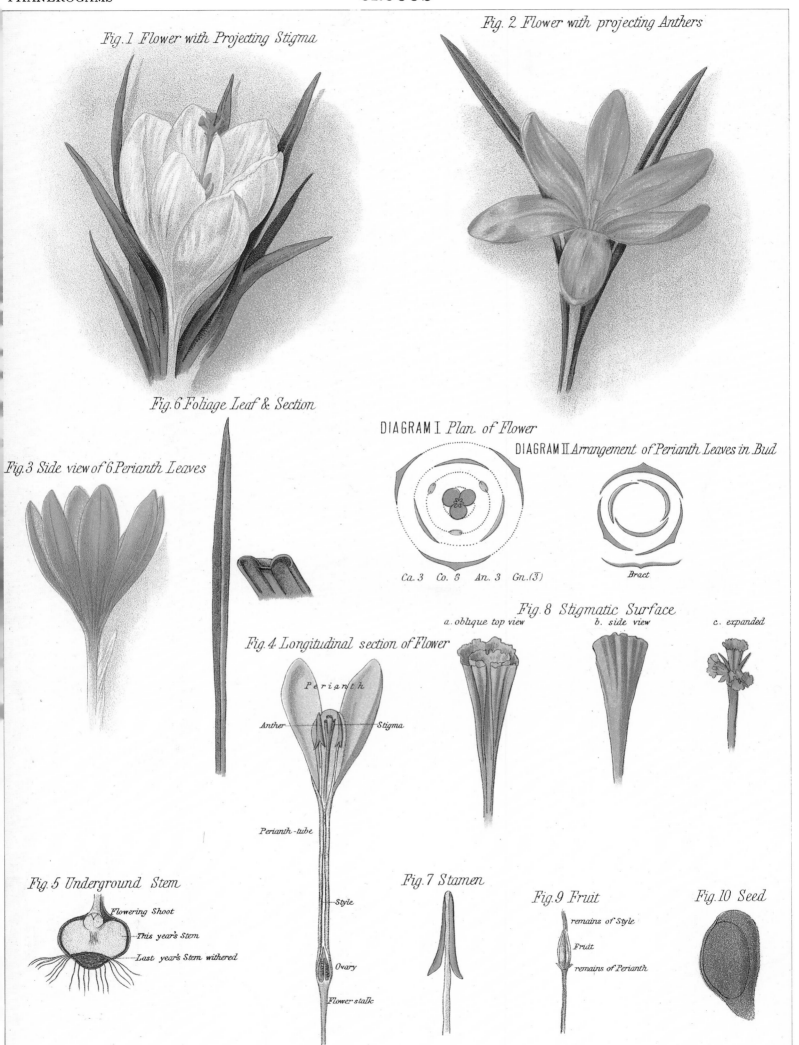

Fig.1 Flower with Projecting Stigma

Fig. 2 Flower with projecting Anthers

Fig. 6 Foliage Leaf & Section

DIAGRAM I *Plan. of Flower*

DIAGRAM II *Arrangement of Perianth Leaves in Bud*

Fig.3 Side view of 6 Perianth Leaves

Ca. 3   Co. 3   An. 3   Gn.(3̄)

Bract

Fig. 8 Stigmatic Surface

a. oblique top view   *b. side view*   *c. expanded*

Fig. 4 Longitudinal section of Flower

Perianth

Anther   Stigma

Perianth-tube

Fig.5 Underground Stem

Flowering Shoot

This year's Stem

Last year's Stem withered

Fig.7 Stamen

Fig.9 Fruit

Fig.10 Seed

Style

remains of Style

Fruit

remains of Perianth

Ovary

Flower stalk

Engraved, Printed and Published by W. & A.K. Johnston, Edinburgh & London.

PLATE IX.

COMMON ORCHIS (*Orchis mascula*).

Orchids are remarkable, in many respects, for the curious shapes of the flowers, the Peculiar structure of their parts, and the numerous and beautiful contrivances for cross-fertilisation. The common or purple Orchis occurs in shady situations, and flowers early in April. The underground stem is in the form of a Tuber, which in this species is ovoid, or it may be divided at the base into finger-like processes. There are two Tubers, a young one storing up material for next year, while the old one is providing for the present. The young Tuber arises as a lateral bud, growing in size as the old one decays, and thus the plant is carried on from year to year. The flower and its arrangement will be noticed in connection with the Figures.

As the Orchid ends the Monocotyledons, space has been found to show the germination of the Date. The Date belongs to the Palm family, but is here introduced to show the well-developed primary or tap-root, a structure with which Monocotyledons are not usually credited.

ROOT AND STEM

Fig. 1 Dig up Tubers at various seasons, before, during, and after flowering, and examine.

The old Tuber is shrivelled, and dark in colour, while the young one is firmer and paler. The relative sizes will vary according to the time at which they are dug up.

Root-fibres arise from the base of the flowering stem, and are thus adventitious.

Fig. 2 Vertical section of Tuber preserved in spirit.

The old Tuber lies beneath flowering stem, and has been pretty largely rained of its substance to afford nourishment to it, as well as to give rise to the young Tuber.

The young Tuber is now plump and in good condition, and bears a bud at

DIAGRAM OF THE UNOPENED FLOWER

(*a.*) Orchid—Calyx of three coloured Sepals.

Corolla of three coloured Petals, alternating with sepals.

Andrœcium of one Stamen, the so-called Auriculæ on each side of it representing Staminodes.

Gynœcium of three united Carpels.

(*b.*) Lady's Slipper or Cypripedium is distinguished by having two Anthers, not, however, corresponding to any of those in Orchis, but from their position forming two of an inner whorl of stamens.

A comparison of Lady's Slipper with other Orchids, and a consideration of monstrous flowers, has led to the view that the original type of Orchid flower was one in which there were six Perianth- segments and six Stamens in two whorls, as represented by the

Class. Monocotyledon.

Division. Petaloideæ

Order. Orchidaceæ.

GERMINATION OF DATE

Fig. 15 The Seed, or so-called Stone of the Date, was planted in a small pot and kept in a hot-house. In about two months some of the seeds planted germinated, as shown in *b* and *d*.

(*a.*) Stone taken from Date.

There is a little hollow on surface of seed, showing position of Embryo. Cut through at that spot.

its summit, which is a preparation for the flowering stem of next year. The young Tuber, at least in its early stages, exhibits indications of its first root at the base, but the future rapid growth of the tuber causes this primary root to disappear.

FLOWER

Fig. 3 Flower in front view.

Sepals, three, one median and two lateral.

Petals three, the lower one forming a platform on which insects may alight. Stamen, one, and Anther two-lobed. Stigmas, three, two lateral and one median, modified into the Rostellum (Lat. *a little beak*).

Ovary, beneath and not seen in this view.

Fig. 4 Remove sepals and two of the formula Ca. 3, Co. 3, An. 3 + 3, Gn. (3).

FOLIAGE AND FLORAL LEAVES

Fig. 6 Foliage-leaf, with parallel veins, and shining surface spotted with dark purple.

Fig. 7 Bract coloured, with central nerve, broad base, and pointed tip.

Fig. 8 Sepal, blunt at tip.

Fig. 9 In a ripe flower insert the point of a pencil for instance, so as to rupture rostellum, and on withdrawing the pencil, one or two pollinia will be found adhering to it.

Pollinium, consisting of a club-shaped pollen-mass borne on a stalk, with a sticky gland at the base.

Fig. 10 In a young unopened flower it is interesting to note that the Ovary is untwisted and that the *lip* is *uppermost* (as shown in Diagram). In expanding, how-ever, the twisting of the ovary

CLASSIFICATION.

Perianth, irregular, superior.

Andrœcium and Gynœcium, united.

Pollen-grains in club-shaped masses.

Ovary, inferior, one-chambered.

SEED. { Cover, a thin skin.
Embryo, small.
Endosperm, large and horny.

(*b, c.*) Germinating seed—*c*, in its natural position and in vertical section.

One end of the single Cotyledon remains in the seed, absorbing the endosperm, while the other end lengthens and carries with it the other parts of the embryo out

petals, so as to expose central portion of flower; *a* and *b* show the essential organs and their relative positions. Anther-lobes open lengthways, exposing the pollen-masses, and there is a Connective between, which arches over at the top.

Fig. 5 Make a vertical section of the flower used in Fig. 4.

The relative position and structure of the parts have evidently reference to the visits of insects. The entrance to the spur is guarded by the Rostellum, in which, as in a cup, lies the sticky base of each pollen-mass.

The stigmatic surfaces project immediately beneath and by the side of the rostellum, so that the upright pollen-mass, when it becomes horizontal on the insect's head, will strike against it.

turns the parts of the flower right round, and the lip comes to occupy its inferior position.

The stalk-like ovary shows the flower to be sessile, and the Inflorescence is therefore a spike.

Figs. 11 and 12 Transverse sections of Ovaries.

The ovary is one-chambered, containing numerous ovules arranged along the walls in three principal rows.

FRUIT AND SEED

Fig. 13 The Fruit has the remains of perianth adherent to it, and opens by three valves or lobes, leaving the ribs still standing between.

Fig. 14 Detach one of the Seeds from wall of fruit, and examine under microscope.

The Seed consists of a Cover, which is irregularly netted, and an Embryo, which is a roundish undifferentiated mass of tissue.

Ovules, numerous; placentation, parietal.

Fruit, capsular.

Seed, without endosperm.

of the seed. The primary root is developed with its root-cap, and leaves are formed within the sheath of the cotyledon.

(*d.*) The young leaves have burst through the sheath of the cotyledon and the Primary root has become largely developed, giving rise to numerous Rootlets. The primary root has a coil at the base, because it had reached the bottom of the flower-pot.

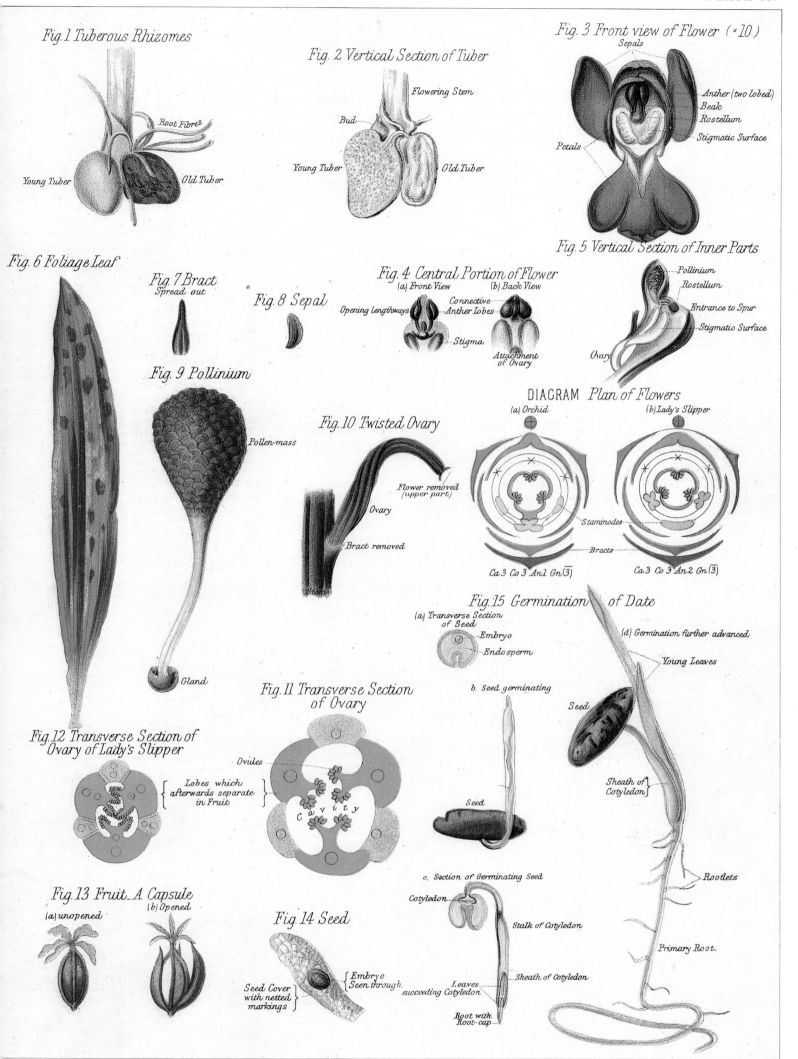

Fig. 1 Tuberous Rhizomes

Root Fibres

Young Tuber   Old Tuber

Fig. 2 Vertical Section of Tuber

Flowering Stem

Bud

Young Tuber   Old Tuber

Fig. 3 Front view of Flower (×10)

Sepals

Anther (two lobed)
Beak
Rostellum
Stigmatic Surface

Petals

Fig. 5 Vertical Section of Inner Parts

Fig. 6 Foliage Leaf

Fig. 7 Bract
Spread out

Fig. 8 Sepal

Fig. 4 Central Portion of Flower
(a) Front View   (b) Back View

Opening lengthways

Connective
Anther Lobes

Stigma

Attachment
of Ovary

Pollinium
Rostellum

Entrance to Spur

Stigmatic Surface

Ovary

Fig. 9 Pollinium

Pollen-mass

DIAGRAM Plan of Flowers
(a) Orchid   (b) Lady's Slipper

Fig. 10 Twisted Ovary

Flower removed
(upper part)

Ovary

Bract removed

Stem

Staminodes

Bracts

Ca 3 Co 3 An1 Gn(3)   Ca 3 Co 3 An 2 Gn(3)

Gland

Fig. 15 Germination of Date

(a) Transverse Section
of Seed

Embryo

Endosperm

(d) Germination further advanced

Young Leaves

b. Seed germinating

Seed

Fig. 11 Transverse Section
of Ovary

Fig. 12 Transverse Section of
Ovary of Lady's Slipper

Ovules

Lobes which
afterwards separate
in Fruit

Cavity

Seed

Sheath of
Cotyledon

c. Section of Germinating Seed

Cotyledon

Rootlets

Stalk of Cotyledon

Fig. 13 Fruit_A Capsule

(a) unopened   (b) Opened

Fig. 14 Seed

Seed Cover
with netted
markings

Embryo
Seen through.

Leaves
succeeding Cotyledon

Root with
Root-cap

Sheath of Cotyledon

Primary Root.

Engraved, Printed and Published by W. & A.K. Johnston, Edinburgh

PLATE X.

BIRCH (*Betula*), HAZEL (*Corylus*), OAK (*Quercus*), and WILLOW (*Salix*).

These four well-known Trees, chosen to illustrate the simpler forms of flowers among Dicotyledons, have this in common, that the flowers are small and simple, male and female being separate and arranged in different spikes which fall away after flowering: hence commonly called Catkins. The Male Flower consists of Stamens, and the Female of Carpels, to which may be added a Perianth more or less obvious. There are also frequently a number of investing Bracts connected with the flowers which have an interest in the detailed comparative study of plants, but for our present purpose are mere accessories—not essentials.

The Birch and Alder, Oak and Hazel, are wind-fertilised, and the pollen is therefore dry and powdery, falling from the male catkins like showers of fine dust, and the male and female flowers are on the same tree. But in the Willow, which is insect-fertilised, the golden-yellow pollen is not dry and powdery, and the two kinds of flowers are on separate trees.

COMMON BIRCH (*Betula alba*), flowers in spring.

Fig. 1 Male and Female Catkins on the same tree, the female being smallest.
Fig. 2 Detach a scale from male catkin and examine.
There are two small scales overlapped by a larger one, and each of the three bears its own stamens.
Fig. 3 Detach a small scale with its accompanying stamens from inside of large scale.
There are two Stamens with branching filaments.
Fig. 4 Stamen detached, showing Filament branching.

Fig. 5 Detach one of the scales from female catkin.
Three scaly bracts are united at time of flowering, each with a female flower in its axil.
Diagram I.—There are three flowers in a group, with three overlapping scales, the largest in the middle.
(*a.*) Male Flower—each consists of two Stamens, the filaments of which fork, and so give rise to the appearance of four Stamens.
(*b.*) Female Flower—each consists of two Carpels united.

Diagram II.—Alder (*Alnus*).
(*a.*) Male Flower—each consists of four unbranched Stamens and a Perianth of four Segments.
(*b.*) In the Female group the middle flower is absent.
Fig. 6 Winged Fruit—in the ripe catkin the scaly bracts are united and bear three winged fruits.
Fig. 7 Make a vertical section of the fruit parallel to the wings.
Only one of the two Ovules has ripened into Seed, the other becoming aborted.

COMMON HAZEL (*Corylus Avellana*), flowers in early spring.

Fig. 8 Male and Female Inflorescence on same tree, the female being small and bud-like with the crimson stigmas projecting.
Fig. 9 Detach scale from Male Inflorescence—outer view (not inner as on Plate).
Wedge-shaped and hairy, with two smaller scales appearing on each side.
Fig. 10 Examine inner side of scale.
Male flower consisting of four Stamens with forked filaments, so that there are apparently eight stamens.
Fig. 11 Stamen detached and magnified.
Filament forked, and Anthers hairy at the tip.
Fig. 12 Female Inflorescence enlarged.
Fig. 13 Remove some of the outer scales and observe that they are barren, while the inner are fertile.
Fig. 14 Single flower detached from scale.
Female flower consisting of two united

Carpels, as indicated by the two long, separate Styles. There are indications of minute teeth surrounding upper part of Ovary, and these may be regarded as a very rudimentary Perianth.
Diagram III.—(*a.*) Male Flower consisting of four branched Stamens. There are three scaly Bracts, but only a single flower appears to be developed.
(*b.*) Female Flower consisting of two united Carpels, with a rudimentary Perianth. There are three small Bracts surrounding the flower, united towards their base and deeply cut at their margins, forming the "husk" of the fruit.
Fig. 15 Fruit—a Nut. A Filbert, for instance, may easily be procured and examined.
Split the nut-shell in two lengthways, as shown, without injuring the seed.
Shell hard and woody with scar *at*

bottom, to which fruit-stalk was attached, and mark left *at top* by the styles.
Seed usually single, attached to bottom of shell by a brown, fibrous cord stretching from top of seed. This cord originally formed the axis between the two chambers of the Ovary, but by the excessive development of one seed at the expense of all the rest, this has been displaced to one side.
Fig. 16 Soak seed for a little in boiling water with a little washing-soda added, then the two coats of the seed may be removed—an outer brown and an inner white—and the two cotyledons parted from one another.
Two fleshy Cotyledons.
Short Radicle at top.
Plumule continuous with radicle, and forming a terminal bud.

OAK (*Quercus Robur*), flowers in spring.

Fig. 17 Male and Female Inflorescence on same tree—the male slender and pendulous with numerous flowers, the female stouter and upright.
Fig. 18 Male flower with lobed

Perianth and ten Stamens, the filaments of which are not forked.
Figs. 19 and 20 Female flower entire and in section.

Investment or cupule of numerous bracteoles.
Perianth, toothed.
Ovary, Style, and three-lobed Stigma.

WILLOW (*Salix Caprea*), flowers in spring—the earliest of all British Willows.

Fig. 21 The Fruit of the Oak is the well-known Acorn.
The woody cup or cupule consists of numerous overlapping scales, and the acorn is simply a Nut.
In the Birch and Hazel there were two Ovules, only one of which usually forms a perfect Seed; but in the Oak there are six Ovules, and yet only one

seed finally survives.
Fig. 22 Seed with usually two Cotyledons, but sometimes, as in this case, with three.
Fig. 23 Male Inflorescence, a bushy, soft mass of golden-yellow Stamens.
Fig. 24 Detach a single Flower with its accompanying Bract.
Two Stamens constitute the flower,

with a small Disc at the base.
Fig. 25 Female Inflorescence, elongated and of a silver-grey colour.
Fig. 26 Detach a single Flower from the central axis.
Two united Carpels constitute the flower.
Fig. 27 The capsular Fruit splits along the midrib of each carpel, and the

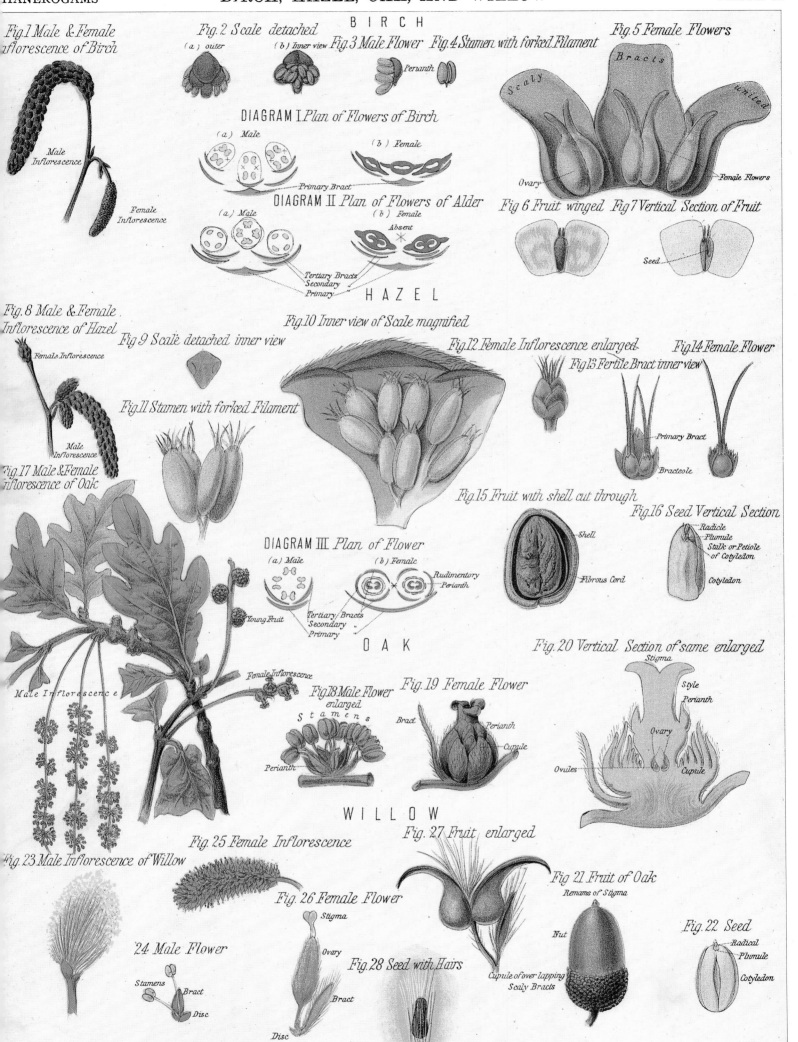

BIRCH

Fig.1 Male & Female inflorescence of Birch

Fig.2 Scale detached
(a) outer
(b) Inner view

Fig.3 Male Flower

Fig.4 Stamen with forked Filament
Perianth

Fig.5 Female Flowers
Bracts
Scaly
united
Ovary
Female Flowers

Male Inflorescence

Female Inflorescence

DIAGRAM I. Plan of Flowers of Birch
(a) Male
(b) Female
Primary Bract

DIAGRAM II. Plan of Flowers of Alder
(a) Male
(b) Female
Absent
Tertiary Bracts
Secondary
Primary

Fig 6 Fruit winged

Fig 7 Vertical Section of Fruit
Seed

HAZEL

Fig.8 Male & Female Inflorescence of Hazel
Female Inflorescence
Male Inflorescence

Fig 9 Scale detached inner view

Fig.10 Inner view of Scale magnified

Fig.11 Stamen with forked Filament

Fig.12 Female Inflorescence enlarged
Fig.13 Fertile Bract inner view
Fig.14 Female Flower
Primary Bract
Bracteole

Fig.15 Fruit with shell cut through
Shell
Fibrous Cord

Fig.16 Seed Vertical Section
Radicle
Plumule
Stalk or Petiole of Cotyledon
Cotyledon

Fig.17 Male & Female inflorescence of Oak

DIAGRAM III. Plan of Flower
(a) Male
(b) Female
Rudimentory Perianth
Tertiary Bracts
Secondary
Primary
Young Fruit

OAK

Male Inflorescence

Female Inflorescence

Fig.18 Male Flower enlarged
Stamens
Perianth

Fig.19 Female Flower
Bract
Perianth
Cupule

Fig.20 Vertical Section of same enlarged
Stigma
Style
Perianth
Ovary
Ovules
Cupule

Fig.21 Fruit of Oak
Remains of Stigma
Nut
Cupule of over lapping Scaly Bracts

Fig.22 Seed
Radical
Plumule
Cotyledon

WILLOW

Fig.23 Male Inflorescence of Willow

Fig.24 Male Flower
Stamens
Bract
Disc

Fig.25 Female Inflorescence

Fig.26 Female Flower
Stigma
Ovary
Bract
Disc

Fig.27 Fruit enlarged

Fig.28 Seed with Hairs

Engraved, Printed and Published by W. & A.K. Johnston, Edinburgh.

two valves curl over at the top, exposing the hairy Seeds.

Fig. 28 Each Seed is enveloped by a pencil of silky hairs springing from the base.

CLASSIFICATION.

Class. Dicotyledon.
Leaves net-veined.
Embryo with two cotyledons.

Orders. Betulaceæ (Birch and Alder).
Male and Female flowers on same tree.
Female flowers without perianth.
Ovary, two-chambered, with one Ovule in each chamber.
Fruit, a flattened nut, usually winged and without investment.

Corylaceæ (Hazel).
Male and Female flowers on same tree.
Female flowers with rudimentary perianth.
Ovary, two-chambered, with one Ovule in each.
Fruit, a nut, with leafy investment.
Cupuliferæ (Oak)
Male and Female flowers on same tree.
Male and Female flowers with perianth.
Ovary, three-chambered, with two Ovules in each.
Fruit, a nut, with cupule.
Salicaceæ (Willow).
Male and Female flowers on different trees.
Disc, representing Perianth.
Ovary, one-chambered with numerous Ovules.
Fruit, capsular, splitting into two valves.
Seeds, numerous, with silky hairs.

PLATE XI.

WHITE WATER-LILY (*Nymphæa alba*) and YELLOW WATER-LILY (*Nuphar luteum*).

These are water-plants, growing in lakes or ponds with floating leaves and large solitary flowers. The leaves and flowers are borne on long stalks, so as to reach the surface of the water, and the stalks are permeated by large air-cavities.

The White Water-lily is specially interesting, as showing a gradual passage from Sepal to Petal and from Petal to Stamen.

The Yellow Water-lily has an alcoholic odour like brandy, hence it sometimes gets the name of brandy-bottle.

FLOWER

Fig. 1 Flower-bud showing four Sepals green on the outside.

Fig. 2 Partially opened Bud, halved from below upwards.

Flower-stalk with air-cavities.

Sepals, less green than in unopened bud.

Petals and Stamens apparently inserted on Ovaries, but really attached to Receptacle, which is developed around, and adherent to the carpels.

Carpels with ovaries, partly above and partly below insertion of stamens.

Diagram I.—Calyx, of four Sepals. Corolla, of numerous Petals, gradually getting smaller as they approach the Stamens.

Andrœcium, of numerous Stamens.

Gynœcium, of numerous Carpels.

Fig. 3 Flower-bud of Yellow Water-lily showing five greenish-yellow Sepals.

Fig. 4 Bud halved lengthways showing superior Ovary.

Diagram II.—Calyx of five Sepals. Corolla, of a variable number of petals, often thirteen.

Andrœcium, of numerous Stamens.

Gynœcium, of numerous superior Carpels.

FOLIAGE- AND FLORAL-LEAVES

Fig. 5 Foliage-leaf, large and heart-shaped.

Fig. 6 Floral leaves of White Water-lily, showing transition from Sepal to petal.

(*a.*) Sepal, quite green.

(*b.*) Petal, white, but otherwise resembling sepal.

(*c.*) Regular Petal

Fig. 7 Stamens showing transition from petals to Stamens.

(*a.*) Stamen, which is essentially a petal-bearing anther.

(*b.*) Regular stamen.

FRUIT AND SEED

Fig. 8 The Fruit consists of the numerous carpels, surrounded by a fleshy Receptacle upon which the petals and stamens were spirally arranged.

It ripens under water and afterwards splits up irregularly to allow the escape of the seeds.

Fig. 9 Vertical section of Seed. The Seed contains a small Embryo with large Endosperm. This endosperm is not only developed as usual in the Embryo-sac, but Nucellus outside the embryo-sac also becomes loaded with nutritious matter, and this is sometimes called Perisperm.

CLASSIFICATION.

Class. Dicotyledon.

Division. Polypetalæ.

Sub-division. Thalamifloræ.

Order. Nymphæaceæ.

Water-plants.

Leaves, usually large and floating.

Flowers, regular.

Petals and Stamens, indefinite.

Carpels, indefinite.

Fruit, berry-like.

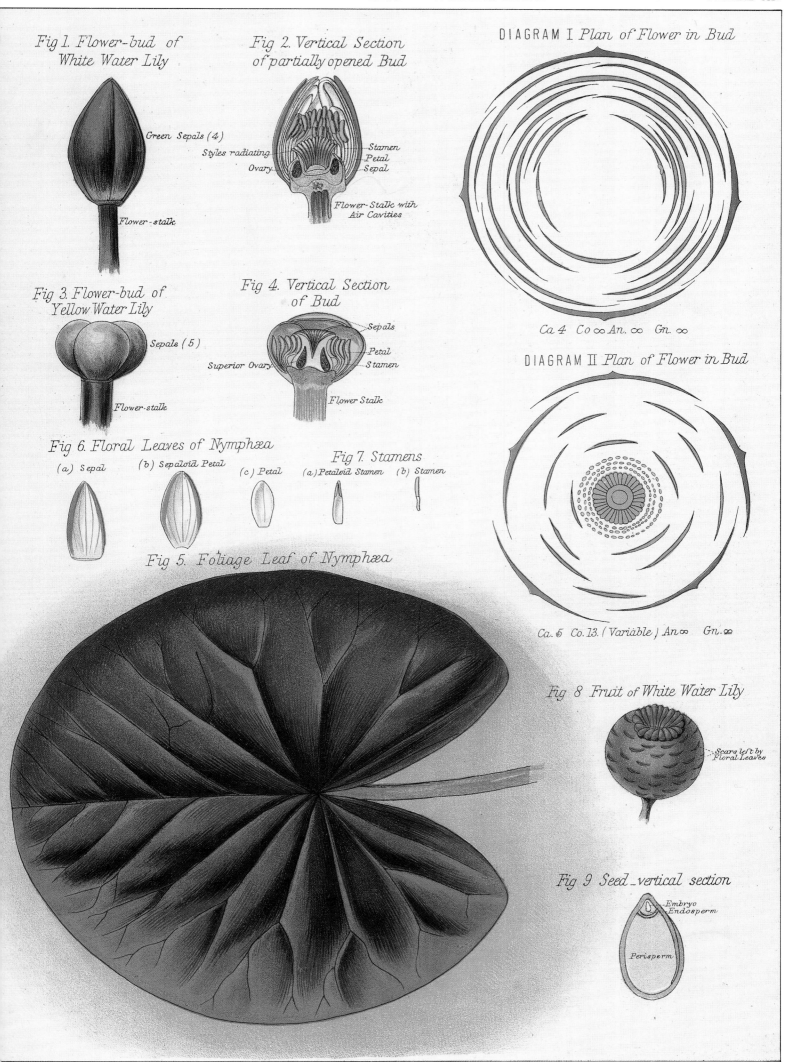

Fig 1. Flower-bud of White Water Lily

Green Sepals (4)

Flower-stalk

Fig 2. Vertical Section of partially opened Bud

Styles radiating
Ovary
Stamen
Petal
Sepal

Flower-Stalk with Air Cavities

DIAGRAM I Plan of Flower in Bud

Ca 4 Co ∞ An. ∞ Gn. ∞

Fig 3. Flower-bud of Yellow Water Lily

Sepals (5)

Flower-stalk

Fig 4. Vertical Section of Bud

Sepals
Petal
Stamen
Superior Ovary

Flower Stalk

DIAGRAM II Plan of Flower in Bud

Ca. 5 Co. 13. (Variable) An ∞ Gn. ∞

Fig 6. Floral Leaves of Nymphæa

(a) Sepal   (b) Sepaloid Petal   (c) Petal

Fig 7. Stamens

(a) Petaloid Stamen   (b) Stamen

Fig 5. Foliage Leaf of Nymphæa

Fig 8 Fruit of White Water Lily

Scars left by Floral Leaves

Fig 9 Seed_vertical section

Embryo
Endosperm

Perisperm

Engraved, Printed and Published by W. & A.K. Johnston, Edinburgh.

PLATE XII.

BUTTERCUP (*Ranunculus*) and COLUMBINE (*Aquilegia*).

(Columbine after Baillon.)

Buttercups are very common, but they are not on that account to be lightly passed over. The Flower shows the four sets of organs very distinctly, and the parts in each are separate. The Leaves are also very instructive as showing how the much-divided compound leaf gradually gets simpler and simpler as the flower is approached, until there is no difficulty in passing from them to the sepals. In the White Water-lily the passage of one *floral*-leaf into another was shown, but no attempt was made to connect the ordinary *foliage*-leaves with them; in fact there is often a difficulty in doing so, especially where the leaves are compound, for you invariably find the leaves of the flower to be simple. The Buttercup shows the process of simplification very beautifully, and it may also be observed in the white-flowered garden *Peony*, belonging to the same Order as the Buttercup.

The simple flower of the Buttercup has many contrivances worth noticing. It is of a golden colour to attract insects; it has a nectary at the base of each petal to entice them into the recesses of the flower; the outer stamens shed their pollen before the inner, and before the carpels are ready to receive it, in order that insects may carry the pollen from younger flowers, to those more advanced, in which the carpels are mature; and, finally, the whole flower is beautifully spread out to sun and sky, enabling it, with the help of its minutely divided leaves, to get the full benefit of its surroundings.

BUTTERCUP

FLOWER

Fig. 1 Halve the expanded flower by cutting from below upwards.
Flower-stalk expanding into Receptacle which is conical, and to which the various parts of the flower are attached.
Sepals inserted on receptacle below carpels, soon falling off. Petals inserted on receptacle, with little scale at base protecting nectar from excessive evaporation.
Stamens inserted on receptacle, and spirally arranged.
Carpels inserted at top of conical receptacle, each with one Ovule, and spirally arranged.
Diagram I.—Make transverse section of Bud, just above the base, in order

to cut through the various parts. Gently separate the parts with dissecting needle and make out their relative position.
Calyx of five free Sepals, imbricate.
Corolla of five free Petals, imbricate.
Androecium of numerous free Stamens.
Gynoecium of numerous free Carpels.
FOLIAGE- AND FLORAL-LEAVES
Fig. 2 Foliage-leaves gradually passing into floral-leaves.
This gradation of leaves may not all occur on one plant, so several plants should be examined.
Fig. 3 Floral-leaves.
Green Sepal, hairy outside.
Coloured Petals, notched and unnotched.

Fig. 4 Filament of Stamen continued along the back or outer face of stamen.
Fig. 5 Carpel with small point of attachment, and consisting of swollen Ovary, short Style and hooked Stigma.
Fig. 6 Side wall of Ovary removed, showing single Ovule in the cavity.

FRUIT AND SEED

Fig. 7 Fruit entire and in vertical section.
Fruit-cover or Pericarp enclosing Seed.
Seed consisting of—
Membranous coat.
Endosperm, white and solid.
Embryo or rudimentary plant towards base.

COLUMBINE

The scientific name *Aquilegia* (Lat. *aquila,* an eagle), and the common name, *Columbine* (Lat. *columba,* a dove), have both reference to the form of the petals, since one of the petals with a sepal on each side resembles a bird.

Fig. 8 Section of Flower as in Fig. I.
Flower-stalk expanded at top.
Sepals, sometimes greenish, but usually coloured, hence called petaloid.
Petals with spur projecting below.
Stamens in several whorls above one another.
Carpels inserted on top of receptacle, each with numerous Ovules.
Diagram II.—Plan of Flower.
Calyx of five free petaloid Sepals.

Corolla of five free spurred Petals, alternating with the Sepals.
Androecium of ten whorls of Stamens of five each, arranged in ten radiating rows. The innermost and uppermost ten Stamens are reduced to flattened scales, and being barren are called Staminodes.
Gynoecium of five free Carpels, opposite the Petals.
Fig. 9 Fruit.
Each Carpel opens along its inner

face to discharge the seeds.
A dry fruit, consisting of a single carpel, containing a number of seeds, and opening lengthways along its inner or ventral face is called a *Follicle.*
Fig. 10 a, b Seed consisting of—
Cover, which forms a projecting ridge on one side, ending in a *scar* or place of attachment.
Endosperm, large and fleshy. Embryo towards apex, with two Cotyledons and Radicle pointing to Micropyle.

BANE-BERRY

Fig. 11 Inflorescence—a Raceme.

Fig. 12 Fruit—a Berry; containing a number of Seeds.

Fig. 13 Single Seed with its covering or Testa.

It may be remarked that in Baneberry, where the Carpels are reduced to their lowest number viz., one, the fruit becomes an attractive Berry, which is eaten by animals, and so the Seeds are deposited under the most favourable conditions.

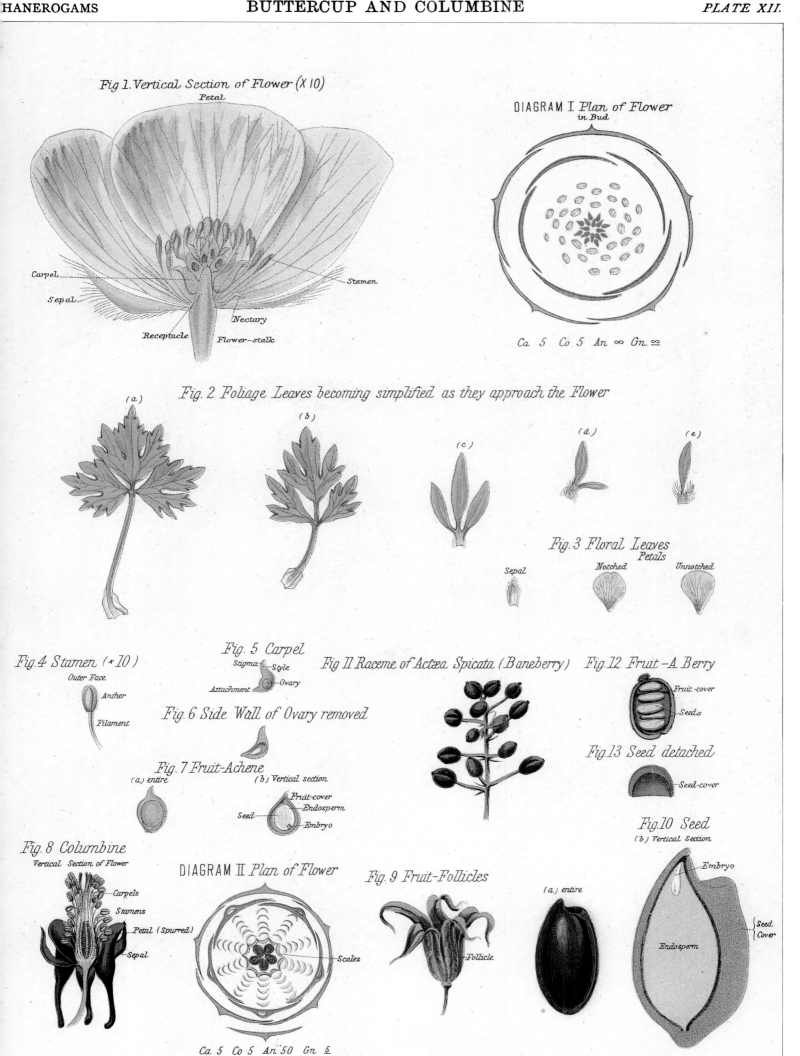

Fig 1. Vertical Section of Flower (X 10)

Petal

Carpel

Sepal

Stamen

Nectary

Receptacle

Flower-stalk

DIAGRAM I *Plan of Flower* in Bud

Ca 5 Co 5 An ∞ Gn. ∞

Fig. 2 *Foliage Leaves becoming simplified as they approach the Flower*

(a)   (b)   (c)   (d)   (e)

Fig. 3 *Floral Leaves*

Sepal   Petals   Notched   Unnotched

Fig. 4 Stamen (× 10)

Outer Face

Anther

Filament

Fig. 5 Carpel

Stigma   Style

Attachment   Ovary

Fig. 6 Side Wall of Ovary removed

Fig. 7 Fruit-Achene

(a) entire   (b) Vertical section

Fruit-cover

Endosperm

Seed

Embryo

Fig II Raceme of Actæa Spicata (Baneberry)

Fig. 12 Fruit – A Berry

Fruit-cover

Seeds

Fig. 13 Seed detached

Seed-cover

Fig.10 Seed

(b) Vertical Section

Embryo

Seed Cover

Endosperm

Fig. 8 Columbine

Vertical Section of Flower

Carpels

Stamens

Petal (Spurred)

Sepal

DIAGRAM II *Plan of Flower*

Scales

Ca 5 Co 5 An 50 Gn 5

Fig. 9 Fruit-Follicles

(a) entire

Follicle

Engraved, Printed and Published by W. & A.K. Johnston, Edinburgh.

PLATE XIII.

BARBERRY (*Berberis vulgaris*) and POPPY (*Papaver Rhoeas*).

BARBERRY

The common Barberry is remarkable for its leaf-spines and its irritable stamens.

The Leaf-spines (see Cryptogams, Pl. XVI.) are hard woody pointed structures, bearing in their axils the branches reduced to tufts of leaves.

The Stamens stand out from the Carpel and lie in the hollow of the petals. If a stamen is touched at the base, with a pin for instance, it curves forward towards the centre of the flower; and it is evident that when an insect visits the honey-glands, situated at the base of the petals, it will irritate the stamens, get dusted with the pollen, and possibly be hurried off in alarm to the next flower.

The connection of the Barberry with Rust of Wheat is shown in treating of that Fungus.

Fig. 1 Inflorescence—a Raceme, as in Baneberry.
Fig. 2 Flower showing twelve honey-glands—in pairs—at base of each petal, and the Stamens close to the petals.
Diagram I.—Barberry—Parts of the flower in three's; Gynœcium being single.

Diagram II.—Epimedium—Parts of the flower in two's; Gynœcium being single.
Fig. 3 Stamen with Anther opening by Valves.
The irritability of the stamens can easily be tested in species of Barberry

or Mahonia, common in shrubberies.
Fig. 4 Fruit—a Berry, as in Baneberry.
Fig. 5 Seed in vertical section.
Seed cover.
Endosperm.
Embryo occupying the axis of the seed.

POPPY

The Field Poppy, so common in fields and waste places, has a conspicuous scarlet flower. If the flower is examined while still wrapped up in the two sepals, it will be found that the anthers fit exactly between the stigmatic rays; and as the *inner* stamens open *first* by lateral slits, the pollen is necessarily dusted over the rays of the stigma which stand up like so many ribs in the centre of the flower. The Stigma is not quite mature, and the pollen is just so much dainty food, spread out on a table as it were, and arranged along radiating lines. When the sepals fall away and the flower expands the stamens have diverged, as in Fig. 2. An insect attracted by the scarlet naturally alights on the solid centre, and finds the pollen it is in quest of. It is arranged along certain lines, and just as the lines and bands of many flowers are supposed to be honey-guides, so these stigmatic rays may be of the nature of pollen-guides. There is abundance of pollen produced by the numerous stamens; and the insects, no doubt while feasting themselves, will carry pollen on their bodies from one flower to another.

FLOWER
Fig. 1 Flower-bud showing the two Sepals which fall off as the flower expands, and the crumpled petals beneath.
Fig. 2 Take an expanded flower, and make a section through it.
Peduncle, hairy.
Petals, larger and smaller, inserted beneath ovary.
Stamens, inserted beneath ovary.
Carpels, united.
Diagram III.—Calyx of two free hairy Sepals.
Corolla of four free Petals, in two whorls of two each.
Andrœcium of numerous Stamens in alternating whorls.
Gynœcium of numerous united Carpels, as indicated by the partial partitions of the ovary.

FOLIAGE-AND FLORAL-LEAVES
Fig. 3 Foliage-leaf with ascending lobes and bristle at the tip of each,
Fig. 4 Floral-leaves—inner side.
(*a.*) Sepal, concave.
(*b. c.*) Outer and inner Petals, the outer pair largest.
Fig. 5 Stamens with anthers opening laterally.

FRUIT AND SEED
Fig. 6 Fruit—a Capsule which opens by pores.

Fig. 7 Seeds with netted markings.
Figs. 8 and 9 Section of seed showing Embryo and Endosperm.
Embryo turned out with the fine hairs of a small brush.
Fig. 10 **Fruit of Celandine (Chelidonium) opening by two valves.**
Diagram IV.—The edges of the carpels are infolded, nearly meeting in the centre and the ovules are attached to the surface (not to the edges) of the inturned carpels.
Diagram V.—Fruit of Celandine consisting of two carpels, and forming a siliquose fruit.

CLASSIFICATION.

Class. Dicotyledon.
Division. Polypetalæ.
Sub-division. Thalamiflowæ.
Order. Berberideæ.
Flower with Bract.

Stamens definite, and Anthers opening by valves.
Fruit, a Berry usually.
Seed with endosperm.
Order. Papaveraceæ.

Flower, regular.
Petals, four.
Stamens, indefinite.
Fruit, a Capsule.
Seed with endosperm.

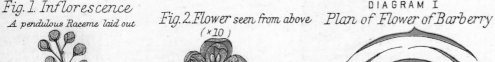

BARBERRY

DIAGRAM I
Plan of Flower of Barberry

DIAGRAM II
Plan of Flower of Epimedium

Fig. 1. Inflorescence
A pendulous Raceme laid out

Fig. 2. Flower seen from above
(× 10)

Fig. 4. Fruit - a Berry

Fig. 3. Stamens
(× 10)

Fig. 5. Seed vertical section
Seed-cover
Endosperm
Embryo

Ca 3+3 Co 3+3 An 3+3 Gn 1

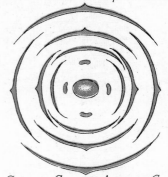

Ca $\underline{2+2}$ Co 2+2 An 2+2 Gn 1
repeated

POPPY

Fig. 1. Flower-bud
Sepals
Petals

Fig. 2. Vertical Section of Flower
Smaller Petal
Larger Petal
Stamens
Peduncle

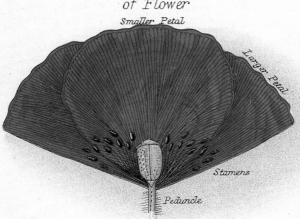

DIAGRAM III
Plan of Flower

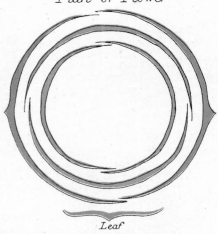

Leaf

Ca.2 Co 2+2 An. ∞ Gn. ∞

Fig. 3. Foliage Leaf

Fig. 4. Floral Leaves - inner view

(a) Sepal

(b) Outer Petal

(c) Inner Petal

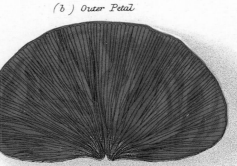

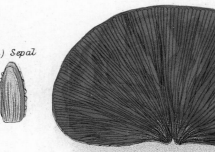

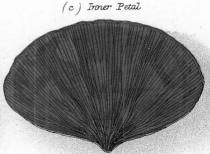

Fig. 8. Seed of Opium Poppy (magnified) vertical section
Seed-cover Endosperm
Embryo

Fig. 10. Fruit of Chelidonium dehiscent

DIAGRAM IV *Transverse Section of Poppy Fruit*

Fig. 5. Stamens (×10) *Fig. 6. Fruit - a Capsule*

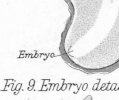

Fig. 9. Embryo detached

Fig. 7. Seeds (× 10)

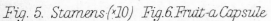

DIAGRAM V *Transverse Section of Chelidonium Fruit*

Engraved, Printed and Published by W. & A.K. Johnston, Edinburgh & London.

PLATE XIV.

FUMITORY (*Fumaria officinalis*)
and WALL-FLOWER (*Cheiranthus Cheiri*).

FUMITORY

The common Fumitory may be readily obtained, generally from May onwards, in all sorts of waste places and corn and other fields. It is a weak straggling herb, with finely divided leaves, and a peculiar shaped irregular flower. The flower is of a pale rose-colour and inconspicuous and said to be fertilised without the agency of insects. The form and arrangement of the different parts are evidently suggestive of some purpose.

FLOWERS

Fig. 1 Inflorescence—a Raceme, and flowers with Bracts.
Figs. 2 and 3 Make a vertical section of the flower from the base, holding it between finger and thumb.
Bract, a modified leaf with a flower in its axil.
Pedicel, short in flower, elongating in fruit.
Sepals, small and scale-like.
Petals, one of the outer bulging at the base.
Stamens and Carpels best seen separate.
Diagram I.—The part of the flower turned towards the axis may be conveniently termed *dorsal,* or *posterior,* and the opposite part towards the bract (when present) will be *ventral,* or *anterior.*
Calyx, two sepals become lateral by a twisting of the flower-stalk.
Corolla, two outer petals (anterior and posterior) large, two inner small.
Androecium, two stamens, each splitting into three anthers.
Gynoecium, two united carpels, as indicated by the lobed stigma.

FOLIAGE- AND FLORAL-LEAVES

Fig. 4 Foliage-leaf much divided.
Fig. 5 Bract with broad base of attachment.
Fig. 6 Sepal with indented margin.
Fig. 7 Petals detached—inner view.
(a.) Anterior petal flat.
(b.) Posterior petal saccate, having a dilated base.
(c.) Inner petals united at tip.
Fig. 8 Stamen with flattened out filament bearing three anthers.
Fig. 9 Carpel with stigma lobed.

FRUIT AND SEED

Fig. 10 Fruit—an Achene.
Fig. 11 Hold the minute fruit between finger and thumb, and cut section lengthways.
Fruit-cover or Pericarp.
Seed consisting of minute embryo with endosperm.
Diagram II.—Fruit in Corydalis, a two-valved capsule, with numerous parietal seeds.

CLASSIFICATION.

Class. Dicotyledon.

Division. Polypetalæ.

Sub-division. Thalamifloræ.

Order. Fumariaceæ
Flowers, irregular.
Stamens, two, each with three anthers.
Ovary, one-chambered.
Fruit, one-seeded Achene or many-seeded Capsule.
Seed, with endosperm.

Genera. Fumaria and Corydalis, the two British genera.

WALL-FLOWER

Wall-flower is a universal favourite no less from its beautiful colours than from its sweet smell. It may be had for examination at almost any season of the year. The cross-like arrangement of the petals gives the name to the Order—Cruciferae—which includes, not only ornamental plants, such as Wall-flower and Stock, but many useful vegetables, such as Turnip and Cabbage, Cress and Cauliflower.

LEAVES AND FLOWERS

Fig. 1 Inflorescence—a Raceme with generally a bract at the base, but individual flowers without bracts.
Foliage-leaves alternate.
Opened flowers outer, unopened towards centre.
Fig. 2 Make a vertical section of fully opened flower, so as to pass through lateral sepals which bulge at the base.
Receptacle, the slightly expanded end of flower-stalk.
Sepals, inserted upon receptacle.
Petals, inserted upon receptacle.
Stamens—long and short—inserted upon receptacle.
Diagram III.—In a Flower-bud examine arrangement and relation of parts—
Calyx, in two whorls of two sepals each—the anterior and posterior overlapping the two lateral sepals.
Corolla, a whorl of four petals, alternating with sepals. Androecium, in two whorls—outer whorl of two short stamens, opposite to lateral sepals, and inner whorl of four long stamens.
Gynoecium of two united carpels.
Fig. 3 Foliage-leaf, lance-shaped, entire.

FLORAL LEAVES

Fig. 4 Lateral sepals, bulging at the base to accommodate the bending of the two short stamens; this bending in turn being due to a little gland on their inner side.
Fig. 5 Petals, with long claws, and blade or limb bent at an angle to it.
Fig. 6 (a, b, c) Stamens—
Filament terminating at base of lance-shaped anther.
Anther opening lengthways on inner face.
Fig. 7 Gynoecium with elongated Ovary, short Style and bi-lobed Stigma.

FRUIT AND SEED

Fig. 8 Fruit—a Siliqua, opening by two valves from below upwards.
Diagram IV—Seeds in two longitudinal rows.
The septum is not formed by the united edges of the two carpels, but by the placentas meeting, and thus forming a spurious partition.
Fig. 9 Seed, with short wing.
Fig. 10 After the seed-cover is removed, nothing is left by the embryo, thus the seed is without endosperm.
Embryo—the Radicle is lateral to the two Cotyledons.

CLASSIFICATION.

Class. Dicotyledon.

Division. Polypetalæ.

Sub-division. Thalamifloræ.

Order. Cruciferæ.
Leaves, alternate.
Flowers, regular and without bracts.
Petals, arranged cross-wise.
Stamens, four long and two lateral short.
Carpels, united and two chambers formed.
Fruit, a siliqua or silicula.
Seed, without endosperm.

Genus. Cheiranthus.

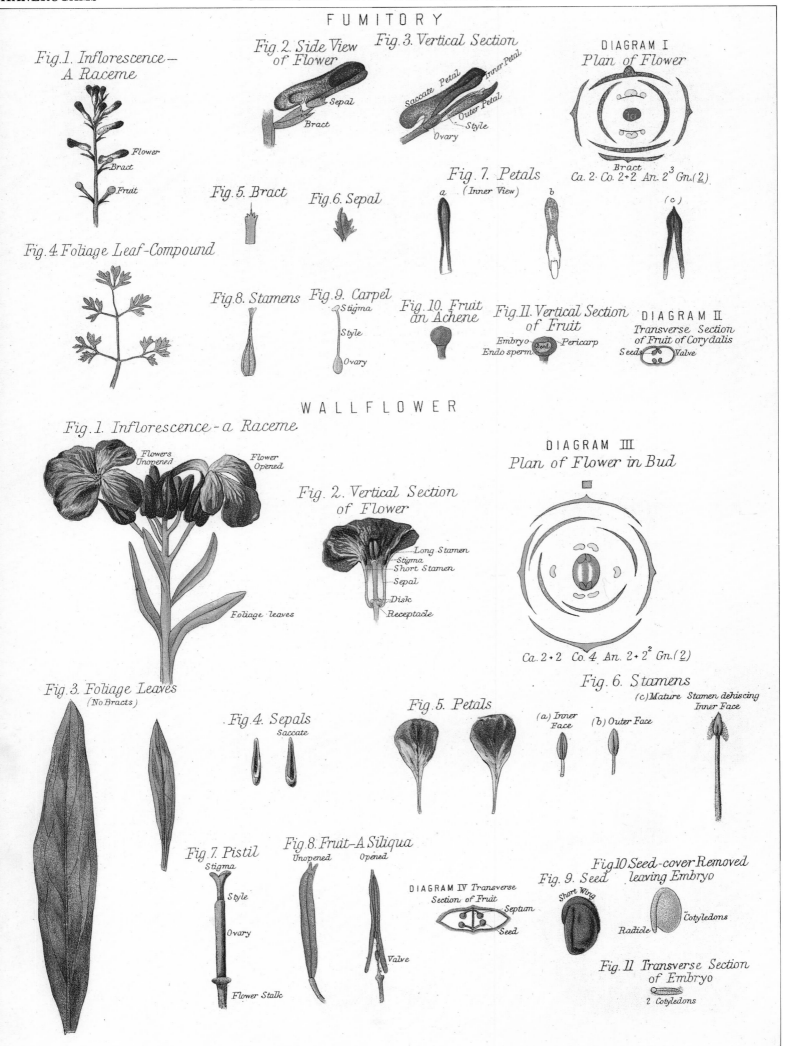

FUMITORY

Fig.1. Inflorescence—A Raceme

Flower
Bract
Fruit

Fig.2. Side View of Flower

Sepal
Bract

Fig.3. Vertical Section

Saccate Petal
Inner Petal
Outer Petal
Style
Ovary

DIAGRAM I
Plan of Flower

Bract
Ca. 2· Co. 2+2 An. 2^3 Gn.($\underline{2}$)

Fig.5. Bract

Fig.6. Sepal

Fig. 7. Petals
(Inner View)
a   b   (c)

Fig.4. Foliage Leaf-Compound

Fig.8. Stamens

Fig.9. Carpel
Stigma
Style
Ovary

Fig.10. Fruit
an Achene

Fig.11. Vertical Section of Fruit
Embryo
Endosperm
Seed
Pericarp

DIAGRAM II
Transverse Section of Fruit of Corydalis
Seeds
Valve

WALLFLOWER

Fig.1. Inflorescence - a Raceme

Flowers Unopened
Flower Opened

Foliage leaves

DIAGRAM III
Plan of Flower in Bud

Ca. 2+2 Co. 4 An. 2+2^2 Gn.($\underline{2}$)

Fig. 2. Vertical Section of Flower
Long Stamen
Stigma
Short Stamen
Sepal
Disk
Receptacle

Fig.3. Foliage Leaves
(No Bracts)

Fig.4. Sepals
Saccate

Fig.5. Petals

Fig. 6. Stamens
(c) Mature Stamen dehiscing Inner Face
(a) Inner Face
(b) Outer Face

Fig.7. Pistil
Stigma
Style
Ovary
Flower Stalk

Fig.8. Fruit–A Siliqua
Unopened   Opened
Valve

DIAGRAM IV Transverse Section of Fruit
Septum
Seed

Fig. 9. Seed
Short Wing

Fig.10 Seed-cover Removed leaving Embryo
Radicle
Cotyledons

Fig. 11 Transverse Section of Embryo
2 Cotyledons

Engraved, Printed and Published by W. & A.K. Johnston, Edinburgh & London.

PLATE XV.

CHICKWEED (*Stellaria media*),
MAIDEN PINK (*Dianthus deltoides*),
and CAMPION (*Lychnis vespertina*).

CHICKWEED

The common name of Chickweed is applied to two different genera of the same order—the one being Stellaria, which is easily known by the line of hairs on stem and branches, and the other Cerastium, distinguished as Mouse-ear Chickweed. Stellaria has been chosen for representation which is common on roadsides and waste places at almost any season of the year, and though small it forms a very good example of a large and varied class of plants. The flowers are not very conspicuous, the petals being overtopped by the sepals, and the pollen is ripe before the stigmas are ready to receive it. The inner stamens are often absent, and even the outer are sometimes reduced to three.

STEM AND LEAVES

Fig. 1 Stem, swollen at the nodes, with a line of hairs on alternate sides. Leaves, opposite, and successive pairs forming right angles with each other. Branches, formed in the axil of each leaf, hence two spring from a node.

FLOWERS

Figs. 1 and 2 Inflorescence—the main axis terminates in a flower, and two lateral axes below that are similarly terminated by a flower, and so on. Generally when an axis produces a flower at its apex its growth is closed; hence such an Inflorescence is called *Definite*.
When a definite inflorescence produces *two* lateral axes of equal value in this way, it is called a Cyme of two branches, or a *Dichotomous Cyme*.

Fig. 3 Sepals, longer than petals. Petals, bifid. Stamens, with slender filament arising from receptacle beneath ovary. Carpels, united; Styles, free.
Diagram.—Calyx, of five free sepals. Corolla, of five free petals. Andrœcium, of five long stamens alternating with petals, and five short alternating with five long. Gynœcium, of three united carpels.

FOLIAGE- AND FLORAL-LEAVES

Fig. 4 Lower Foliage-leaves with stalk; upper, sessile.

Fig. 5 (a) Free Sepal, with broad base of attachment.
(*b*) Petal, deeply cleft.
Fig. 6 Stamen, with glandular swelling at base of filament.
Fig. 7 Gynœcium, with globular Ovary, and three distinct Styles.
Fig. 8 Placentation, free-central, because ovules are attached to a central axis *free* from wall of ovary

FRUIT AND SEED

Fig. 9 Fruit a dry, dehiscent Capsule, opening by six valves, and containing numerous seeds.
Figs. 10 and 11 Seed, with curved Embryo enveloping Endosperm.

MAIDEN PINK

Figs. 12 and 13 Pink, in its first condition with stamens mature, and projecting; second condition, with stigmas mature, and occupying position of the shrivelled-up stamens.

CAMPION

Campion, like the generality of flowers which expand by night, is *white*; since white is a colour which reflects even the faint light existing at night-time, thus rendering objects of that colour as conspicuous as possible. It also smells in the evening in order to guide and attract insects.

In Chickweed, the male and female organs exist, but there is a tendency to reduction in the stamens, and the pollen is shed before the stigmas of the flower are mature. In Pink, male and female organs also exist, but the pollen is shed while the stigmas are not only immature but concealed. In Campion, the separation of the male and female organs has gone further, since the male and female flowers are produced on separate plants.

Figs. 14 and 15 Male Flower, with ten Stamens—five long, alternating with sepals, and five short, alternating with petals. Corona, at junction of claw and blade of petal, scale-like—essentially a ligular appendage, occupying same position and at right angles to leaf as in Grasses.
Axis of flower, developed between sepals and petals.
Fig 16 Female Flower, with five curling stigmas, thus offering a large surface for the reception of pollen.

CLASSIFICATION.

Class. Dicotyledon.

Division. Polypetalæ.

Sub-division. Thalamifloræ.
Order. Caryophyllaceæ, or Pinks.

Stem, with swollen nodes.
Leaves, opposite and entire.
Inflorescence, definite.
Flowers, regular.
Stamens, definite.
Ovules, many, and Placentation free-central.
Fruit, a capsule (usually).
Seed, with endosperm.

Genera. Stellaria, Cerastium, Dianthus, Lychnis.

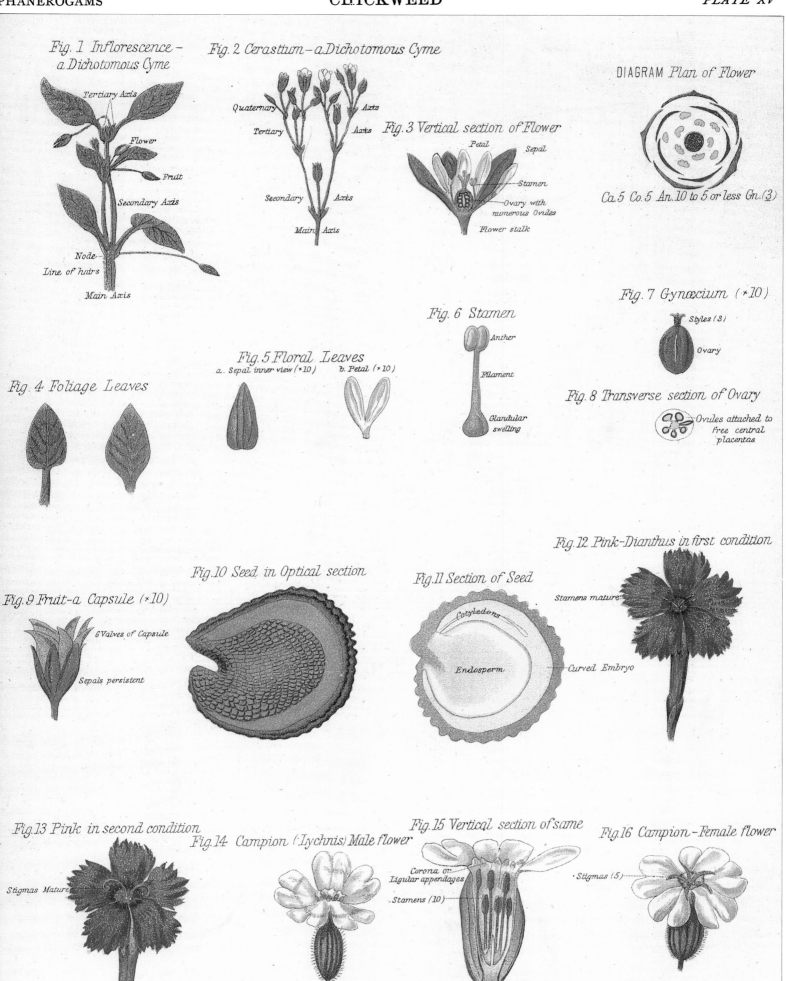

Fig. 1 Inflorescence - a Dichotomous Cyme

Tertiary Axis

Flower

Fruit

Secondary Axis

Node

Line of hairs

Main Axis

Fig. 2 Cerastium - a Dichotomous Cyme

Quaternary   Axis

Tertiary   Axis

Secondary   Axis

Main Axis

Fig. 3 Vertical section of Flower

Petal   Sepal

Stamen

Ovary with numerous Ovules

Flower stalk

DIAGRAM *Plan of Flower*

Ca.5 Co.5 An.10 to 5 or less Gn.(3)

Fig. 4 Foliage Leaves

Fig. 5 Floral Leaves

a. Sepal inner view (×10)   b. Petal (×10)

Fig. 6 Stamen

Anther

Filament

Glandular swelling

Fig. 7 Gynœcium (×10)

Styles (3)

Ovary

Fig. 8 Transverse section of Ovary

Ovules attached to free central placentas

Fig. 9 Fruit - a Capsule (×10)

6 Valves of Capsule

Sepals persistent

Fig. 10 Seed in Optical section

Fig. 11 Section of Seed

Cotyledons

Endosperm

Curved Embryo

Fig. 12 Pink - Dianthus in first condition

Stamens mature

Fig. 13 Pink in second condition

Stigmas Mature

Fig. 14 Campion (Lychnis) Male flower

Fig. 15 Vertical section of same

Corona or Ligular appendages

Stamens (10)

Fig. 16 Campion - Female flower

Stigmas (5)

Engraved, Printed and Published by W. & A.K. Johnston, Edinburgh & London.

PLATE XVI.

HERB-ROBERT (Geranium Robertianum).

Herb-Robert is a very common member of the Crane's-bill family, so called from the form of the fruit. It appears in flower towards the end of April, and I have met with it on to the end of December. It attracts notice by its disagreeable smell, and the bright colour of the flower; and in the autumn, when its foliage assumes a tint to match the flower, the whole plant becomes a conspicuous object. The stem forks a deal, and is very brittle at the joints. The leaves are in pairs as well as the flowers, and are deeply segmented. Honey-glands are situated at the base of the petals, and insects entering for the sake of the honey will encounter the stigmas or the anthers at the entrance.

STEM, LEAVES AND FLOWERS

Fig. 1 Compound leaf with five leaflets, which are again much divided. The leaf as it approaches the flower is seen to become not only smaller but simpler.

Fig. 2 Stem brittle at the joints. Leaves with long stalks and membranous stipules.

Flower, bent—thus protecting the honey better from being acted on by rain.

Fruit, the long and tapering style persisting as the beak.

Fig. 3 Cut a flower through from the base upwards—

Sepals, hairy, arising from receptacle.

Petals, arising from receptacle, pointed at base and expanded at top.

Stamens, long and short, also arising from receptacle.

Carpels, united.

Diagram I.—Calyx of five free sepals. Corolla of five free petals, alternating with sepals.

Andrœcium of five outer, shorter stamens *opposite* to petals, and five longer, inner stamens.

Gynœcium of five carpels, as shown by the five stigmas, alternating with inner stamens.

Nectaries, in the form of five small glands alternating with petals. If these nectaries be regarded as modified stamens, then the alternation of the different parts of the flower would be quite regular—sepals with petals; petals with nectaries or outermost row of modified stamens; outer with middle, short stamens; middle with inner, long stamens; and inner with carpels.

FLORAL-LEAVES

Fig. 4 Sepal with a long awn.

Fig. 5 Petal with a narrow claw and expanded blade.

Fig. 6 Stamen with flattened-out filaments.

Fig. 7 Gynœcium with Ovary, Style, and five distinct Stigmas. There are two Ovules superposed in each chamber of the ovary, one of which grows largely, while the other shrivels up.

Fig. 8 Cut across ovary to see Placentation.

Ovules attached to a central axis, with partitions between each ovule. This is called Axile Placentation.

FRUIT AND SEED.

Fig. 9 The sepals persist at the base of the Fruit, as in Fig. 1, but spread out when fully ripe.

The carpels split from below upwards, and to prevent the jerk separating them entirely from the central axis, each ovary is fastened to the base of the stigma by two silky hairs. These hairs are sufficiently strong to keep the ovaries in place till the wind wafts them to new quarters, so by this beautiful and delicate contrivance the seeds are properly scattered.

Fig. 10 Seed, smooth.

Fig. 11 Take the seed between finger and thumb, and make a section lengthways and another cross-wise. Embryo occupies the whole of the seed, and has its cotyledons much folded.

CLASSIFICATION.

Class. Dicotyledon

Division. Polypetalæ.

Sub-division. Thalamifloræ.
Order. Geraniaceæ (*Gr.* geranos,

a crane, from the beak-like prolongation of the carpels).
Leaves, stipulate.
Stamens, definite.
Placentation, axile.
Fruit, capsular

Seed, without endosperm.

Genus. Geranium.

Species. Robertianum.

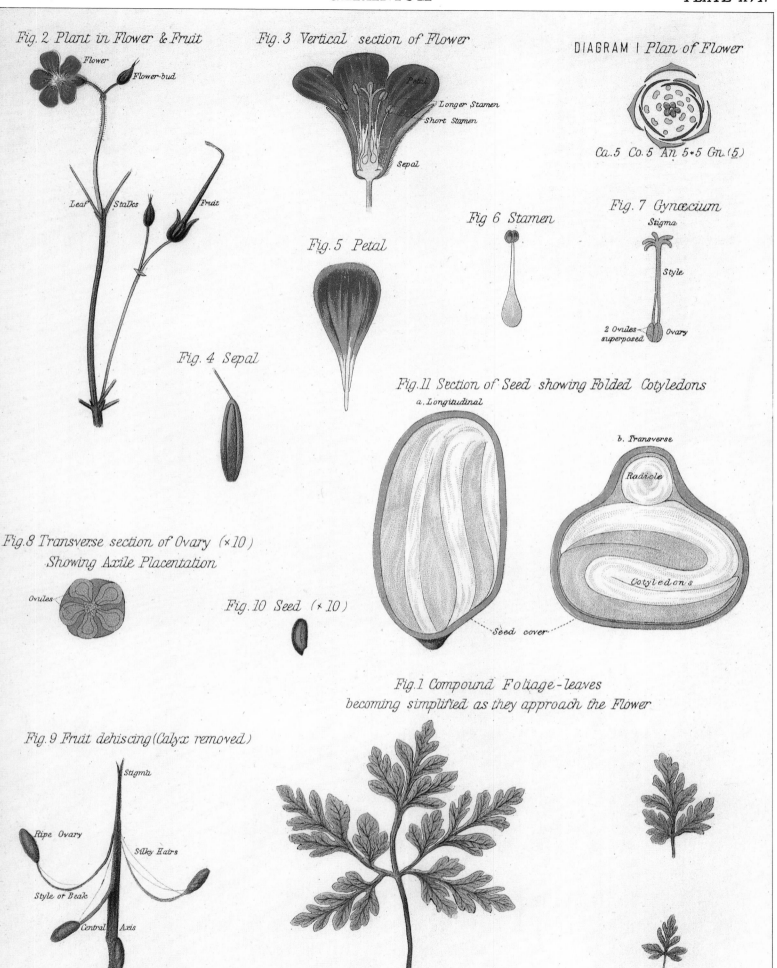

Fig. 2 Plant in Flower & Fruit

Flower

Flower-bud

Leaf   Stalks   Fruit

Fig. 3 Vertical section of Flower

Petal

Longer Stamen

Short Stamen

Sepal

DIAGRAM I *Plan of Flower*

Ca. 5   Co. 5   An 5+5   Gn. (5)

Fig 6 Stamen

Fig. 5 Petal

Fig. 7 Gynæcium

Stigma

Style

Ovary

2 Ovules superposed

Fig. 4 Sepal

Fig. 11 Section of Seed showing Folded Cotyledons

a. Longitudinal

b. Transverse

Radicle

Cotyledons

Seed cover

Fig. 8 Transverse section of Ovary (×10)
Showing Axile Placentation

Ovules

Fig. 10 Seed (×10)

Fig. 1 Compound Foliage-leaves
becoming simplified as they approach the Flower

Fig. 9 Fruit dehiscing (Calyx removed)

Stigma

Ripe Ovary

Silky Hairs

Style or Beak

Central Axis

Engraved, Printed and Published by W. & A.K. Johnston, Edinburgh & London.

PLATE XVII.

SWEET VIOLET (*Viola odorata*)
and PANSY (*Viola Tricolor*).

The fragrant odour of the one and the brilliant colouration of the other have rendered these flowers universal favourites, but to the botanist they have an additional charm in the beautiful mechanical arrangement of parts for ensuring cross-fertilisation—that is, the transference of the pollen from one flower to the stigma of another.

As there are many other flowers with equally remarkable contrivances it may prove interesting and instructive to ask ourselves and answer for ourselves some of those questions which this very flower—the Sweet Violet—suggested to the mind of Sprengel, who was one of the first during the last century, to perceive the relations between flowers and insects. After examining the flower in order to understand the position and arrangement of the different parts, he asked himself, What is the meaning of all this? and proceeded to write down questions and answers similar to the following:-

I. *Why does the flower bend over?*—To protect the honey from rain, and to place the stamens so that the pollen will fall into the space between the ovary and the free end of the stamens.

2. *Why has the corolla a spur?*—To make room for the appendages of the Anthers, and to hold the nectar they secrete.

3. *Why is the lower petal expanded?*—To serve as an alighting place for insects.

4. *Why have some of the anthers appendages?*—To secrete nectar.

5. *Why is the base of the style bent and thin?*—To enable the insect readily to bend it, as if straight it would be more difficult to bend.

6. *Why is the pollen more powdery than usual?*—To fall out of the anther more readily into the box formed by the membranous connectives.

The object of the whole contrivance is evidently to get an interchange of pollen through the agency of insects—the honey, the colour, and the smell all being so many inducements to attract them. The insect on alighting crawls between the style and the petal to reach the nectar. In so doing it comes in contact with the stigma and leaves there any pollen about its head brought from another flower. At the same time it bends the flexible style which moves the ovary, thus pressing back the anthers surrounding the ovary, and tapping the pollen-box, as it were. As the anthers slightly overlap, this motion is communicated all round, and the pollen collecting in the lower anthers will be jerked out by the necessary wagging of their appendages. The converging spoon-shaped connectives (Fig. 7) regulate the distribution of the pollen on the insect's head, so that when it visits the next flower, the bulk of the pollen will be left upon the open mouth of the stigma ready to receive it. The lower lip of the stigma will clearly prevent the insect, as it withdraws its head, from leaving any of the flower's own pollen, since the lip will close and none will stick.

Fig. 1 Leaf of Pansy—Stipules, large and leafy.

Figs. 2 and *3* Vertical section of Pansy and of Sweet Violet.

Bracts; minute, near bend of flower-stalk in Pansy, about middle of flower-stalk in Sweet Violet.

Sepals, attached to receptacle so as to leave posterior ends, free.

Petals, of different size and shape; the lowest the largest and prolonged into a spur.

Stamens, surrounding the ovary, with little membranous orange tips, and the two lower anthers with appendages projecting into the spur.

Carpels, consisting of swollen Ovary, bent Style, and hollow Stigma, with the opening directed downwards.

Diagram.—Calyx, of five free Sepals, unequal in size.

Corolla, of five free petals, unequal in size.

Andrœcium, of five free Stamens,

with large curved anthers overlapping one another.

Gynœcium, of three united Carpels.

Fig. 4 Bract with indications of stipules.

Fig. 5 Sepal with auricles representing stipules.

Fig. 6 Petals—two lateral with a brush of hairs, and lower with double brush and spur.

Fig. 7 Stamen with very short Filament, anther-lobes opening inwards and connective forming a large scoop.

Fig. 8 Gynœcium with swollen Ovary, bent Style, and hollow Stigma.

Fig. 9 Ovary composed of three carpels, united by their in-turned edges, which bear the Ovules. Here there is a single chamber and the ovules are attached to the wall of the ovary, so that the placentation is said to be *parietal*.

Fig. 10 In Narcissus the Ovule was

shown on the eve of fertilisation, here—in Viola—it is shown directly after fertilisation. The pollen-tube has spread out on the Embryo-sac and, by virtue of some influence conveyed by the pollen-tube to the embryo-cell through the synergida, fertilisation has been effected and an *Embryo* formed. The contents of the embryo-sac also break up into a number of *Endosperm* cells by a process of free-cell formation.

It may be noted that, whereas in Narcissus only a single layer of cells formed the apex of the Nucellus, here there are several layers.

Figs 11 and *12* Fruit, a Capsule splitting up into three valves along what corresponds to the midrib of each carpellary leaf.

Fig. 13 Seed taken between finger and thumb may be readily halved.

Embryo, at the attached end of seed.

Endosperm, abundant.

CLASSIFICATION.

Class. Dicotyledon.

Division. Polypetalæ.

Sub-division. Thalamifloræ.

Order. Violaceæ.
Leaves, stipulate.
Flowers, irregular.
Stamen with Connectives produced beyond Anthers.

Placentation, parietal.
Fruit, a three-valved capsule.

Genus. Only one British genus, Viola.

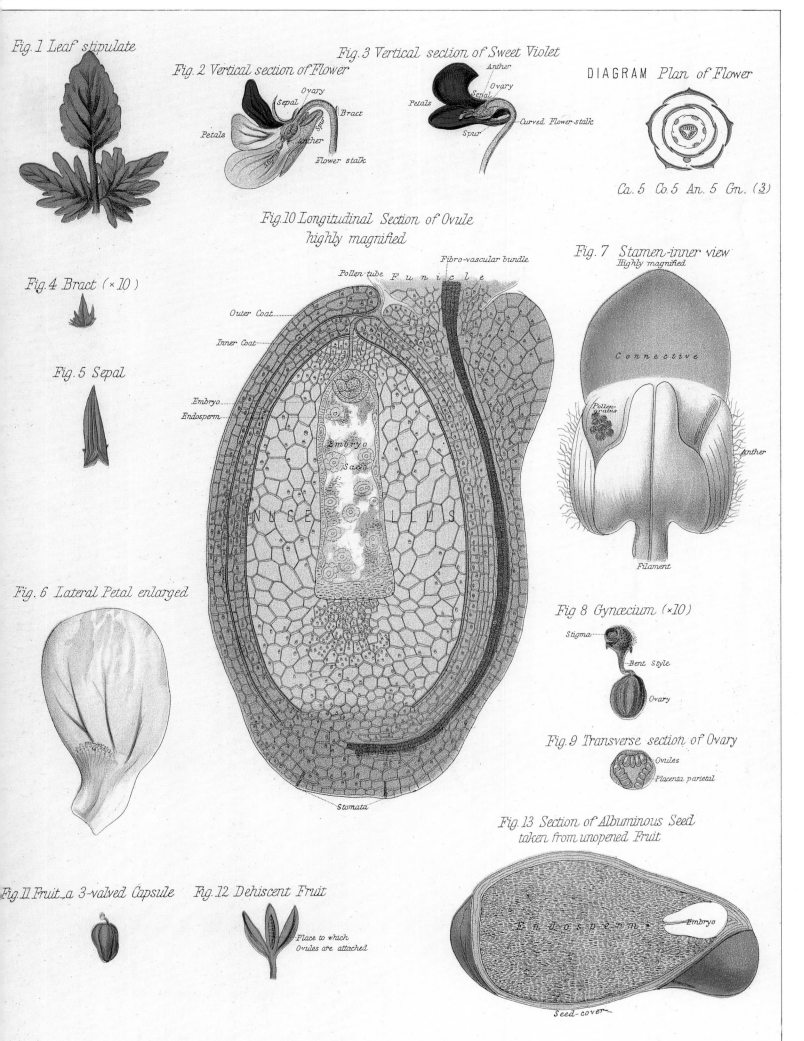

Fig. 1 Leaf stipulate

Fig. 2 Vertical section of Flower

Ovary
Sepal
Petals
Bract
Spur
anther
Spur
Flower stalk

Fig. 3 Vertical section of Sweet Violet

Anther
Ovary
Sepal
Petals
Spur
Curved Flower stalk

DIAGRAM Plan of Flower

Ca. 5 Co. 5 An. 5 Gn. (3)

Fig. 4 Bract (×10)

Fig. 5 Sepal

Fig. 10 Longitudinal Section of Ovule
highly magnified

Fibro-vascular bundle
Pollen tube F u n i c l e
Outer Coat
Inner Coat
Embryo
Endosperm
Embryo
Sac
N U C E L L U S
Stomata

Fig. 7 Stamen-inner view
Highly magnified

Connective
Pollen-grains
Anther
Filament

Fig. 6 Lateral Petal enlarged

Fig. 8 Gynæcium (×10)

Stigma
Bent Style
Ovary

Fig. 9 Transverse section of Ovary

Ovules
Placenta parietal

Fig. 11 Fruit a 3-valved Capsule

Fig. 12 Dehiscent Fruit

Place to which
Ovules are attached

Fig. 13 Section of Albuminous Seed
taken from unopened Fruit

Endosperm
Embryo
Seed-cover

Engraved, Printed and Published by W. & A.K. Johnston, Edinburgh.

PLATE XVIII.

COW-PARSNIP or HOGWEED (*Heracleum Sphondylium*).

(Fig. 3 after Muller.)

Umbellifers are so named from the arrangement of their flowers, their stalks standing out from a central spot like the wires of an umbrella. The Order is a very extensive one—including useful forms, such as Carrots and Parsnips, Celery and Parsley, or poisonous forms, such as Hemlock and Fool's Parsley; and in keeping with this distribution the attractions and inducements held out to insects are neither few nor small. The flowers, though small individually, are associated together in such a way as collectively to present an imposing appearance. Further, the outer flowers of the umbel have their corollas larger and much more developed than those towards the centre; so the outer flowers, with plenty of room to expand, attract insects by their size and thus entice them to visit the less conspicuous flowers in the centre. Not only is there attraction, but there is inducement in the shape of honey. In the centre of each flower is a ring-like disc secreting nectar, which is thus not only central in position but also circular, to admit of free access to it from any and every part of the flower. As a further precaution against self-fertilisation the pollen is shed before the stigmas are ready to receive it.

The Fruit of Umbellifers is very characteristic, and important for purposes of classification, and even the smell of the plant may be of use in the same direction.

Fig. 1 Inflorescence—a compound Umbel with numerous rays. The primary umbel usually possesses a few Bracts at its base, and each of the secondary umbels has a whorl of bracts.
Fig. 2a Outer flower with the three outer Petals largely developed, and the two inner small.
b Inner flower with all the Petals equally small.
Fig. 3 Flower of Wild Chervil showing the first or Male condition, when the anthers are ripening and the stigmas still undeveloped; and the more advanced or Female condition, when the stamens are gone and the stigmas appear.
Fig. 4 Make vertical section of flower, between the two styles, to show insertion of parts.
Sepals, minute teeth arising from vary.
Petals, inserted upon ovary.
Stamens, inserted upon ovary, at the base of disc (not seen in this section).
Carpels with the flower-stalk prolonged between them.
Disc, at top of ovary and attached to styles.
Diagram.—Calyx of five Sepals, represented by five small teeth. Corolla of five free Petals, alternating with the sepals. Androecium of five Stamens, alternating with petals. Gynoecium of two united Carpels.
Fig. 5 Stem—hairy, hollow except at the nodes, and grooved.
Fig. 6 and 7 The Foliage-leaves are large, and the leaf-stalk forms a sheath at its base. (Fig. 7 shows a leaf consisting wholly of sheath.)
Fig. 8 Bract, small and pointed.
Fig. 9 Stamen with curved Filament, attached to the back of the Anther by its tip.
Fig. 10 Take an Ovary well-developed, and make a vertical section, cutting through the two styles, and a transverse section in the region of the ovules.
One Ovule in each chamber suspended from the top.
Fig. 11 Fruit of two carpels, each containing a seed, and called a Cremocarp (Gr. *cremos,* I suspend). The forked axis in the middle separates and suspends each half of the fruit, which is called a Mericarp (Gr. *meros,* a part).
a. Outer face with five ridges and furrows between.

RIDGES { Two Marginal / Two Intermediate / One Median

FURROWS—In the underlying tissue are the four oil-canals.
b. Inner face with two oil-canals.
c. Occasionally there are five oil-canals on the outer face, and the fifth furrow is made by the forking of the median ridge.
Fig. 12 If a Mericarp is soaked the cover can be easily removed, exposing the Seed. Then the seed can be cut in two, showing the small embryo and large endosperm.
Fig. 13 Minute embryo may be turned out of seed with a needle and examined.

CLASSIFICATION.

Class. Dicotyledon.

Division. Polypetalæ.

Sub-division. Calycifloræ.

Order. Umbelliferæ.

Stem, hollow except at nodes.
Leaves, sheathing.
Inflorescence, umbellate.
Petals, five, inserted at base of disc.
Stamens, five, incurved, inserted upon the ovary.

Ovary, two-chambered.
Ovules, pendent, one in each carpel.
Fruit, dry, indehiscent, separating into two, by the splitting of the longitudinal axis.
Seed with endosperm.

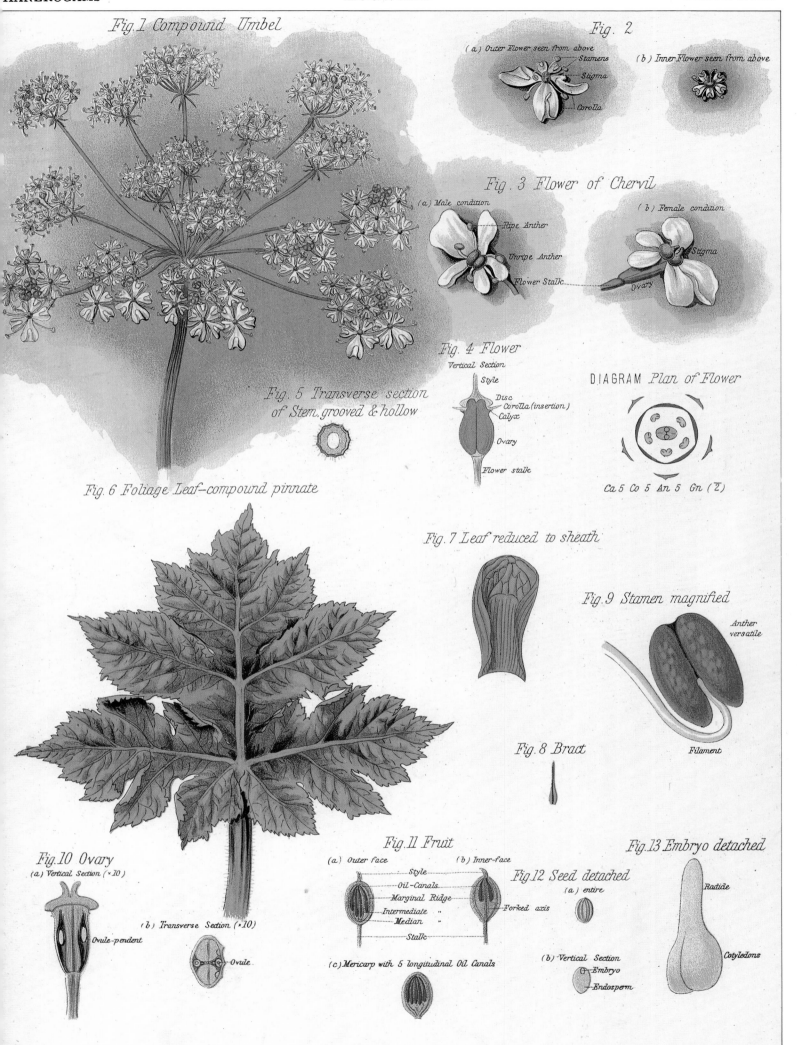

Fig. 1 Compound Umbel

Fig. 2
(a) Outer Flower seen from above
Stamens
Stigma
Corolla
(b) Inner Flower seen from above

Fig. 3 Flower of Chervil
(a) Male condition
Ripe Anther
Unripe Anther
Flower Stalk
(b) Female condition
Stigma
Ovary

Fig. 4 Flower
Vertical Section
Style
Disc
Corolla (insertion)
Calyx
Ovary
Flower stalk

Fig. 5 Transverse section of Stem, grooved & hollow

DIAGRAM Plan of Flower
Ca 5 Co 5 An 5 Gn (2)

Fig. 6 Foliage Leaf—compound pinnate

Fig. 7 Leaf reduced to sheath

Fig. 9 Stamen magnified
Anther versatile
Filament

Fig. 8 Bract

Fig. 10 Ovary
(a) Vertical Section (×10)
Ovule-pendent
(b) Transverse Section (×10)
Ovule

Fig. 11 Fruit
(a) Outer face
Style
Oil-Canals
Marginal Ridge
Intermediate ..
Median ..
Stalk
(b) Inner-face
Forked axis
(c) Mericarp with 5 longitudinal Oil Canals

Fig. 12 Seed detached
(a) entire
(b) Vertical Section
Embryo
Endosperm

Fig. 13 Embryo detached
Radicle
Cotyledons

Engraved, Printed and Published by W. & A.K. Johnston, Edinburgh

PLATE XIX.

BLACKBERRY or BRAMBLE (*Rubus fruticosus*).

The Bramble is a straggling and prickly shrub of common occurrence in hedges and woods. It flowers in autumn and produces the well-known fruit. It is very variable in its characters, giving rise to quite a host of sub-species, some even treating these varieties as distinct species. The leaf is very variable and shows all the intermediate gradations from the *simple* leaf to the *compound* leaf of five leaflets. The simple leaf develops two leaflets, and becomes Fig. 2c; then the lower leaflets may become lobed, as in Fig. 2b, and the division may extend till it reaches the midrib, thus forming five leaflets as in Fig. 2a. This passage from the inferior leaves of the stem with five leaflets, through three leaflets, till nearer the flower the simple leaf appears, is very interesting as bearing on the simplicity of the floral leaves.

The Flower is much visited by insects, and the stamens ripen from the outside inwards, so that the stigmas will usually have received their pollen before the inner anthers have opened.

STEM
Fig. 1 Stem with hooked prickles. These Prickles are superficial structures like hairs, but as they are not derived entirely from the epidermis, but from the underlying tissue as well, they are distinguished as Emergences.

LEAF
Fig. 2 Compound Leaves becoming simpler as they approach the flower.
(*a.*) Compound digitate leaf with five leaflets.
Stipules adherent to base of stalk.
(*b.*) Leaf with three leaflets, the lower two partly divided.
(*c.*) Compound leaf with three leaflets.

FLOWER
Fig. 3 Longitudinal median section of flower.

Receptacle, laterally expanded to support the sepals, petals, and stamens, and produced in the middle to bear the numerous carpels.
Sepals inserted on receptacle.
Petals with narrow base of attachment.
Stamens with minute anthers.
Carpels, seated on the elevated convex Receptacle.
Diagram.—In Flower-bud examine the arrangement of sepals and petals by gently separating them with needle, then make transverse section of bud to complete plan.
Calyx of five Sepals with imbricate arrangement.
Corolla of five Petals with imbricate arrangement, and alternating with sepals.
Andrœcium of numerous Stamens in alternating whorls.

Gynœcium of numerous distinct Carpels.
Fig. 4 Sepal continuous with the laterally expanded receptacle.
Fig. 5 Petal concave with short and narrow claw and expanded blade.
Fig. 6 Stamen with filament expanding into connective.

FRUIT AND SEED
Figs. 7 and 8 Fruit entire and in vertical section.
The Receptacle has elongated and become conical, bearing the numerous fleshy *drupes*.
Each little globular drupe has an outer skin or epicarp covering a juicy pulp or mesocarp, enclosing a little stone or endocarp.
Calyx and withered Stamens persist.
Fig. 9 Embryo.

CLASSIFICATION.

Class. Dicotyledon.

Division. Polypetalæ.

Sub-division. Calycifloræ.

Order. Rosaceæ.
Leaves, usually stipulate and alternate.
Flowers, regular.
Receptacle, laterally extended.
Petals free, on margin of receptacle.

Stamens free and indefinite usually, also inserted towards margin of receptacle.
Carpels free, one or more.
Seeds without endosperm.

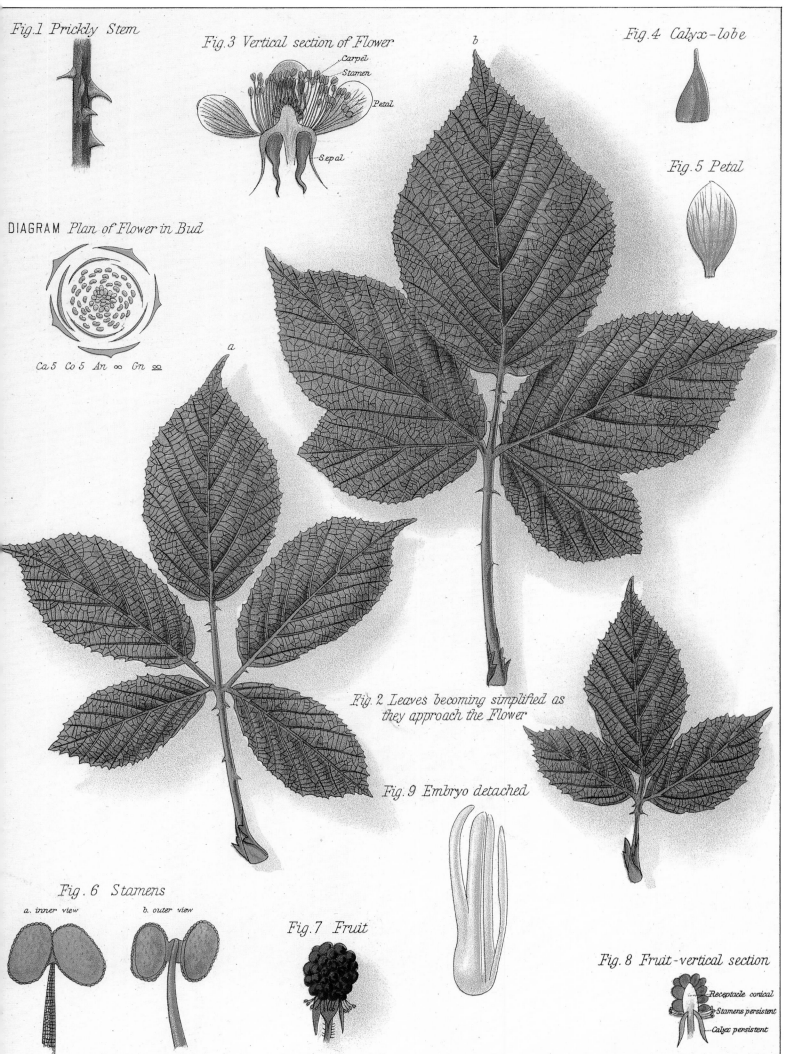

Fig.1 Prickly Stem

Fig.3 Vertical section of Flower
Carpel
Stamen
Petal
Sepal

Fig.4 Calyx-lobe

Fig.5 Petal

DIAGRAM *Plan of Flower in Bud*

Ca 5 Co 5 An ∞ Gn ∞

a

b

Fig. 2 Leaves becoming simplified as
they approach the Flower

Fig. 9 Embryo detached

Fig. 6 Stamens

a. inner view   b. outer view

Fig. 7 Fruit

Fig. 8 Fruit-vertical section
Receptacle conical
Stamens persistent
Calyx persistent

Engraved, Printed and Published by W. & A.K. Johnston, Edinburgh & London.

PLATE XX.

ROSE, STRAWBERRY, SPIREA, APPLE, CHERRY, LADY'S MANTLE.

The large and important Natural Order of the Rosaceæ may be conveniently divided into five Series, based principally upon the number of the Carpels and the nature of the Fruit. There is a sixth Series which is exceptional and peculiar.

I. ROSEÆ.—Type, Dog Rose (*Rosa canina*) or Sweetbrier (*Rosa rubiginosa*).

Fig. 1 Sweetbriar Rose in vertical section.
Receptacle, *hollow*. The so-called Calyx-tube is simply the end of the Floral Axis hollowed out to protect the Ovaries, hence the sub-division Calyciflorae was founded on a misconception.
Sepals, arising from margin of receptacular cup.
Petals, arising from margin of receptacular cup.
Stamens, arising from margin of receptacular cup.
Carpels contained in hollow receptacle, the stigmas projecting beyond it.
Diagram.—Calyx of five Sepals.
Corolla of five Petals.
Androecium of numerous Stamens.
Gynoecium of numerous Carpels.
Figs. 2 and 3 Fruit of Dog Rose entire and in section.
The receptacular cup has become fleshy, and the enclosed single-seeded fruits are Achenes enveloped in hairs.

II. FRAGARIEÆ or DRYADEÆ.—Type, Bramble (*Rubus fruticosus*) or Strawberry (*Fragaria vesca*).

Fig. 4 Strawberry flower in vertical section.
Receptacle, *convex*.
Sepals from lateral expansion of receptacle.
Petals from lateral expansion of receptacle.
Stamens from lateral expansion of receptacle.
Carpels, studded over elevated receptacle.
Fig. 5 Base of Flower.
The Sepals have Stipules as well as the leaves, and these form an Epicalyx or Calyculus.
Diagram.—Calyx of five Sepals.
Corolla of five Petals.
Androecium of numerous Stamens.
Gynoecium of numerous Carpels.
Fig. 6 Strawberry.
The receptacle has become swollen and succulent and the little Achenes are almost imbedded in it.
In the Bramble (*Rubus*) the fruits which are little drupes, have become succulent while the relatively small receptacle is dry.
In the Silver-weed (*Potentilla*) both fruits and receptacle are dry.

III. SPIRÆACEÆ.—Type, Meadow-sweet (*Spiræa Ulmaria*).

Fig. 7 Spiræa in vertical section—with a few Stamens only shown.
Receptacle a *flat expansion*, slightly raised in the centre.
Sepals and Petals arising from margin of receptacle.
Stamens arising from the flat receptacle.
Carpels, attached to slightly raised central portion of receptacle.
Fruit of five Follicles.
Diagram.—Calyx of five Sepals, persistent in fruit.
Corolla of five Petals.
Androecium of numerous Stamens or reduced to twenty.
Gynoecium of five Carpels usually, or more.

IV. POMEÆ.—Type, Apple (*Pyrus Malus*).

Fig. 8 Apple-flower in vertical section.
Receptacle hollow and closed at the top.
Sepals, Petals, and Stamens arising close together.
Carpels adherent to hollow receptacle.
Diagram.—Calyx of five Sepals.
Corolla of five petals.
Androecium from fifteen to twenty Stamens.
Gynoecium, not more than five Carpels.
Fig. 9 Apple in transverse and vertical section.
The swollen succulent receptacle has enveloped the five carpels now ripened into fruit, and each has a cartilaginous lining.
Seeds, two in each carpel, sometimes one aborts.
Calyx, persistent at the top of receptacle.

V. AMYGDALEÆ—Type, Cherry (*Prunus Cerasus*).

Fig. 10 Cherry-flower in vertical section.
Receptacle, hollow.
Sepals, Petals, and Stamens from margin of receptacle.
Single Carpel in centre.
Diagram.—Calyx of five Sepals.
Corolla of five Petals.
Androecium from ten to twenty Stamens.
Gynoecium of one Carpel.
Figs 11 and 12 Cherry a Drupe containing one Seed, enclosed within the innermost stony portion, surrounded by a succulent part, and covered by a skin.

VI. SANGUISORBEÆ—Lady's Mantle (*Alchemilla vulgaris*).

Fig. 13 Lady's Mantle, entire and in section.
Receptacle, hollow.
Calyx of four Sepals with an Epicalyx.
Corolla, absent.
Stamens, four, arising from beneath disc.
Carpel, one.
The members in this Series are very variable, but generally the Carpels are not more than four, and the stamens are sometimes indefinite.
Fig. 14 Simple leaf of Apple with Stipules at the base.
Fig. 15 Compound leaf of Rose with leaflets arranged pinnately.
Fig. 16 Rose-bud showing the Sepals compound like the leaf, but gradually becoming simpler as they pass inwards to the Petals.

Summary.—In the Rose the Carpels are indefinite and one-ovuled, and the receptacular cup becomes fleshy on ripening, forming the well-known Hip. The Anthers and Stigma are mature at the same time.

In the Strawberry the Carpels are still indefinite and one-ovuled, but instead of being in a cup are on an elevation, and the swollen elevated receptacle becomes excessively succulent. Stigma mature before Anthers, hence called Protogynous (Gr. *protos*, first; *gonos,* seed).

In Meadowsweet the Carpels are reduced to five (sometimes more), and the slightly convex receptacle bears Follicles which contain *several* Seeds and *open* along one face.

In the Apple the Carpels are five (never more) and two-ovuled, enclosed in a receptacular cup which becomes much larger and more succulent than in the Rose. Stigma mature before Anthers.

In the Cherry the Carpels are reduced to their lowest—one, and the Fruit, in the form of a Drupe, has reached its highest perfection.

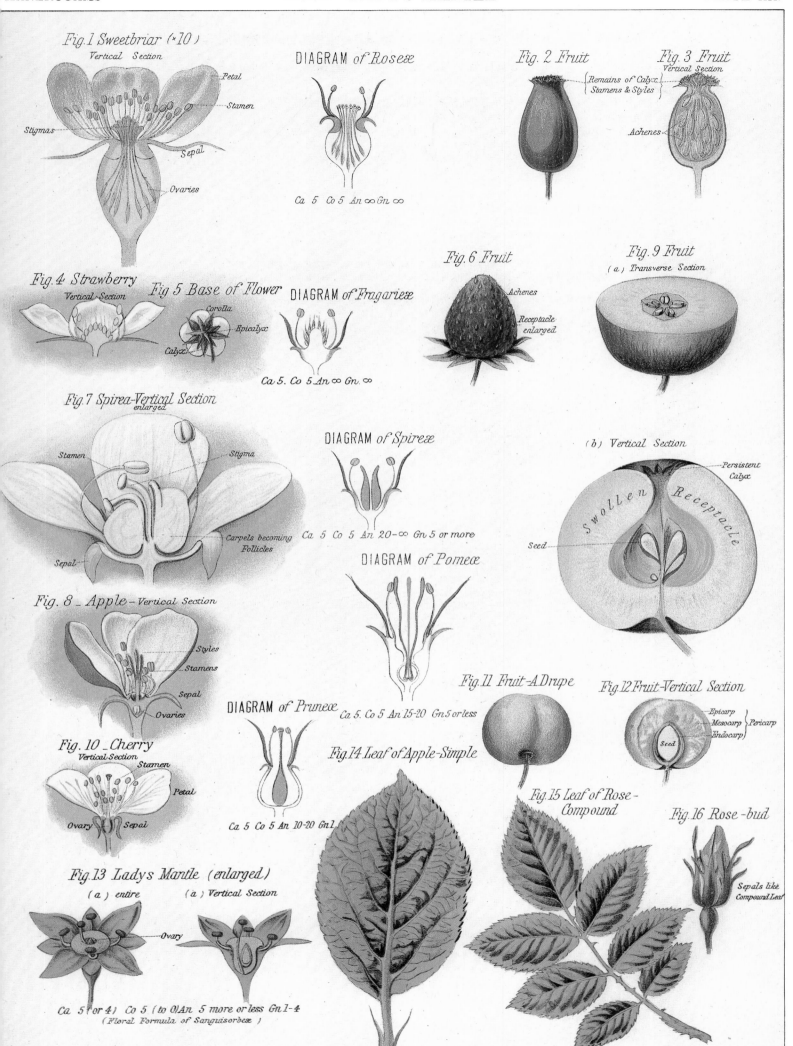

Fig. 1 Sweetbriar (×10)
Vertical Section
Petal
Stamen
Stigmas
Sepal
Ovaries

DIAGRAM of Roseæ
Ca 5 Co 5 An ∞ Gn ∞

Fig. 2 Fruit
Remains of Calyx, Stamens & Styles

Fig. 3 Fruit
Vertical Section
Achenes

Fig. 4 Strawberry
Vertical Section

Fig 5 Base of Flower
Corolla
Epicalyx
Calyx

DIAGRAM of Fragarieæ
Ca 5. Co 5 An ∞ Gn. ∞

Fig. 6 Fruit
Achenes
Receptacle enlarged

Fig. 9 Fruit
(a) Transverse Section

Fig. 7 Spirea-Vertical Section
enlarged
Stamen
Stigma
Carpels becoming Follicles
Sepal

DIAGRAM of Spireæ
Ca 5 Co 5 An 20-∞ Gn 5 or more

DIAGRAM of Pomeæ
Ca 5. Co 5 An 15-20 Gn 5 or less

(b) Vertical Section
Persistent Calyx
Swollen Receptacle
Seed

Fig. 8 - Apple - Vertical Section
Styles
Stamens
Sepal
Ovaries

DIAGRAM of Pruneæ
Ca 5 Co 5 An 10-20 Gn 1

Fig. 11 Fruit - A Drupe

Fig. 12 Fruit - Vertical Section
Epicarp
Mesocarp } Pericarp
Endocarp
Seed

Fig. 10 - Cherry
Vertical Section
Stamen
Petal
Ovary
Sepal

Fig. 14 Leaf of Apple - Simple

Fig. 15 Leaf of Rose - Compound

Fig. 16 Rose - bud
Sepals like Compound Leaf

Fig. 13 Ladys Mantle (enlarged)
(a) entire
(a) Vertical Section
Ovary

Ca 5 (or 4) Co 5 (to 0) An 5 more or less Gn 1-4
(Floral Formula of Sanguisorbeæ)

Engraved, Printed and Published by W. & A.K. Johnston, Edinburgh.

PLATE XXI.

LEGUMUNOSÆ—SWEET PEA (*Lathyrus odorata*), principally.

This large and important Order is only known to us in Britain as having irregular butterfly-shaped flowers, but in tropical regions the flower assumes a more or less regular form. The Order is thus capable of division into sections:— 1. Mimoseæ—represented by Acacia, or Mimosa—the Sensitive Plant, having regular flowers; 2. Cæsalpinieæ—represented by Cassia—having irregular flowers but not butterflied; and 3. Papilionaceæ—our British representatives—having flowers of the well-known Pea type, with a corolla fancifully resembling a butterfly, hence called *papilionaceous*.

The action of insects alighting on the Pea flower, for instance, may be imitated by pressing down the wings, and the keel goes along with them, thereby exposing the anthers and stigma.

MOSEÆ.—Flower, regular. Petals, valvate. Stamens, definite or indefinite.

Fig. 1 and *Diagram* I.—Calyx of five united Sepals.
Corolla of five Petals. Andrœcium of numerous free
Stamens. Gynœcium of one Carpel.

CÆSALPINIEÆ.—Flower, irregular. Petals, imbricate. Stamens, definite.

Fig. 2 and *Diagram* II.—Calyx of five free Sepals.
Corolla of five free Petals. Andrœcium of ten or less free
Stamens. Gynœcium of one Carpel.

PAPILIONACEÆ—Flower, irregular. Petals, imbricate.

Fig. 3 Compound leaf with Stipules which arise from the base of leaf-stalk and not from stem.
There are two ordinary leaflets, then the next Pair are modified into coiled *tendrils* and the end of the leaf-stalk is prolonged into branching tendrils. Here the leaf or part of it is modified into an organ of support, enabling the weak stem to ascend.
Fig. 4 The Pea flower in its natural position presents its standard to the breeze, so that it may act as a fluttering flag to attract insects, and as a shelter to the more delicate inner parts. But when an insect alights on the wings which are of the nature of a platform, the wings and keel are depressed, and the anthers and stigma are exposed, but return again to their old position when the pressure is removed. The insect, while searching for pollen or nectar in the staminal tube, will undoubtedly carry away some pollen amongst its hairs and leave it on visiting other flowers.
Fig. 5 Cut the flower in two from the base upwards.
Sepals, united about half-way down and inserted on receptacle.
Petals—Standard is towards the main

floral axis and therefore *dorsal* in position.
Wings, one on each side, therefore *lateral* in position.
Keel, of two partially united petals, is away from the main floral axis and therefore *ventral* in position.
Stamens, one free, rest united into a tube.
Carpel in the middle, arising from receptacle.
Diagram III.—Calyx of five united Sepals.
Corolla of five Petals. Dorsal petal or Standard overlaps the rest in bud. Andrœcium of ten Stamens—dorsal stamen free, other nine united. Gynœcium of one Carpel, and the Ovules are out-growths from its margins.
Fig. 6 Petals of unequal size and shape.
(*a*) Standard laterally expanded, and tightly clasping rest of flower at base.
(*b*) Wing with interlocking processes at base for keel.
(*c*) Keel in natural position enclosing Stamens and Carpel, and forming a tight fit with keel.
Fig. 7 Stamens.
Filaments united for the greater part of their length into a Staminal tube.

Dorsal filament free to about base.
Fig. 8 Fruit—a Pod or Legume, from which the Order derives its name. The Calyx still persists, also the slender Style and even the withered Stamens.
Figs. 9 and 10 Steep some peas for a night in water, when they may be conveniently examined.
On the outer surface of Sweet Pea observe elongated *scar* in the centre indicating its point of attachment inside the fruit, a small opening below, through which moisture can be squeezed, indicating the *micropyle*. In section of Garden Pea observe that when the skin is removed nothing is left but the Embryo consisting of Stem-bud or Plumule.
Primary root or Radicle pointing towards micropyle.
Seed-leaves or Cotyledons.
Fig. 11 Germination.
The Radicle has elongated, producing the primary root or Tap-root, with its Rootlets.
The Plumule also grows upwards, producing at first the insignificant small leaves gradually growing larger as you ascend the stem.

CLASSIFICATION.

Class. Dicotyledon.

Division. Polypetalæ.

Sub-division. Calycifloræ.

Order. Leguminosæ.
Leaves, usually compound and stipulate.
Flower, irregular.
Corolla, papilionaceous.

Stamens, ten.
Carpel, superior and solitary.
Fruit, generally a Legume.
Seed, without endosperm.

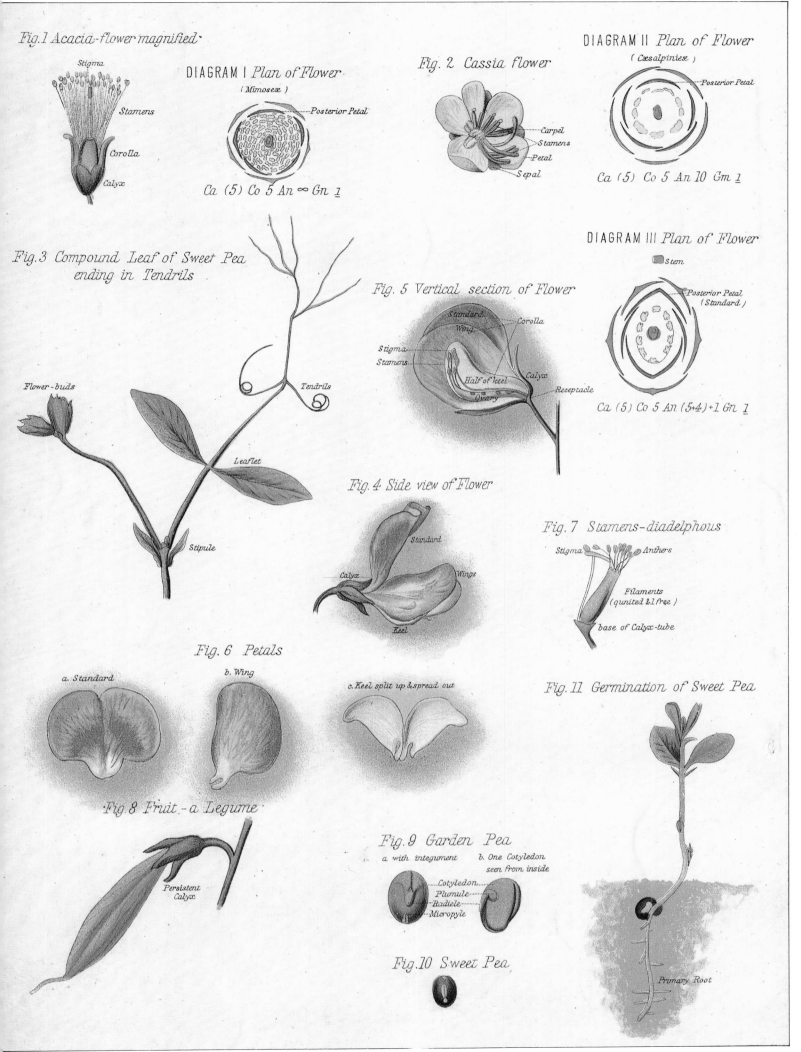

Fig. 1 Acacia-flower magnified·

Stigma

Stamens

Corolla

Calyx

DIAGRAM I *Plan of Flower*

(*Mimoseæ*)

Posterior Petal

Ca (5) Co 5 An ∞ Gn 1

Fig. 2 Cassia flower

Carpel

Stamens

Petal

Sepal

DIAGRAM II *Plan of Flower*

(*Cæsalpinieæ*)

Posterior Petal

Ca (5) Co 5 An 10 Gm 1

Fig. 3 Compound Leaf of Sweet Pea
ending in Tendrils

Flower-buds

Tendrils

Leaflet

Stipule

DIAGRAM III *Plan of Flower*

Stem

Posterior Petal
(*Standard*)

Ca (5) Co 5 An (5+4)+1 Gn 1

Fig. 5 Vertical section of Flower

Standard

Wing

Corolla

Stigma

Stamens

Half of keel

Ovary

Calyx

Receptacle

Fig. 4 Side view of Flower

Standard

Calyx

Wings

Keel

Fig. 7 Stamens-diadelphous

Stigma

Anthers

Filaments
(9 united & 1 free)

base of Calyx-tube

Fig. 6 Petals

a. Standard

b. Wing

c. Keel split up & spread out

Fig. 11 Germination of Sweet Pea

Fig. 8 Fruit - a Legume·

Persistent
Calyx

Fig. 9 Garden Pea

a. with integument   b. One Cotyledon
seen from inside

Cotyledon

Plumule

Radicle

Micropyle

Fig. 10 Sweet Pea

Primary Root

Engraved, Printed and Published by W. & A.K. Johnston, Edinburgh

PLATE XXII.

PRIMROSE (*Primula vulgaris*) and HEATH (*Erica*).

PRIMROSE

The Primrose might be dismissed with the convenient expression, "too well-known to need description;" but, although certainly known, it by no means follows that it is generally understood and appreciated, for in it there is to be seen a wonderful adaptation of means to ends, which Darwin was the first thoroughly to appreciate and to explain. If the flowers are examined on several different plants it will be found that they vary: those on one plant having the knob-headed stigma at the entrance to the corolla-tube, and those on another having the stamens in that position. These two different forms of flowers are respectively called Long-styled and Short-styled. A glance at Fig. 2 will show that an insect visiting the long-styled flower, and thrusting its proboscis down the tube, will carry away pollen so placed that, on visiting a short-styled flower, it will come in contact with the stigma, and thus ensure cross-fertilisation. Reversing the order of its visit, from short-styled to long-styled, the insect would still produce the same effect.

The Pollen-grains, too (Fig. 4), are adapted for their respective duties. In the long-styled flower they are smallest because they are intended to be transferred to the stigma of the short-styled flower, and so have to produce a shorter pollen-tube than the other.

The Primrose appears in early spring (Primula, from Lat. *primus,* first) at a time when insect life is still scarce; and yet so perfect is the adaptation of its various parts to secure cross-fertilisation—with the minimum of waste, so attractive is its flower and scent, and so well-chosen its situation on sloping bank or sheltered glade that it not only manages to thrive, but often overspreads the hedge-bank with its blossoms like so many golden stars.

Fig. 1 Form and Habit of the plant. The wrinkled Leaves stand out from the base in radiating fashion, and the Flowers also radiate from a centre, having long flower-stalks. Here the Umbel is sessile, but in Cowslip it is stalked.
Figs. 2 and 3 Slit up a Long-styled and Short-styled form of flower from the base, and compare them. Stigma of one about the same height as the Anthers of another.
Fig. 4 Dust pollen on slides from the Anthers of the respective flowers, and observe different relative size in each case.
Fig. 5 Vertical section of Ovary, showing a free central column, to which the Ovules are attached.
Fig. 6 Fruit—met with in July. Capsule of five valves opening by ten teeth, and containing numerous Seeds.
Fig. 7 Seed halved. Seed-cover raised into little elevations. Embryo surrounded by Endosperm.

CLASSIFICATION.

Class. Dicotyledon.

Division. Gamopetalæ.
Calyx and Corolla present.
Petals, united.

Order. Primulaceæ.
Corolla, regular.
Stamen, attached to corolla-tube, *opposite* petals.
Ovary, superior, one-chambered.

Ovules, numerous; Placentation, free-central.
Fruit, capsular.
Seed with endosperm.

HEATH

Heath is sufficiently common to give its name to large tracts of country where it protects the surface of otherwise barren wastes. It flowers during the summer months, when its modest bloom delights the eye and "sheds beauty o'er the lonely moor." Heather (Calluna) blooms in autumn, and the flower differs from that of Heath (Erica), principally in the Calyx being longer than the Corolla, and having four bracts at its base. Rhododendron is a well-known allied ornamental shrub, with large and showy flowers.

Fig. 8 Form and Habit of the Plant. The Stem is upright and much branched. The Leaves are in close-set whorls of four, and the Flowers are arranged in crowded racemes.
Figs. 9 and 10 Flower entire and in section.
Calyx of four sepals and coloured.
Corolla is bell-shaped, with four broad lobes.
Stamens, eight; anthers outside of corolla tube, and each opening by two pores.
Carpels, four, united, with Style projecting beyond anthers.
Fig. 11 Flower of Rhododendron in section.
Calyx, represented only by minute teeth.
Corolla of five lobes, deciduous and irregular.
Stamens, ten.
Carpels, five, united.
Diagram II.—Calyx of four Sepals.
Corolla of four united Petals.
Andrœcium of eight Stamens, four opposite to sepals and four opposite to Petals.
Gynœcium of four united Carpels.
Fig. 12 Transverse section of Ovary. The Ovary is divided into four chambers, with numerous Ovules in each, springing from the Axis.
Fig. 13 Fruit of Rhododendron—a Capsule.
The Carpels separate in the form of five valves, the sides of which are formed by the split septa. In Heather the Capsule splits similarly, but is four-valved; while in Heath the splitting of the valves takes place along the *midrib* of each carpellary leaf.

CLASSIFICATION.

Class. Dicotyledon.

Division. Gamopetalæ.

Order. Ericaceæ.
Corolla, regular.
Stamens, free from corolla.
Ovary, superior, many-chambered.

Ovules, usually numerous; placentaion, axile.
Fruit, capsular or berried.
Seed with endosperm.

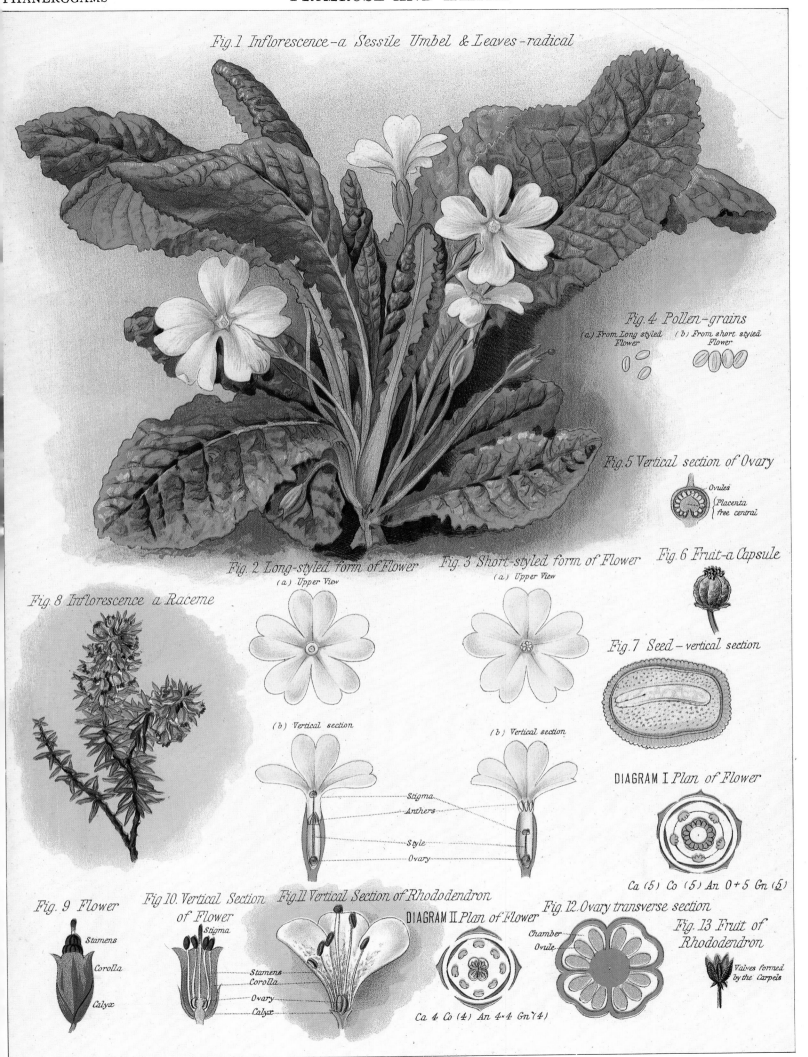

Fig.1 Inflorescence–a Sessile Umbel & Leaves–radical

Fig. 4 Pollen-grains
(a) From Long styled Flower   (b) From short styled Flower

Fig. 5 Vertical section of Ovary
Ovules
Placenta free central

Fig. 2 Long-styled form of Flower
(a) Upper View
(b) Vertical section

Fig. 3 Short-styled form of Flower
(a) Upper View
(b) Vertical section

Fig. 6 Fruit–a Capsule

Fig. 7 Seed – vertical section

Fig. 8 Inflorescence a Raceme

Stigma
Anthers
Style
Ovary

DIAGRAM I Plan of Flower
Ca (5) Co (5) An 0 + 5 Gn (5)

Fig. 9 Flower
Stamens
Corolla
Calyx

Fig 10. Vertical Section of Flower
Stigma
Stamens
Corolla
Ovary
Calyx

Fig.11 Vertical Section of Rhododendron
DIAGRAM II Plan of Flower
Ca 4 Co (4) An 4+4 Gn (4)

Fig. 12 Ovary transverse section
Chamber
Ovule

Fig. 13 Fruit of Rhododendron
Valves formed by the Carpels

Engraved, Printed and Published by W. & A.K. Johnston, Edinburgh.

PLATE XXIII.

WHITE DEAD-NETTLE (*Lamium album*) and SAGE (*Salvia*).

(Figures of Sage from Dodel-Port, after H. Muller.)

DEAD-NETTLE

The common white Dead-nettle owes, no doubt, much of its widespread character to the perfect adaptation of its structure to fertilisation by insects. The contrivances for ensuring cross-fertilisation will now be glanced at. The lower lip of the corolla is expanded, thus forming a platform for insects. The upper lip arches over the stamens like an umbrella, protecting them from rain and preventing the pollen from being carried away, at the same time sheltering the tube of the corolla, at the base of which lies the honey. The ring of upwardly directed hairs near the bottom of the tube will exclude small insects from the honey. The stamens are arranged in parallel series of different lengths, and thus the pollen is not widely dusted over the insect's body, but confined to parts where it will most easily come in contact with the stigma. The stigma, too, hangs down beneath the anthers, and the stigmatic surface is turned outwards, so that any of the flower's own pollen falling down, will only fall upon the back of it, and produce no effect.

When an insect visits a flower of this construction, it alights upon the platform, attracted by the white flowers peeping out from the green foliage; and as it wedges its head into the tube for honey, the pollen on its back is sure to brush against the under surface of the stigma. As the stigma lies lower than the anthers, it will come against it first, and so leave the foreign pollen upon it. When backing out, the insect will receive a fresh coating of pollen from the stamens, and be ready to repeat the process over again on the next flower it visits.

STEM, LEAVES, AND FLOWERS

Fig. 1 Stem, square.
Leaves, opposite, and alternately on opposite sides of the square stem.
Figs. 2 and 3 Flowers in the axils of leaves; the tufts in each axil being a dichotomous cyme condensed.
With a pair of scissors slit up the front face of the flower, that is, the ventral surface, and lay out the parts so as to display interior.
Sepals, separating from each other about half way into long, thin points.
Petals upper lip notched; lower lip with central lobe, and a little tooth at each side.
Stamens, attached to throat of corolla, but their fibro-vascular cords may be traced to the base, and thus their relative position to the other parts of the flower fixed.
Carpels, with forked stigma; the stigmatic surface turned away from the Anthers.

Diagram.—Plan of Flower—
Calyx, bell-shaped, of five united Sepals—one dorsal two lateral, and two ventral.
Corolla, two-lipped; upper lip of two united Petals, and lower lip of three (the upper lip is divided in the Ground Ivy, and the little teeth of the lower lip are known in some flowers to grow out into regular lobes; hence, from this and their alternating position, the two lips together are considered five united Petals).
Andrœcium, of four Stamens; two long and two a little shorter (in some instances a fifth rudimentary stamen is found).
Gynœcium, of two united Carpels.

FLORAL-LEAVES

Fig. 4 Stamen, showing filament expanding into connective.

Fig. 5 Gynoecium.
The ovary is four-lobed, and this might be taken as indicating four Carpels without an explanation. There are really two carpels, as denoted by the bifid stigma, which meet by their edges in the middle, and each carpel bears two ovules, thus making four altogether. The midrib of each carpel grows out towards the centre, and becomes attached to it, thus making the double chamber into four. Then the dorsal side of each carpel, that is, the midrib portion, grows excessively, so that the style becomes sunk in the middle, and apparently rises from the *base* of the ovary.

FRUIT AND SEED

Fig. 6 Fruit, consists of four little Nutlets
Seed, entirely taken up with Embryo.
Fig. 7 Embryo, removed and enlarged.

SAGE.

Figs. 8, 9, and *10* In Sage, the *contrivances* for cross-fertilisation are carried to even a higher degree of perfection than in Dead-nettle, as the amount of fertilising material at command is less, there being only two stamens.

In Dead-nettle the two Anther-lobes were obliquely divided, but in Sage they are completely separated (Fig. 9). The Connective diverges to such an extent that this separation takes place, and the upper anther-lobe only bears pollen, while the lower is rudimentary and a mere pad. An insect visiting the flower (as in Fig. 9) strikes against this lower rudimentary lobe, and the upper anther-lobe swings round, dusting the insect's back with pollen. As an effectual preventative against self-fertilisation, the anthers are mature before the stigmas are ready, and on ripening the stigmas come to occupy the position formerly held by the anther-lobes, so that an insect carrying the pollen from one flower will leave it on the stigma of another.

CLASSIFICATION.

Class. Dicotyledon.

Division. Gamopetalæ.

Order. Labiatæ.

Stem, square.
Leaves, opposite.
Inflorescence, condensed cymes.
Corolla, two-lipped.
Stamens, two long and two short.

Carpels with four-lobed Ovary and bifid Style.
Ovules, one in each lobe.
Fruit, of four little Nutlets.
Seed, without endosperm.

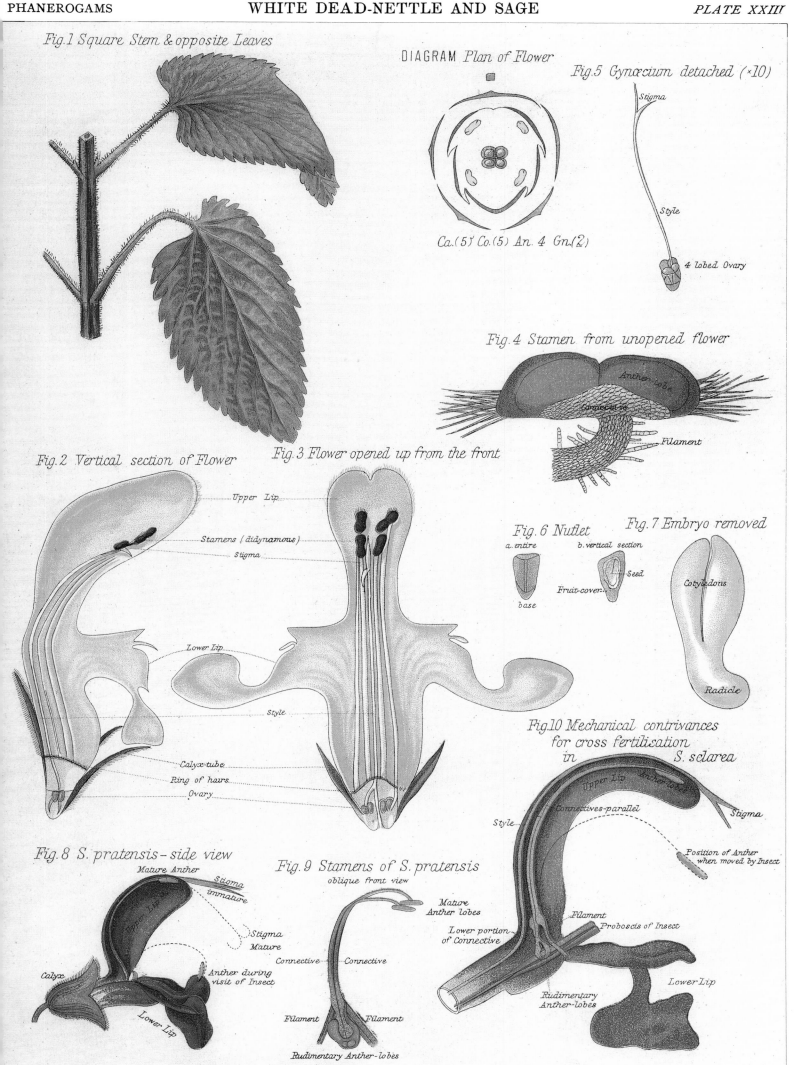

Fig.1 Square Stem & opposite Leaves

DIAGRAM *Plan of Flower*

Fig.5 Gynœcium detached (×10)

Stigma

Style

4 lobed Ovary

Ca.(5) Co.(5) An. 4 Gn.(2)

Fig.4 Stamen from unopened flower

Anther-lobe

Connective

Filament

Fig.2 Vertical section of Flower

Fig.3 Flower opened up from the front

Upper Lip

Stamens (didynamous)

Stigma

Fig.6 Nutlet

a. entire   b. vertical section

Fig.7 Embryo removed

Seed

Fruit-cover

base

Cotyledons

Radicle

Lower Lip

Style

Calyx-tube

Ring of hairs

Ovary

*Fig.10 Mechanical contrivances
for cross fertilisation
in S. sclarea*

Upper Lip Anther-lobes

Style

Connectives-parallel

Stigma

Position of Anther
when moved by Insect

Fig.8 S. pratensis – side view

Mature Anther

Stigma
immature

Fig.9 Stamens of S. pratensis
oblique front view

Mature
Anther lobes

Lower portion
of Connective

Filament

Proboscis of Insect

Upper Lip

Stigma
Mature

Calyx

Anther during
visit of Insect

Connective   Connective

Lower Lip

Filament   Filament

Rudimentary Anther-lobes

Rudimentary
Anther-lobes

Lower Lip

Engraved, Printed and Published by W. & A.K. Johnston, Edinburgh & London.

PLATE XXIV.

FOX-GLOVE (*Digitalis purpurea*).

The purple Fox-glove is a well-known plant, coming into flower about June, and occurring usually on the rough and rugged slopes of the hill-sides. The shape of the flower has suggested both the common and the scientific name. Folk's-glove has reference to its resemblance to the finger of a glove, and Digitalis (Lat. *digitus,* a finger) implies the same. The leaves are used in medicine, and the flowers are adapted for insect-visitation. The Anthers ripen first, and in doing so change from a transverse to a longitudinal position, thus enabling the bee as it enters the bell to carry off the pollen, spread over a larger linear surface of its body.

There are several members of the same Order equally well-known and cultivated, such as Snapdragon, Musk, and Calceolaria, while the Speedwells, usually blue, are among the commonest of spring, summer, and even autumn flowers.

LEAVES AND FLOWERS

Fig. 1 Inflorescence—a Raceme, and each flower in the axil of a bract. The unopened flowers towards the top are more or less of a whitish colour, and occasionally the mature flower remains white. It is no uncommon thing to find the axis, under cultivation, terminated by a flower which, under these circumstances, develops its lobes at the margin of the bell regularly, and not irregularly, as in the lateral flower.

Fig. 2 Take a flower with the lips still closed, and make a longitudinal section, cutting from the base upwards. Sepals, inserted on receptacle. Petals, inserted on receptacle. Stamens, attached to corolla but traceable to their attachment beneath ovary. The filaments are bent, and the unopened anthers lie transverse to the filaments. Ovary, superior, with a long style lying close to the petals.

Fig. 3 Take a fully expanded flower and lay open Corolla. Anthers are now open, and instead of being transverse they are longitudinal.

Diagram I.—Calyx of five Sepals, unequal in size and united at base. Corolla of five united Petals, the upper lip being slightly notched in the middle, representing two petals, and the lower lip three-lobed, representing three petals. Andrœcium of four Stamens, two long and two short. A rudimentary fifth stamen is found in the Snapdragon, sometimes developing into a complete one. Gynœcium of two united Carpels, as indicated by the two-lobed stigma.

Fig. 4 Foliage Leaves, long-stalked towards the root, becoming sessile higher up. Bracts, leafy.

Fig. 5 Sepal or Calyx-lobe, broad base and pointed tip.

Fig. 6 Transverse section of Ovary (mounted in glycerine). There are two chambers, and a central axis between, to which the numerous Ovules are attached. The united edges of the two carpellary leaves form the swollen axis, so that the Placentation is axile.

Fig. 7. and *Diagram II.*—Speedwell, or Veronica shows a reduction in the number of parts.

Calyx of four Sepals, the posterior one being suppressed. Corolla of four Petals united at the base, so as to form what is called a rotate corolla. The lower lip is three-lobed, and the upper lip undivided. Stamens reduced to two. Carpels, two united.

FRUIT AND SEED

Fig. 8 Fruit of Speedwell entire, and in vertical section. Capsule is laterally compressed, the seeds are attached to a central axis and the two valves separate to allow seeds to escape.

Figs. 9 and *10* Fruit of Fox-glove entire, and in transverse section. Capsule is pear-shaped, and the two valves separate by splitting from the top downwards.

Fig. 11 Seed in vertical section. The embryo occupies the axis of the seed, and is surrounded by Endosperm.

Fig. 12 The Capsule of Snapdragon opens by pores, and the Seeds are curiously marked with depressions, surrounded by walls with jagged surfaces.

CLASSIFICATION.

Class. Dicotyledon

Division. Gamopetalæ.

Order. Scrophulariaceæ.

Corolla, irregular. Stamens, four, two long and two short; sometimes two. Ovary, superior, two-chambered.

Ovules, numerous; placentation, axile. Fruit, capsular. Seed with endosperm.

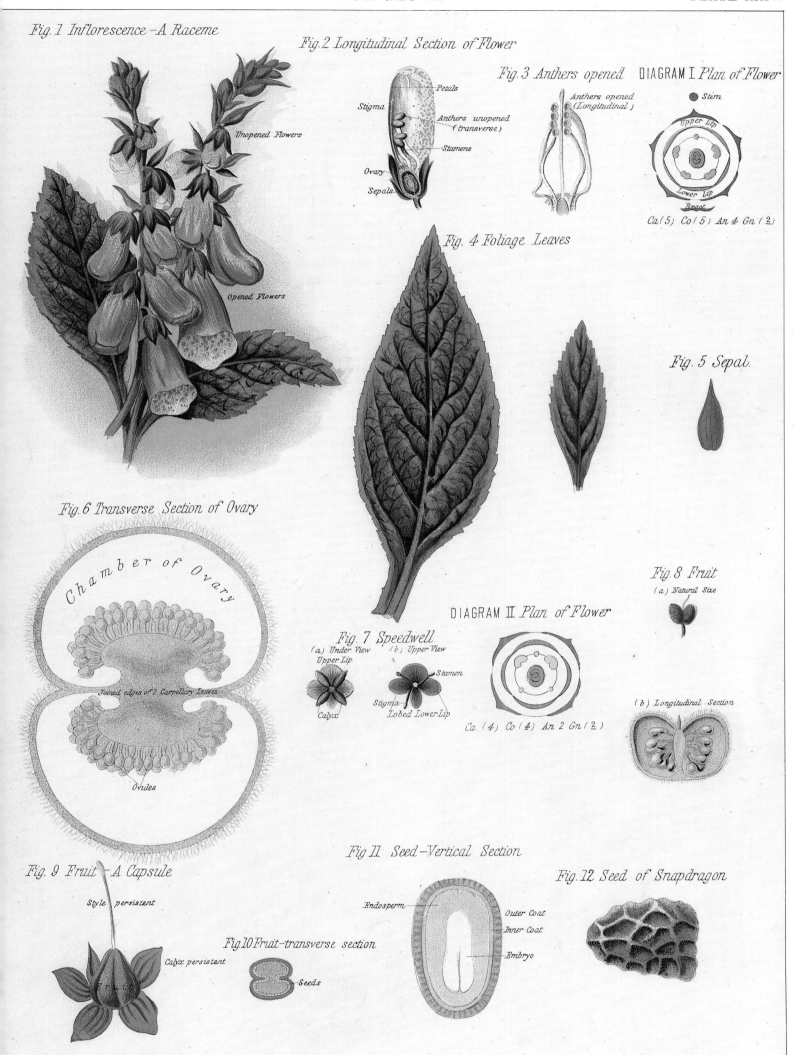

Fig.1 Inflorescence – A Raceme

Unopened Flowers

Opened Flowers

Fig.2 Longitudinal Section of Flower

Stigma

Petals

Anthers unopened
(transverse)

Stamens

Ovary

Sepals

Fig.3 Anthers opened

Anthers opened
(Longitudinal)

DIAGRAM I Plan of Flower

Stem

Upper Lip

Lower Lip

Bract

Ca (5) Co (5) An 4 Gn (2)

Fig. 4 Foliage Leaves

Fig. 5 Sepal.

Fig.6 Transverse Section of Ovary

Chamber of Ovary

Joined edges of 2 Carpellary Leaves

Ovules

Fig. 7 Speedwell

(a) Under View   (b) Upper View

Upper Lip

Stamen

Stigma

Calyx

Lobed Lower Lip

DIAGRAM II Plan of Flower

Ca. (4) Co (4) An 2 Gn (2)

Fig. 8 Fruit

(a) Natural Size

(b) Longitudinal Section

Fig. 9 Fruit – A Capsule

Style persistent

Calyx persistent

Fruit

Fig.10 Fruit-transverse section

Seeds

Fig 11 Seed–Vertical Section

Endosperm

Outer Coat

Inner Coat

Embryo

Fig. 12 Seed of Snapdragon

Engraved, Printed and Published by W. & A.K. Johnston, Edinburgh

PLATE XXV.

DAISY (*Bellis perennis*)
and DANDELION (*Taraxacum dens-leonis*).

The Daisy and Dandelion are the commonest representatives of a Natural Order which is the largest known, and universal in its distribution. The flowers are arranged in great numbers side by side on the extremity of a stalk—flattened or conical—and from having such compound heads of flowers, they are reckoned composite plants or *Compositæ*. The large numbers and wide distribution of this Order are associated with a condensation of parts carried to its greatest possible extent. Not only are the flowers as a whole, as closely packed as possible into a Head, but the individual flowers have their various parts bound together in closest union. This compactness gives a completeness to the whole for insect-fertilisation, inasmuch as a number of flowers are likely to be fertilised by one visit of the insect.

The Daisy and Dandelion are types of the two great divisions of this Order—the Daisy having tubular flowers, except the outer row; and a watery juice; while the Dandelion has strap-shaped or ligulate flowers and a milky juice.

DAISY

Fig. 1 Slit up a Flower-head from its base upwards.
Flowers, sessile, on a common Receptacle which is conical.
Bracts, forming a single whorl.
The outer Flowers are strap-shaped and constitute the Ray, while the inner are tubular and form the Disc.
The flowers open from the outside inwards, so that the youngest are towards the centre.
Fig. 2 Detach a single flower from the Ray, and magnify it.
(*a.*) Ordinary form, magnified.
(*b.*) Occasional form, more highly magnified.
Calyx may be represented by a short tuft of hairs called the Pappus.
Corolla, in one piece, tubular at the base, gradually flattening out, and

ending in two small lobes. In some, however, there are distinct indications of five small lobes, thus showing the five-fold nature of the corolla.
Stamens, absent.
Gynœcium of two united Carpels, as indicated by the bi-lobed stigma; but in the flower with five-lobed corolla, the stigma was also five-lobed. The Ovary is elongated.
The Ray-flower is thus seen to be Female, and consists of a probable remnant of a Calyx, a Corolla of five united Petals, and a Gynœcium of five united Carpels.
Fig. 3 Remove a flower from the Disc, and magnify it.
The Corolla is tubular and distinctly five-lobed, usually, and the Stigma is

two-lobed; but there are no hairs crowning the Ovary.
Fig. 4 Open up tubular Corolla with dissecting needle, and spread it out as much as possible.
The flower is now seen to be bi-sexual.
The Stamens have short Filaments attached to corolla, and the Anthers are united so as to form a tube round the style.
Fig. 5 Look for specimens without Ray-flowers, with much enlarged common Receptacle studded over with small Fruits, or possibly lying in the cup-like whorl of bracts.
(*a, b*) Fruit is an Achene, as on examination it will be found to be one-seeded, dry, and does not open.

DANDELION.

Fig. 6 Flower-head unopened, with portion of Stalk.
The stalk is usually leafless, but sometimes bears a reduced one.
There is an outer set of recurved bracts, and an inner upright set.
Fig. 7 Flower-head slit up.
Common Receptacle is a flat expansion of a hollow stalk.
Flowers are all strap-shaped, and the outer open first.
Fig. 8 Detach an outer mature flower and an inner less mature flower.
(*a*) Calyx, represented by Pappus, well-developed.
Corolla with five distinct teeth.
Stamens with short Filaments, and

long Anthers united to form a tube.
Gynœcium of two united Carpels, the lobes of the Stigma curling over and fertilising themselves, if insect should fail to do so.
(*b*) At this stage the Stigma projects beyond the Corolla, and has mere indications of two lobes.
Fig. 9 Carefully remove the wall of the Ovary with needles, and expose single Ovule.
Figs. 10 and 11 The Fruit is very unlike that of the Daisy, in being conspicuous, and having a stalk bearing a tuft of hairs.
These hairs catch the faintest breath of wind, and so disperse the fruit.

Fig. 12 Cut the fruit in two, and expose seed.
There is one seed filling up the cavity, without endosperm. *Fig. 13* The ordinary Foliage-leaf is deeply segmented, the apex of the triangular segments pointing downwards.
The occasional Leaf on Stalk is much smaller, less segmented, and altogether simpler.
Fig. 14 The bracts may be traced through all gradations from a lobed leaf, as on stalk, till next the flower it becomes thoroughly simple, and even some of the petals are intermediate between bract and petal.

CLASSIFICATION.

Class. Dicotyledon.

Division. Gamopetalæ.

Order. Compositæ.

Flowers, sessile, and in heads.
Corolla, in one piece, ligulate or tubular.
Stamens, epipetalous; anthers forming

a tube.
Ovary, inferior, with one Ovule.
Fruit, an achene.
Seed without endosperm.

Daisy (Figs 1-5)   Dandelion (Figs 6-14)

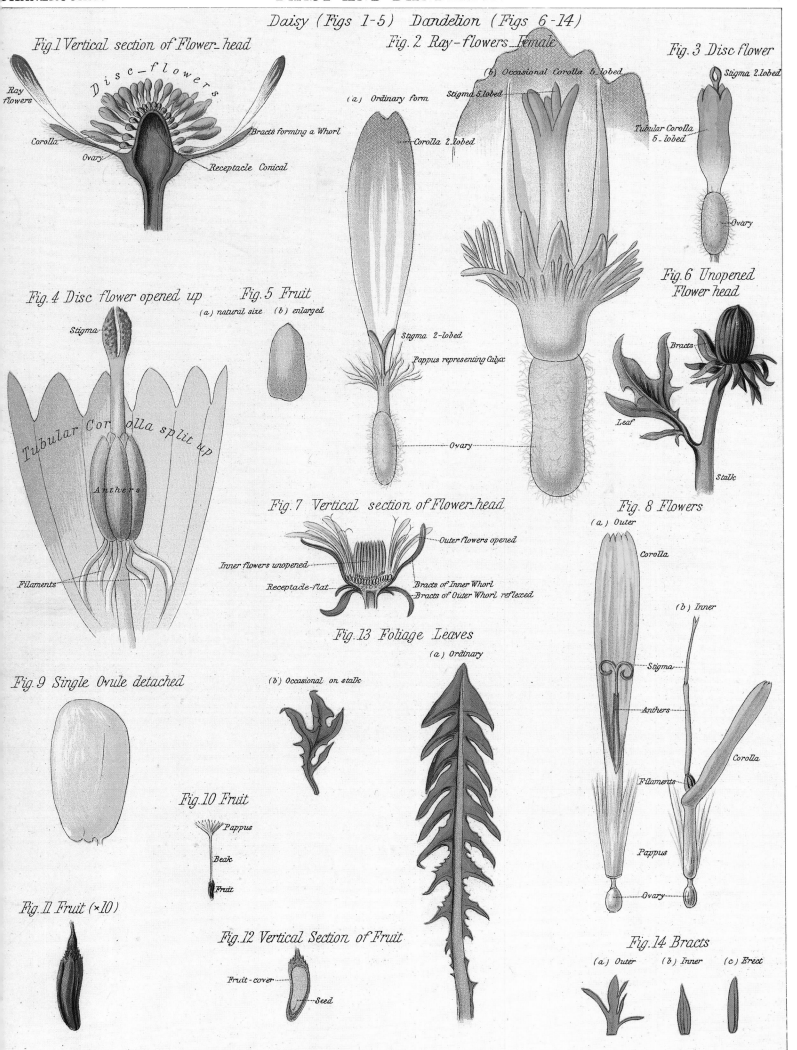

Fig.1 Vertical section of Flower-head

Disc-flowers

Ray flowers

Corolla

Ovary

Receptacle Conical

Bracts forming a Whorl

Fig. 2 Ray-flowers—Female

(a) Ordinary form

(b) Occasional Corolla 5-lobed

Corolla 2-lobed

Stigma 5-lobed

Stigma 2-lobed

Pappus representing Calyx

Ovary

Fig. 3 Disc flower

Stigma 2-lobed

Tubular Corolla 5-lobed

Ovary

Fig. 4 Disc flower opened up

Stigma

Tubular Corolla split up

Anthers

Filaments

Fig. 5 Fruit

(a) natural size   (b) enlarged

Fig. 6 Unopened Flower head

Bracts

Leaf

Stalk

Fig. 7 Vertical section of Flower-head

Outer flowers opened

Inner flowers unopened

Receptacle-flat

Bracts of Inner Whorl

Bracts of Outer Whorl reflexed

Fig. 8 Flowers

(a) Outer

Corolla

(b) Inner

Stigma

Anthers

Corolla

Filaments

Pappus

Ovary

Fig. 13 Foliage Leaves

(a) Ordinary

(b) Occasional on stalk

Fig. 9 Single Ovule detached

Fig.10 Fruit

Pappus

Beak

Fruit

Fig.11 Fruit (×10)

Fig.12 Vertical Section of Fruit

Fruit-cover

Seed

Fig.14 Bracts

(a) Outer   (b) Inner   (c) Erect

Engraved, Printed and Published by W. & A.K. Johnston, Edinburgh

PLATE XXVI.

PARASITES AND INSECTIVOROUS PLANTS.

In a work dealing with typical forms of plant-life it would be unpardonable entirely to overlook the subjects of the present Plate. They are not treated, however, with great fullness, because the object in view was rather to call attention to them, than to make a detailed study of them. I have endeavoured to represent them in such a way that they may be easily recognised when met with, and carefully examined.

In the case of Insectivorous Plants, students often either do not know them or overlook them from their relatively small size. They are accustomed to such magnified drawings and have such exalted notions of Traps, Tentacles, and Bladders, that the little Sundew of our moors, for instance, is hardly within their range of vision. To obviate this, each plant or a conspicuous portion of the plant is given in its natural size. The three British genera here figured were all obtained from around Edinburgh—Sundew from the neighborhood of Balerno, and Butterwort and Bladderwort from Gullane—and the little that is given about them may tempt the student to seek further information in the late Mr Darwin's well-known work on "Insectivorous Plants."

The mode of Nutrition is the principal thing to be noted in each case, and it will be seen that not merely living and decayed vegetable matter may be absorbed by plants, but even *digestion* and absorption of living and decayed animal matter can be accomplished.

MISTLETOE (*Viscum album*).

The MISTLETOE with its berried Fruit is a familiar object at Christmas-time, but it is in summer that the Flower is met with. It is parasitic on trees, such as the Apple and Hawthorn, but rarely on the Oak. The berries are used for making bird-lime, hence the name of the plant Viscum (Lat. *viscus*, bird-lime). The seeds are often sown on the branches of trees by birds, which eat the fruit for the sake of its succulent and viscid cover, and afterwards cleaning their bill, leave the seed behind sticking to the tree. The seed begins to germinate generally after it has slipped round to the under surface of the branch, and puts forth rootlets which bore through the bark and pass towards the centre along the softest parts—the medullary rays. It thus becomes blended with the tissues of the plant on which it grows, and by means of this organic connection feeds upon it, frequently killing the branch on which it has settled. The Mistletoe is a parasite which does not live wholly at the expense of others, but does something for itself by means of its green leaves. The Dodder (*Cuscuta*), however, produces no leaves, not even seed-leaves, but twines round its host—such as the Clover—and sucks the substance out of it. There are plants even, such as the Bird's-nest Orchid (*Neottia*), which grovel in decay, and live upon decayed vegetable matter, such as decaying leaves and the like. Such are distinguished as Saprophytes (Gr. *sapros*, rotten; *phuton*, a plant).

Fig. 1 Branch of Fir-tree, in section, showing sucking roots running through it.
Figs. 2 and 3 Male and Female Plants distinct.
Male Inflorescence consists of three flowers, each flower having usually four Perianth-leaves and the sessile Anthers inserted upon them.
Female Inflorescence also of three flowers, each with four Perianth-leaves and a relatively large inferior Ovary.
Fig. 4 Fruit, a berry, easily cut through.
The fruit-cover is pulpy and sticky, and the single seed frequently contains more than one embryo, usually two, embedded in the endosperm.

BLADDERWORT (*Utricularia*—Lat. *Utriculus*, a little bottle).
(*Fig. 8 after Cohn.*)

BLADDERWORT occurs in stagnant water and in ditches which are foul and therefore swarming with minute animal life. It flowers about July.

Figs. 5 and 6 The flowering stem rises above the surface of the water and bears a few yellow flowers. The flower has an upper and an under lip, with a well-marked prominence on the latter, and altogether has a general resemblance to the flower of Snapdragon.
Fig. 7 The Leaf is much divided and the divisions continually fork. The Bladders are borne on short stalks and vary in number.
Fig 8 The Bladder consists of a transparent membrane and the specimens examined were of a pale purple tint. Small animals, such as Cyclops, Insect larvae, etc., gain admission by following the bristles at the entrance, and thereby opening a folding door in the shape of the free edge of an elastic valve ; this shuts after them so that they are entrapped. The Bladders do not secrete, but only *absorb*, the decayed matter by means of four-armed processes covering the interior.

BUTTERWORT (*Pinguicula vulgaris*—Lat. *pinguis*, fat).

BUTTERWORT grows in damp places, sometimes near to the stagnant waters containing

130

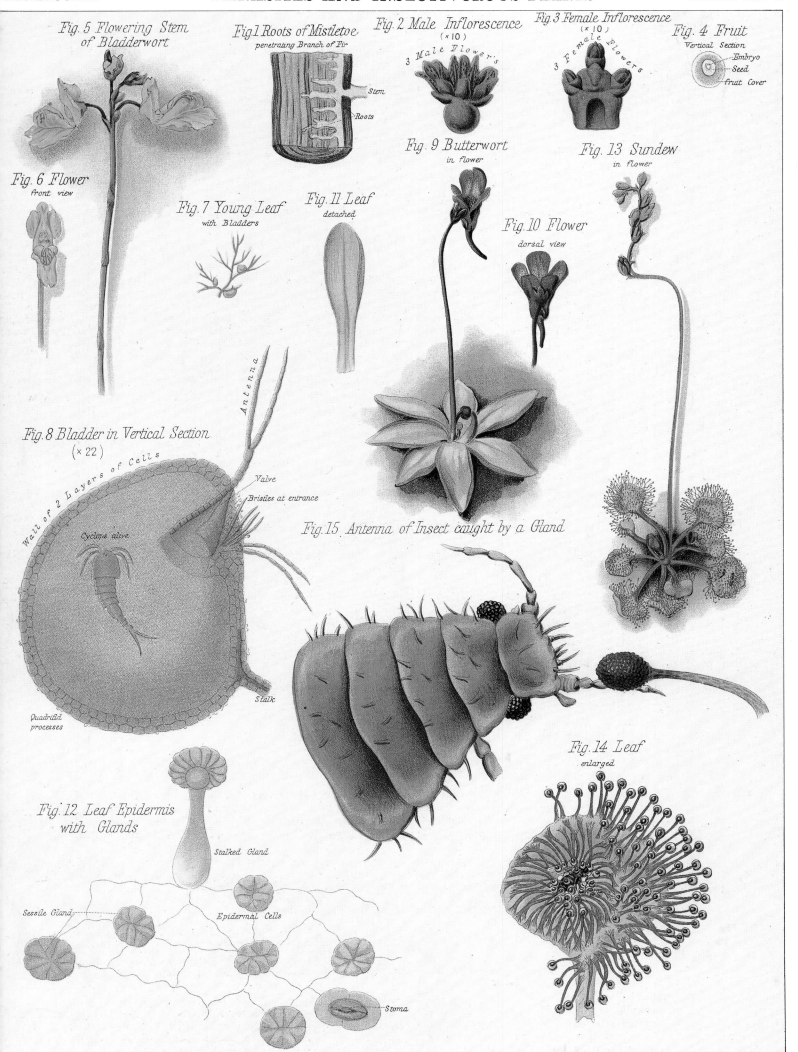

Fig. 5 Flowering Stem of Bladderwort

Fig. 1 Roots of Mistletoe
penetrating Branch of Fir
Stem
Roots

Fig. 2 Male Inflorescence (×10)
3 Male Flowers

Fig. 3 Female Inflorescence (×10)
3 Female Flowers

Fig. 4 Fruit
Vertical Section
Embryo
Seed
Fruit Cover

Fig. 9 Butterwort
in flower

Fig. 13 Sundew
in flower

Fig. 6 Flower
front view

Fig. 7 Young Leaf
with Bladders

Fig. 11 Leaf
detached

Fig. 10 Flower
dorsal view

Fig. 8 Bladder in Vertical Section
(×22)
Wall of 2 Layers of Cells
Antenna
Valve
Bristles at entrance
Cyclops alive
Quadrifid processes
Stalk

Fig. 15 Antenna of Insect caught by a Gland

Fig. 12 Leaf Epidermis with Glands
Stalked Gland
Sessile Gland
Epidermal Cells
Stoma

Fig. 14 Leaf
enlarged

Engraved, Printed and Published by W. & A.K. Johnston, Edinburgh

Utricularia, but flowering earlier, usually in May.

Figs. 9 and 10 One or more stalks arise from the centre of the radical leaves, and each bears a terminal drooping, violet flower with a projecting spur.
Fig. 11 The leaves have usually incurved margins and are embedded in the boggy ground, so that they are on a level with the surface, and creeping things may readily get on to them When plucked up by the root the leaves soon bend back and almost meet by their tips, and this folding is the same which keeps them flat when growing.
Fig. 12 Bend a leaf about the finger, and remove a thin portion of the surface with a sharp razor, and examine to see the glands on the surface.

There are two kinds of glands—those which stand out on a stalk and those which are sessile. These glands secrete a viscous fluid, and when small flies, etc., venture on the leaf, the margins arch over them, and the secretion acts upon them until they are dissolved. Here a process of digestion takes place.

DROSERA ROTUNDIFOLIA (Gr. *drosos*, dew).

The SUNDEW derives its name from the glistening appearance of the fluid drops at the tip of each of the tentacles of the leaves.

It occurs on boggy ground and wet moors, and the moss serves as a sponge to keep up a supply of water. It flowers about July.

Fig. 13 The Leaves are arranged in the form of a rosette, and the scape bearing several flowers has a characteristic bend towards the top. The flowers are comparatively small, and the white petals are almost enclosed by the sepals, merely peeping forth a little at the top.
Fig. 14 The Leaf is beset with numerous tentacles, each terminated by a gland, and surrounded by a colourless viscid secretion. An insect alighting on the centre of the leaf is speedily enveloped by the infolding tentacles, and the copious secretion poured forth by the glands not only weakens its struggles but shortly smothers it. Thus quietly resting on the leaf which forms a trough for its reception, the soft parts of the insect are gradually dissolved and absorbed by the Leaf, which again expands its tentacles to glitter in the sun and attract more prey.
Fig. 15 This is a case where the antenna was caught by a gland, and it would appear that the insect is bound hand and foot, as it were, by the inner, shorter tentacles and the outer longer tentacles gradually fold over and seal its doom.

There are two ways in which a plant may feed, either by taking in *inorganic* substances and converting them into the organic material of which it is already composed, or by taking in *organic* materials and working them up into its own substance.

The first mode is that adopted by plants possessed of chlorophyll, or an allied colouring matter. This chlorophyll is commonly regarded as a carbonic-acid decomposing-apparatus; but quite recently it has been suggested that it is the living protoplasm underlying it which performs this work, while chlorophyll merely serves to mask it, and prevent too rapid action in the presence of sunlight. In this case chlorophyll would be an accompaniment, and not the cause, of decomposition.

The second mode is carried on by plants without chlorophyll, or an equivalent colouring matter; and, as already pointed out, *living* green plants or animals may be preyed upon, in which case the attacking plants are *Parasites*; or *dead* and decayed organic bodies may be used, when they are *Saprophytes.*

Starting with the ordinary Green Plants, every stage of Degradation may be traced.

The *Mistletoe* is only partially parasitic, since it bears green leaves, but the *Dodder* is wholly parasitic. It forms little discs in contact with the stem of the plant it has attacked, from the centre of each of which a rootlet is emitted, and penetrates into the tissues of its host.

Then the next step is from living to decayed matter, as in the case of the brown Bird's-nest Orchid, which absorbs the liquified decaying leaves amongst which it lives. The Bladder-wort, too, absorbs the decayed animal matter, putrifying in its bladders.

But a further stage is reached when the plant is able to bring its food materials into a state of solution as well as to absorb them, and this is accomplished by the Butterwort and the Sundew, which have not only beautiful contrivances for catching their living prey but means for digesting it as well.

CRYPTOGAMS

INDEX TO ILLUSTRATIONS — FOR COMPARATIVE STUDY

PHANEROGAMS

INDEX TO ILLUSTRATIONS — FOR COMPARATIVE STUDY

"D" INDICATES DIAGRAM

135